INTRODUCTION to PRIMARY SCHOOL TEACHING

INTRODUCTION to PRIMARY SCHOOL TEACHING

Edited by **Colin Forster & Rachel Eperjesi**

Sage

S Sage

1 Oliver's Yard
55 City Road
London EC1Y 1SP

2455 Teller Road
Thousand Oaks, California 91320

Unit No 323–333, Third Floor, F–Block
International Trade Tower Nehru Place
New Delhi 110 019

8 Marina View Suite 43–053
Asia Square Tower 1
Singapore 018960

Editor: James Clark
Editorial Assistant: Esosa Otabor
Production Editor: Neelu Sahu
Copyeditor: Sarah Bury
Proofreader: Salia Nessa
Marketing Manager: Lorna Patkai
Cover Design: Naomi Robinson
Typeset by KnowledgeWorks Global Ltd
Printed in the UK

Library of Congress Control Number: 2023940657

British Library Cataloguing in Publication data

A catalogue record for this book is available from the British Library

ISBN 978-1-5297-9807-4
ISBN 978-1-5297-9806-7 (pbk)

At Sage we take sustainability seriously. Most of our products are printed in the UK using responsibly sourced papers and boards. When we print overseas we ensure sustainable papers are used as measured by the Paper Chain Project grading system. We undertake an annual audit to monitor our sustainability.

CONTENTS

ABOUT THE EDITORS AND CONTRIBUTORS

Editors

Much to the surprise of anyone who meets him now, when he was a young man, **Colin Forster** spent two years working as an outdoor activities instructor and it was during this time that he developed an interest in education. He began his primary teaching career in south-west London before moving to Gloucestershire, where he continued to gain school leadership experience. He is currently a senior lecturer in primary education at the University of Gloucestershire, where he has gained considerable experience of primary teacher education leadership and in supporting students, at both undergraduate and postgraduate level, with research projects focused on improving practice. His areas of interest include primary science, behaviour management and action research, and he has undertaken research into children's experience of homework in the primary years and the role of the school-based mentor in supporting student teachers' professional learning.

Rachel Eperjesi knew she wanted to be a teacher from the age of five. However, some rather poor careers advice led her to embark on a medical degree, which quickly resulted in her declaring it 'too messy' and deciding to follow her heart into teaching instead. After completing a BEd Hons, Rachel taught in Foundation Stage and Key Stage 1 (also quite messy) in Gloucestershire, as well as undertaking English consultancy for the local authority. She now works at the University of Gloucestershire, lecturing in primary English and professional studies, as well as leading the School Direct PGCE Primary course. Rachel has supported many students, both undergraduate and postgraduate, with research projects focusing on improving their educational practice.

Contributors

Kevin Day began his career in secondary education as a teacher of physical education before progressing into roles within pastoral care, safeguarding and SENCo. Kevin has been the headteacher of Gloucestershire's Virtual School, supporting the education of children in care.

Currently, he leads Belmont Special School and is the county lead for developing effective approaches to trauma-informed relational practice.

Ruth Hollier is a senior lecturer in primary education and a university teaching fellow at the University of Gloucestershire. Having previously enjoyed a rewarding career as a primary school teacher and deputy headteacher, Ruth now teaches primary mathematics and professional studies across undergraduate and postgraduate initial teacher education courses. Ruth also supports professional development in mathematics for primary teachers through extensive work with the GLOW Maths Hub, for which she is a member of the strategic board.

Emma Howell began her career working as a class teacher in a range of infant and primary schools, specialising as a school mentor, before moving into initial teacher education. After ten years as a senior lecturer in the primary mathematics team, Emma now leads the primary partnership and school experience aspects of initial teacher education at the University of Gloucestershire. Emma continues her interest in primary mathematics through ongoing work with the GLOW Maths Hub.

Simon Hyde-White taught in a variety of primary schools for 20 years before fulfilling his longstanding desire to work with the future generation of teachers by becoming a senior lecturer in primary education at the University of Gloucestershire. Simon delivers the provision for physical education and religious education on the undergraduate and postgraduate initial teacher education courses. He works with local subject leaders in both subjects and has led student research in local primary schools, exploring how best to develop physically literate and religiously literate pupils. He has a lifelong fascination and engagement with both subjects.

Debbie Innes-Turnill has been a teacher and school leader for nearly 30 years. A second degree in psychology, followed by an MSc in advanced child protection studies, enabled her to develop an expertise in the support and protection of vulnerable children and their families. She now lectures on child protection issues at the University of Birmingham. She has a freelance safeguarding consultancy, which advises schools, charities and other organisations in safeguarding culture. She provides a holistic approach to the wellbeing of both children and adults, thinking about their participation to improve practice in keeping them safe. This work is underpinned by her own research interests, related to children living in poverty, safeguarding culture in education, children's experiences of trauma and how their needs are met.

Lynda Kay taught for over 20 years in primary schools and held a variety of roles, including class teacher, SENCo, designated teacher for safeguarding and senior leader. After that, Lynda worked as a specialist SEN advisory teacher before becoming a senior lecturer in inclusion/SEN at the University of Gloucestershire, where she is currently joint course leader for the MA Education and the PG Certificate NASENCo. Lynda is a director of Leading Learning for SEND Community Interest Company, which oversees the work of the National SENCo

Award Provider Partnership Working Group, and has currently returned to school, working as a SENCo one day per week alongside her university work. Lynda's research focuses upon exploring effective pedagogy for children with speech, language and communication needs who present with challenging behaviour in primary schools.

Jackie McNeil taught in a range of primary schools in England and overseas for more than 20 years before becoming a senior lecturer in primary mathematics at the University of Gloucestershire. She is a university teaching fellow and teaches mathematics and professional studies to students on undergraduate and postgraduate initial teacher education courses. As an accredited Continuing Professional Development (CPD) lead for the National Centre for Excellence in the Teaching of Mathematics (NCETM), she also works with primary teachers and teaching assistants through the GLOW Maths Hub, to develop their teaching of mathematics.

Tristan Middleton is a senior lecturer in education, university teaching fellow and academic course leader for the MA Education suite at the University of Gloucestershire. Tristan is the editor of the *International Journal of Nurture in Education* and also a director of Leading Learning for SEND Community Interest Company. Tristan's research and publishing interests include nurture groups, special educational needs, resilience and practitioner support and supervision.

Graham Parton is Head of School for Education and Humanities at the University of Gloucestershire. Before taking up the Head of School role, he was Director of Teacher Education at Leeds Beckett University. Graham has extensive experience of teaching in primary schools in East London and his research interests include technology-enhanced learning and problem-based learning.

Jude Penny worked for 16 years as a primary school teacher and science lead in London, and 12 years at the University of Gloucestershire as a senior lecturer in primary education. She currently teaches on the initial teacher education programmes at the University of South Wales. Jude's specialist areas are science and PSHE and her research interests include dialogic teaching and teachers' questioning. She also has a passion for Philosophy For/With Children (P4wC) and supports accredited training for student teachers.

Ben Screech worked in mainstream and SEND primary settings, in addition to a children's charity before moving into higher education. His main teaching and research specialism is children's literacy and literature, and he completed his PhD in 2018, exploring literary representations of 'othered' young people. Ben is also the project coordinator for the ERAMUS+ project 'Get Readers on the Wavelength of Emotions' (GROWE).

Sian Templeton is an educational psychologist with InsightEPs, having previously worked as a senior lecturer in education at the University of Gloucestershire. In her role as an educational psychologist, Sian currently works with a variety of schools, including mainstream and specialist settings. Sian is particularly interested in supporting children and young people who demonstrate a range of vulnerabilities, and enjoys working with the adults who are closely involved with those children and young people in helping them to fulfil their potential.

Kate Thomson is a senior lecturer in primary education at the University of Gloucestershire, specialising in teaching history and English on undergraduate and postgraduate initial teacher education courses. She began her career teaching in a range of primary schools, before working as an advisory teacher for history and geography in Gloucestershire. Kate now leads the foundation subjects team at the University of Gloucestershire and is a university teaching fellow.

Michelle Walton enjoyed working as a primary school teacher for 16 years in a range of primary schools in Gloucestershire before joining the University of Gloucestershire as a senior lecturer in primary education. Michelle specialises in maths, music and professional studies on the undergraduate and postgraduate initial teacher education courses. As a NCETM-accredited CPD lead, Michelle also supports professional development in mathematics for primary teachers and teaching assistants through work with the GLOW Maths Hub.

Tracey Wire is a senior lecturer in primary education and School Direct Primary PGCE course leader at the University of Gloucestershire. She has over 20 years of experience working in primary and secondary schools and universities. Tracey specialises in teaching history and English with undergraduate and postgraduate initial teacher education students, and has undertaken research focused on younger children's gender and sexual identities and relationships education. Tracey has supported professional development in primary history through the university, Schools History Project and Historical Association.

Chantel Yeates is currently leading her second school as a deputy headteacher. Having a passion for the emotional wellbeing of staff and pupils, and understanding what brings out the best in people, has led to a career working with children with additional needs. Chantel is particularly focused on supporting children who have experienced trauma. Developing an understanding of trauma-informed relational practice is key to her work in her current setting and with the local authority.

ACKNOWLEDGEMENTS

Creating a high-quality edited text is only possible with the support, goodwill and enthusiasm of many people, so we have a number of people we'd like to thank.

First and foremost, we would like to thank all of the contributors to this book for sharing their expertise so willingly and for coming on the journey with us with enthusiasm.

We would like to thank all of our student teachers, from whom we learn so much every year, and to all our colleagues at the University of Gloucestershire.

We would like to thank all our school partners and, in particular, the following colleagues, who have shared key insights and specific case study material for the book: Emily Britton-Drewry, Rob Evans, Liz Geller, Tanya Harris, Alyson Meredith, Sasha Palmer, Gary Tucker and David Walton.

We have had tremendous support from the team at Sage, for which we are very grateful.

Finally, we would like to thank our respective families for their patience and support throughout.

Colin Forster and Rachel Eperjesi

1
INTRODUCTION: THE VALUES AND CHARACTERISTICS OF GREAT TEACHERS

Rachel Eperjesi and Colin Forster

Chapter Objectives

- To consider the life-changing impact that great teaching can have on learners.
- To explore the characteristics and values of great teachers.
- To reflect on how teachers learn and develop their practice.

In this chapter, we consider the impact that teachers and teaching can have on learners, both in the short term and the longer term. We explore some characteristics and values which are common to great teachers, as well as considering how teachers learn and develop their own practice. Finally, we explain how to make effective use of this book to maximise your own learning, as you embark upon this incredible journey of becoming an outstanding primary school teacher.

Becoming a Great Teacher

Throughout this book, we make the assumption that you don't just want to be a teacher, but that you want to be a highly effective teacher, one who has a significant positive impact on learning and on learners themselves. Teaching is a demanding profession, but one which has many rewards; for most teachers, witnessing the positive impact of their teaching is the most significant reward and it motivates them to continue to strive to be the best teacher they can be.

Think back to your own time as a primary school pupil. Which of your teachers can you remember? Can you remember all of them equally, or do some stick in your memory more than others? For most people, their memories of some teachers are clearer than others. They tend to remember any teacher that they had a particularly negative experience with and those that they had a particularly positive experience with; the 'just ok' teachers are easily forgotten. Hopefully, you want to be a really memorable teacher, for all the right reasons.

Life-changing Impact of Great Teaching

The Department for Education (DfE) (2019: 3) suggests that 'the quality of teaching is the single most important in-school factor in improving outcomes for pupils – and it is particularly important for pupils from disadvantaged backgrounds'. Coe et al. (2014: 2) would agree with this, defining great teaching as 'that which leads to improved student progress'. That seems fairly straightforward: good teaching leads to good learning.

Truly great teaching, though, goes beyond simply having an immediate impact on students' progress in academic learning. Truly great teachers not only help children to develop their learning, they also consider the children holistically, to help them become happy, well-rounded, successful individuals. Truly great teachers care deeply about the children in their classes and schools, and want the best for them. Truly great teachers recognise that learning and happiness are linked: children who are not feeling safe, secure or happy find it much more difficult to learn.

Whether considering academic progress or the development of other aspects, such as wellbeing, social skills or emotional intelligence, what we teach children can change not only their day, week, month or academic year, but also, in some cases, their whole lives. Throughout this book, we will consider how you can be a truly great teacher, who nurtures every aspect of a child's development, and how your impact can be life-changing and life-enhancing.

Characteristics and Values of Great Teachers

As we will explore later in this book, all children are unique individuals and the same is true of teachers. Even those who are using the same teaching skills will do so in slightly different ways. Nonetheless, there are some characteristics and values that are common among great teachers.

Research into Teacher Effectiveness

Significant research has been undertaken into teacher effectiveness. One important study, undertaken by management consultants Hay McBer (2000), identified, perhaps obviously, that teaching skills play an important role in teacher effectiveness and these skills will be explored in other chapters in this book. Perhaps less obviously, at least to those with less experience, is that professional characteristics (such as confidence, creating trust and working well as part of a team) and classroom climate (how it feels to be a pupil in that classroom) are also key factors contributing to teacher effectiveness. As part of the research study, pupils identified several dimensions in relation to classroom climate that affected their motivation and capacity to learn, such as fairness and support.

More recently, Coe et al. (2014) also carried out research into great teaching. They identified six key components and, again, while aspects such as quality of instruction and classroom management were identified, so was classroom climate. In establishing a positive classroom climate, our values, and how we communicate those values to pupils, will be highly significant, and that communication is very much about what we do, not just what we say. For example, we can claim to respect and value all pupils as individuals, but if we shout at and belittle a child for finding something difficult, our actions communicate something entirely different.

— Critical Task 1.1 —

As a Learner, What is Important to You?

You are currently in a unique position as you are both a learner and a (student) teacher. Consider your own recent learning experiences and how it felt to be in particular people's 'classrooms' (lecture theatres, training rooms, etc.). What did their actions communicate to you about their values and how did they make you feel? What are the implications of that for your own practice?

Characteristics and Values

It is difficult to establish a definitive list of the characteristics and values of great teachers as various research reports have emphasised different elements. This variation will be partly about personal positions, but also about terminology, with different sources using slightly different terms to mean the same thing.

Bennett (2014: 169) suggests there are five 'virtues' of great teachers: justice, courage, patience, wisdom and compassion. Clearly, justice aligns with fairness, which is one of the classroom climate dimensions identified in the Hay McBer (2000) report. If you reflect on

Bennett's (2014) list, it is easy, we hope, to see how these might impact on a teacher's effectiveness in the classroom, while not being explicitly about teaching skills or approaches. For example, as we will explore later in the book, learning is complex and all pupils are individuals, so we need to be patient when children take longer or need more support to grasp something than we had anticipated. Some pupils may be facing significant challenges in their home lives, which may impact on their capacity to learn or on their wellbeing. Of course, we should treat those pupils with compassion, as indeed we should for all of the pupils in our class.

In our own previous publication, *Teaching the primary curriculum* (Forster and Eperjesi, 2020), we identify some key principles for great teachers to draw on: empathy, partnership (with the children), problem-solving, humility and determination. Again, we can see the connections between empathy and compassion. We need to put ourselves in the shoes of the learner and seek to understand their experience and perspective.

Although undertaken in China, Liu and Meng's (2009: 324) research, which sought views from pupils, parents and teachers, identified the notion of 'teacher ethics' as one of the most important qualities of great teachers. The pupils, parents and teachers involved in the study defined teacher ethics as including patience, humour, consideration, respect, dedication, care about students, the fair treatment of students and building good relationships. As noted, this research was conducted in China, but, as part of the study, the authors also made comparisons with studies carried out in other countries, and found significant similarities.

While it might not be possible to provide a definitive list, the discussion above, as well as your own reflections from Critical Task 1.1, should enable you to identify some key characteristics and values that are common to great teachers. Seek to hold on to these characteristics and to ensure that your own actions are consistent with what you believe to be important.

How Teachers Learn

As a student teacher, you will learn in many of the same ways as experienced teachers. If you are thinking that, by the end of your training, you will know all there is to know about teaching, we are sorry to tell you that is not the case. Teachers continue to learn and develop their practice throughout their entire careers. As developments occur in education, schools and teachers will implement new strategies and approaches in order to try to better meet the needs of the children. Every child is an individual and so teachers will need to be prepared to adapt their practice and try different approaches for individual children, to ensure that all children's progress is maximised.

You have probably already considered that some of your learning as a student teacher will be through lectures, seminars and other learning opportunities led by your teacher training provider. Whatever type of teacher training course you are undertaking, there will be some centre-based training to develop your own knowledge, understanding and skills. However, you will also learn a great deal through the time you spend in school as a student teacher, both through assessed placements and through any other time spent in school. Below, we will explore some of the valuable learning opportunities available to you during your time in school.

Observing Great Teachers

The opportunity to observe experienced teachers can be very positive and powerful, in terms of learning about what effective practice 'looks like'. It is highly likely that your teacher training provider will direct you to observe teaching and learning, particularly in the earlier stages of your training. Observation can be a valuable thing to do at all stages of your teaching journey, including as a qualified teacher.

However, to learn the most from observing experienced teachers, it goes beyond simply watching them. First, it helps to have a specific focus when observing. This doesn't mean that you necessarily ignore other significant things that you notice, but by identifying a focus, you can tailor your observations to your own areas for development as a teacher. For example, if you are finding it difficult to manage transitions (e.g., children moving from the carpet to their tables), you can observe how an experienced teacher does that and then try out the same approach in your own practice.

Second, after you have observed a teaching session, you need to undertake an analysis of it. Carefully consider what you have observed and think about why it was effective. What, specifically, did the teacher do or say that led to the desired outcome? Analysing why an approach is effective is not always easy. As Perkins (2017: 3) suggests, 'good teaching is invisible … like a swan who glides beautifully along the river while, unseen to the observer, there is frantic activity going on underneath the surface'. In this book, we help you to identify the important things to look out for when you are observing an experienced teacher.

Asking Great Questions

You can also learn a great deal from experienced teachers through engaging in discussion with them. This might be about something you have observed or about any aspect of your developing practice. Staff working in schools will want to support you along your journey, but we also need to remember that they are busy people, so keeping those discussions as focused as possible will help you to make the best possible use of your time and theirs.

One of the ways that you can do that is by asking great questions and, just as we will advise for asking children questions, planning the questions you want to ask in advance can be very valuable. Questions that enable you to focus on the detail of effective practice will be most useful. For example, rather than asking, 'How do you manage behaviour?', you might ask a more specific question, such as, 'How do you respond when a child is disrupting the learning of others during whole class lesson introductions?'.

In the early stages, though, asking specific and targeted questions can be challenging, as you don't yet know what it is that you don't know, so you don't always know what to ask. Don't worry: in this book, we suggest some valuable questions to ask, so that you can learn as much as possible through your discussions with experienced teachers.

Reflecting on Practice

If you have already started your teacher training course, then it is highly likely that the importance of reflection has already been shared with you. Feedback from experienced teachers will certainly help you to identify your strengths and those areas that need development, as well as how to improve your practice. However, you will also need to reflect on your own practice, in order to maximise your progress and enable you to achieve your ambition of becoming an effective teacher.

McVittie (2012: 15) provides a good definition: 'Reflection requires being honest in your thinking and an ability to question your experiences and perspectives, which can lead to a greater understanding about a situation, alternative approaches and solutions to problems'. So, to reflect on your practice means to try to take a step back and to view it as objectively as possible, thinking about what went well and what did not go quite as well, and, most importantly, *why* that might be the case. The 'why' will help you to identify not only what you might change, but also how you might change it.

All effective teachers reflect on their practice. For more experienced teachers, it is likely that they do most of that mentally. As a student teacher, in order to learn the skills of reflection on practice, it is highly likely that your teacher training provider will ask you to evaluate your teaching and your progress in a written form, so that, by the end of your training, reflection and self-critique are becoming second nature.

How to Use This Book

In this section, we will consider how to use this book so that it has maximum impact on your developing practice as a teacher and so that you can, in turn, have maximum impact on your learners. Chapters 2 to 19 each address a different aspect of professional practice that you will need to learn about, but this particular book takes a different approach from most other texts of its genre to ensure that your learning from others is as effective as possible.

The Initial Teacher Training Core Content Framework

This book is structured in sections that reflect the five core areas of the *Initial Teacher Training Core Content Framework (CCF)* (Department for Education, 2019): behaviour management, pedagogy, curriculum, assessment and professional behaviours. Within the core areas that have multiple sections, such as pedagogy, we have included a chapter to align with each section. We have also added a sixth section on the 'principles of inclusion' (Chapters 17 to 19) because, while the *CCF* states that it 'deliberately does not detail approaches specific to particular additional needs' in order to 'reflect the importance of quality first teaching' (Department for Education, 2019: 6), our experience of working with student teachers over many years has demonstrated that this is an aspect that many student teachers feel less confident about and is a key element of professional learning. Chapter 20 provides a conclusion to the book, including a consideration of how to thrive in the early stages of your career as a primary school teacher.

The *CCF* 'defines in detail the minimum entitlement of all trainee teachers' and 'draws on the best available evidence' (Department for Education, 2019: 3), so your teacher training provider will have developed a carefully sequenced curriculum that encompasses all the content of the *CCF*, as well as including other elements that your provider considers important for you to learn. Each section of the *CCF* is split into two different types of learning. There are 'Learn that…' statements, which are addressed throughout this book and will also be addressed through the taught elements of your initial teacher training (ITT) programme (e.g., lectures and other types of centre-based training). There are also 'Learn how to…' statements, which you will focus on during your school experience placements. There are two different types of 'Learn how to…' statements: learning from others (e.g., observing expert colleagues, discussion with expert colleagues) and 'taking opportunities to practise, receive feedback and improve' (Department for Education, 2019: 9). Each chapter will suggest ways in which you can engage with these elements of your professional learning while on placement.

Features of the Book

Chapters 2 to 19 share some common features that have been carefully designed to support you in 'learning that…' and 'learning how to…', with particular emphasis on how to learn from expert colleagues. Each of these chapters includes:

- **Critical Tasks**: These are 'thinking tasks', which are designed to encourage you to reflect on what you have read. They usually include a question or two for you to mull over and possibly discuss with your peers. In some instances, but not all, the chapter authors have, towards the end of the chapter, summarised some of their own responses to these critical tasks.
- **Case Studies**: These provide examples from practice to help you to contextualise your learning. They may be examples of children's responses or learning, or examples of effective teaching practice. The chapter authors have provided some expert commentary to support you in reflecting on the significance of the case studies.
- **Observation Guides**: As learning from expert colleagues is such an important aspect of your teacher training, each chapter includes a guide of what to look out for when you are observing others, to help you to understand the details of effective practice.
- **Question Guides**: Each chapter also includes a question guide to support you when you are engaged in discussions with expert colleagues, so that you can ask useful questions to extend your learning.

Chapter Summary

In this chapter, we have considered the importance of striving to be a great primary teacher, and not just a satisfactory teacher, by reflecting on the significant impact that great teaching can have on children: it can be life-changing. We have explored some of the characteristics and values that are common to great teachers, and considered how teachers learn and develop their practice. In particular, we have reflected on some of the valuable learning opportunities available to you while in school as part of your training. We have also explained how to use this book to maximise your own learning as you undertake this exciting journey into primary school teaching.

Further Reading

Department for Education (DfE) (2019) *ITT core content framework.* London: DfE.

As this book is aligned with the *ITT core content framework*, it is sensible for you to familiarise yourself with the framework so that you can see the full range of 'Learn that…' and 'Learn how to…' statements and how these are organised within the five core areas. At the back, you can also see the reference lists which were used to compile the framework, which may lead you to further reading of interest.

Glazzard, J. and Stones, S. (2020) *The ITT core content framework: What trainee primary school teachers need to know.* London: Learning Matters.

Having familiarised yourself with the *ITT Core Content Framework* (Department for Education, 2019), you might then find it helpful to engage with Glazzard and Stones' text, which expands on the content contained with the framework, to help you to interpret it.

Walker, R. (2012) *12 characteristics of an effective teacher: Inspirational stories of teachers who inspired others to become teachers.* Morrisville, NC: Lulu Publishing.

In addition to identifying some of the key characteristics of effective teachers, this book is also testament to the life-changing impact that teachers can have on their learners. It includes multiple stories of how teachers were inspired by their own teachers, exemplifying the key characteristics in practice.

References

Bennett, T. (2014) 'Virtues of great teachers: justice, courage, patience, wisdom and compassion', in A. Pollard (ed.), *Readings for reflective teaching in schools.* London: Bloomsbury Academic, pp. 169–172.

Coe, R., Aloisi, C., Higgins, S. and Major, L.E. (2014) *What makes great teaching? Review of the underpinning research.* Available at: www.suttontrust.com/wp-content/uploads/2019/12/What-makes-great-teaching-FINAL-4.11.14-1.pdf (accessed 9 November 2022).

Department for Education (DfE) (2019) *ITT core content framework*. London: DfE.

Forster, C. and Eperjesi, R. (2020) 'Introduction', in C. Forster and R. Eperjesi (eds.), *Teaching the primary curriculum*. London: Sage, pp. 1–9.

Hay McBer (2000) *Research into teacher effectiveness: A model of teacher effectiveness*. London: Hay Group UK.

Liu, S. and Meng, L. (2009) 'Perceptions of teachers, students and parents of the characteristics of good teachers: a cross-cultural comparison of China and the United States', *Educational Assessment, Evaluation and Accountability*, 21, 313–328.

McVittie, E. (2012) 'Children as reflective learners', in A. Hanson (ed.), *Reflective learning and teaching in primary schools*. London: Learning Matters/Sage, pp. 11–31.

Perkins, M. (2017) *Observing primary literacy* (2nd edn). London: Sage.

SECTION I
BEHAVIOUR MANAGEMENT

2
UNDERSTANDING BEHAVIOUR

Sian Templeton

Chapter Objectives

- To explore some of the underpinning influences on the behaviours that you might see in a classroom context.
- To consider the idea of behaviour as a form of communication which is linked to children's life experiences and their underlying needs.
- To reflect on the implications of these ideas for teaching practice.

In this chapter, we explore contextual and individual factors impacting on children's behaviour in the classroom context. We reflect on how these behaviours can be seen as an important form of communication that reveals information about the various contexts and other influences on a child's development, which in turn influences how they behave in the classroom. We use the bio-ecological model developed by Urie Bronfenbrenner (2005) to help understand the range of possible influences, then explore an education-specific framework to help make sense of these influences within a school setting. Additional support and ideas will be discussed to help with guided observations of children's behaviour while on placement.

Keep in mind as you read this chapter: What is the one thing that I might do differently as a teacher as a result of reading this chapter?

Why is Understanding Behaviour Important?

Teachers come across a range of behaviours in their day-to-day role. Some of the behaviours encountered will be both personally and professionally challenging, with Hibbin and Warin

(2020) suggesting that the challenge is not only experienced by teachers, but by the children demonstrating the behaviours themselves. Understanding that not all behaviour is consciously under the control of any individual child is important in promoting inclusive practice and enabling teachers to make a positive difference to children's lives.

Standard 7 within the *ITT Core Content Framework* (*CCF*) (Department for Education (DfE), 2019) is focused on the effective management of behaviour. However, in order to manage behaviour, we must first understand the underpinning factors which may lead to unwanted behaviours (Ofsted, 2021). A rationale for this more holistic understanding is linked to enabling teachers to have a life-long impact on outcomes for children. Research illustrates the array of poorer outcomes for children who demonstrate difficult behaviours, including poor attainment (Dunlap et al., 2006), mental health difficulties (Powell et al., 2011) and leaving school early, all of which limit a child's opportunity to achieve their potential (Powell et al., 2011).

According to Krause et al. (2020), teachers are coming across a wider range of challenging behaviours than previously experienced in their day-to-day practice, and these behaviours have increased in both severity and frequency. They go on to provide examples of behaviours that teachers might encounter, ranging from low-level behaviours (such as calling out in class time) to physical aggression towards teachers and other students. Evidence shows us that even the low-level behaviours can lead to teacher stress, which Powell et al. (2011) argue then impacts on a teacher's ability to teach. However, the behaviours that we can directly observe are typically underpinned by a variety of different influences and are often indicators of unmet needs. Reyneke (2020) identifies a range of such influences, including, but not limited to, poverty, emotionally distant parents, peer influence and experience of punishment as the primary approach to discipline. In addition to these influences, which might be considered as external to the child, there are also factors linked to the child and their sense of self. Research such as that by Zimmermann et al. (2013) makes the link between a child's self-esteem and their likelihood in engaging in challenging behaviour, while Krause et al. (2020) explain that children who are demonstrating poorly managed behaviour in schools are more likely to experience elevated social and emotional difficulties.

There is evidence that there is a cyclical process, with poor teacher–pupil relationships increasing the likelihood of children engaging in unwanted behaviours in the classroom and children's challenging behaviour damaging teacher–pupil relationships (Reyneke, 2020). The importance of positive relationships is also emphasised by Morris et al. (2013), who established that children who engage in challenging behaviour are more likely to experience success in emotionally warm classroom environments. Using neuroscientific research as an evidence-base, Garvey (2017) also concurs about the importance of positive relationships and how this is a key factor leading to quality outcomes for children. Ideas around brain development and how an understanding of the brain can help with understanding behaviour are discussed later in this chapter, but the importance of relational approaches to helping children manage heightened emotions is widely acknowledged by theorists and practitioners alike.

To support our understanding of potential influences on behaviour that may not be immediately observable, the iceberg metaphor (initially introduced by Eric Schopler in 1994 in an attempt to understand the behaviours of individuals on the autistic spectrum) can be helpful. This metaphor helps to illustrate that we only see the surface behaviour, but there may be several underpinning features which lie beneath the surface, as illustrated in Figure 2.1.

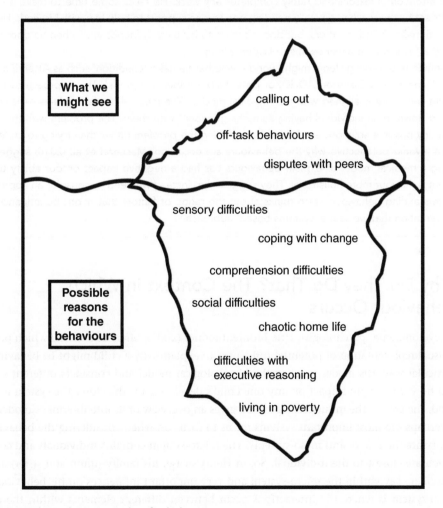

Figure 2.1   The iceberg metaphor for behaviour

Case Study 2.1

The Medical Model: Henry (Part 1)

Henry has recently joined the school in Year 4. He is already well known by all the teachers, and not because of his shining example as a model of good behaviour! He lives with his mum, Ms Sharpe, and younger sister, Rose, who also attends the school and is in Year 2. Rose is a quiet child and largely goes unnoticed around the school. Henry, however, appears to be on the move for most of the time and is known to often interrupt teachers. He struggles to concentrate and pay attention in lessons and rarely completes any work. He takes some time to make a start on tasks set by the teacher, typically needing one-to-one support to help him with his work. He is not intentionally unkind to others, but doesn't seem to have many friends and, when he does start to build a friendship, it never seems to last very long.

Someone observing Henry might wonder whether he has a 'condition' such as Attention Deficit and Hyperactivity Disorder (ADHD) or potentially another 'diagnosis'. This approach to thinking about behaviour is aligned with the 'medical model'. The medical model explains behaviours as being down to an individual having something 'wrong' with them. The problem with this view is that any possible solutions are focused on *treating* the *problem* rather than trying to understand from a wider perspective *why* the behaviours are occurring. MacLeod et al. (2010) suggest that using a medical model to explain behaviours has had a negative impact on our ability to think about behaviour more holistically. They suggest that instead we need to consider an approach to understanding behaviour which thinks about the range of factors that might be influencing the presentation that we see: a 'systems-based' approach.

Why Do They Do That? The Context in Which Behaviour Occurs

A developmental psychologist, Urie Bronfenbrenner (2005), offers us a model which provides a visual representation of potential influences to explain why a child might be behaving in a particular way. His model is called the bio-ecological model and considers different systems and how they might impact on any one child's development; the closer the system is to the child, the greater the influence. Figure 2.2 gives an overview of Bronfenbrenner's model.

Perhaps the most important systems for us to focus on when considering the behaviour of Henry are the micro- and meso-systems. The micro-system contains individuals and contexts which are closest to the individual. So, in Henry's case, his family (mum and sister) and his school are key within the micro-system and very important influences on his behaviour. The meso-system is where the interactions occur between different elements within the micro-system. So, how the school and his family interact will impact on his development, depending on the nature of that interaction. If there is a positive relationship between home and school,

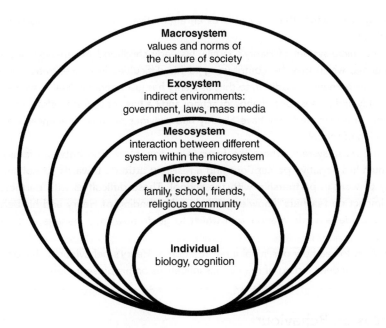

Figure 2.2 Bronfenbrenner's bio-ecological model

with clear lines of communication and a mutual respect, then outcomes are typically optimised. However, if there is resistance and a more acrimonious relationship, then this can have more of a detrimental impact on Henry and the behaviours that are seen in school.

Case Study 2.2

Bronfenbrenner's Model: Henry (Part 2)

Henry's teacher, Connor, calls a meeting with his mum and invites you along so that you can engage in learning from expert input. Henry's mum (Ms Sharpe) arrives late and flustered and is clearly intimidated by coming into school. Initially Ms Sharpe reacts quite abruptly when Connor is outlining the school's concerns about Henry's behaviour. However, after Connor has reassured her, Ms Sharpe starts to calm down and begins to open up a bit about Henry's history. Henry's mum explains that Henry's father was violent to both her and Henry, and that she ended up taking Henry and his sister into a woman's refuge to keep them all safe. She also admits that she struggled at school and feels anxious about coming into school.

Moving away from the 'medical model', we can use Bronfenbrenner's model to help our understanding of possible reasons for Henry's behaviour. We can focus on the micro-system

Continued

and meso-system factors that may give us an alternative explanation for his behaviour in and around school.

Within the *micro-system* of Henry's family, his early childhood experiences are likely to have caused trauma, which may be contributing to his difficulties in concentration when in a busy classroom environment. In addition to this, as Henry has just arrived in Year 4, we can assume that he has already had at least one change of school and he has yet to form helpful relationships with either peers or adults, and may have already had previous negative influences which impact on his perception of school.

Within the *meso-system*, where the focus is on the interaction between family and school, Henry's mum has negative perceptions and a resistant attitude towards school and is therefore less likely to work in partnership with the school. These difficulties with partnership working will also impact on teachers' knowledge and understanding of Henry and his behaviours, and therefore provide less information with which to guide how they manage and respond to his behaviour.

We can start to see how our initial interpretation of Henry's behaviour is changing because of our deepening understanding of the various influences on his presentation.

Influences on Behaviour

Powell et al. (2011) have identified a range of other systemic influences which may impact on the behaviours that we see in the classroom:

- **Individual processes**: These are 'within-child' factors. Examples include their approach to learning, their ability to 'hold on to information' in the short term, how they think and feel about themselves and others, or social skill development and problem-solving skills.
- **Family**: Within-family factors can cover a range of issues, such as poverty, parental difficulties (mental ill-health, involvement in the criminal justice system), punitive approaches to discipline, poor boundaries, emotionally distant parents and chaotic home environments.
- **Peers**: The nature of the peer groups with which a child interacts can impact on behaviours, such as whether they are accepted or rejected and/or attracted to more deviant peer groups.
- **Local community and school**: These factors relate to whether the child has had exposure to anti-social behaviours, an authoritarian approach to discipline by teaching staff, or emotionally distant teachers.

In recognition of the range of influences identified by Powell et al. (2011), both within the child and external to the child, Frederickson and Cline (2015) have developed and refined the Interactive Factors Framework (IFF) (Table 2.1). The IFF is designed to help teachers and other professionals working in and with schools to develop a more holistic understanding of children and the variety of factors which might influence how they are behaving in school. Chapter 18 will include further discussion about this model to support an understanding of children who have special educational needs and disabilities (SEND).

Table 2.1 Interactive Factors Framework, adapted from Frederickson and Cline (2015)

Environmental factors	Within-child factors	
Family, school, community factors (financial stressors, housing, the learning environment, Adverse Childhood Experiences (ACEs), child in care, English as an additional language, peer group dynamics, outside agency involvement)	**Biological factors** (medical conditions, general health, developmental history, diet, sensory needs)	
	Cognitive factors (memory, attention, verbal ability, language and communication skills, academic attainment)	**Affective factors** (self-esteem, confidence, motivation, self-regulation)
	Behavioural factors (care for others, risk-taking behaviours, bullying, absenteeism, ability to develop and maintain friendships, social interactions with adults, attitudes towards others, self-harm)	

Critical Task 2.1

The Interactive Factors Framework (IFF)

With the agreement and support of your teacher mentor, choose a child from your class for whom you feel it would be useful to develop a more holistic understanding of their behaviour. Using Table 2.1, have a go at plotting the different factors which contribute to your understanding of this child.

You will probably find that you can add new information to the IFF as you learn more about your focus child. As you complete the framework over time, see if you can generate some ideas as to why the child may be behaving in that way, and whether or not, as a result of this understanding, you can change how you respond to the behaviours observed. It is worth seeking information from a variety of sources (e.g., from parent/carers, other teachers, your own observations). To support the elicitation of information from parents, it is helpful to take the opportunity to learn from expert colleagues within your school.

Observation Guide 2.1

Communication with Parents

The *CCF* states that student teachers should 'learn how to … build effective working relationships by … observing how expert colleagues communicate with parents and carers proactively' (DfE, 2019: 29–30).

To help develop a more holistic understanding of the unique contexts of the children in your class, the child's parent/carer can provide some really useful information as experts in their own children.

Continued

- Observe how the teacher communicates with a child's parent/carer, particularly when there has been a difficulty during the school day. Note the style and types of questions that the teacher asks in order to elicit the parent/carer perspective.
- Note how the parent/carer responds and how the teacher adapts their style of communication to maintain the relationship and 'hear' the parental voice.

Why Do They Do That? Individual Factors (or Not?)

So far, we have identified the importance of developing a holistic understanding of the behaviours that we observe in children. However, as indicated in both Bronfenbrenner's bio-ecological model and the IFF, there may be some internal factors to the child that are also influencing their behaviour, which we will consider in this section.

The Brain's Response

Neuroscience is increasingly offering a contribution to teacher understanding of how aspects of brain development might contribute to the behaviour of children in their classrooms. However, neuroscience uses a complex conceptual vocabulary that is not always accessible, which can lead to misrepresentation of neuroscientific principles in practice. To help combat this, Garvey (2017) suggests that our focus should be on the neurological processes that underpin cognition (i.e., the processes involved in knowledge acquisition, such as thinking and making sense of experiences). He provides guidance on brain development to show the relevance of neuroscience to education (Table 2.2).

The brain develops in a neuro-sequential manner, which means that our brain stem develops first, followed by our limbic brain, and finally our neocortex, broadly finishing its formation at around 25 years old. However, even when our brains are moving towards the development of all three brain regions, there are still times when situations and events can interfere with a fully functioning neocortex. Siegel and Bryson (2012) explain that, at times of threat, when a child might experience a challenging situation, the reptilian brain drives the child's fight/flight/freeze response: the child might become angry and aggressive or run away or draw into themselves. At this point, they are very unlikely to be fully processing what is happening around them (the neocortex is not working well) and, after the event, their recall of the event may well be rather vague, as the limbic brain is also not functioning well, with a subsequent impact on their memory.

Table 2.2 Brain development, adapted from the work of Garvey (2017)

Brain region	Responsible for...	Associated reasons for behaviours
The brainstem/ reptilian brain	Our bodily functions and our immediate response to our environment This involves the fight/flight/freeze reflex; the reflex is linked to our instinctive physiological response as to whether or not we can beat/ outmanoeuvre the perceived threat	Tiredness, hunger, too cold/ too hot, fear
The limbic/ mammalian brain	Our emotions, memories and sense of self are driven by this part of the brain	Insecurity in relationships and trust in others Difficulties with understanding and interpreting the emotions of others Difficulties with self-regulation of emotions
The neocortex	Our ability to think and engage in rational problem-solving Our ability to sustain attention Our ability to be creative and use our imagination	When this area of the brain is in control we are more likely to be able to rationalise and make decisions about our behaviour

— Critical Task 2.2 —

Reflect On Your Own Experiences

Think about when you first started on your teacher training course.

How did you feel on your first day going to your first lecture?

How much of the information from the first 10 minutes of the lecture did you actually take in/remember?

Most people will have said that they were feeling anxious, nervous and/or excited and that they were very conscious of other people staring at them. Hopefully some of you will have had the experience of a lecturer smiling at you and helping you to feel welcome. You will probably have then looked for a friendly face in the crowd and either sat next to or near them. My guess is that you will not have been able to process the information from those first 10 minutes because you were trying to fit in socially and get your bearings. This is your mammalian brain supporting you, making sure that you feel safe and secure before you can attend to learning.

Now imagine if you were in a similar situation but your experiences of life so far had not been that people could be relied on to make you feel welcome and you could not trust that others would help you to feel safe and secure. How might that have changed your response?

It is easy to make the assumption that school is a safe space for children because, as adults, we know and trust that teachers want to have a positive impact on the children in their class and in fact have a duty to keep the children safe. However, the past experiences of children may have challenged this perspective and, instead of being a place of safety, school and the adults within it are a source of threat. The possible reasons for this perception are discussed below.

Attention Seeking Or Attention Needing?

You have probably heard different adults explaining children's behaviour as 'attention-seeking' behaviours, and consequently offering advice about ignoring the behaviour in an attempt to gradually make the behaviour disappear. There are times when this might be the case, but with our 'understanding behaviour' hat on, then we might also want to consider other explanations for why we are seeing the behaviour. One of these reasons could instead be linked to an unmet *need* for attention. Smith (2018) drew on evidence from a range of academic and professional fields to explore factors which might contribute to unmet emotional needs, specifically linked to Adverse Childhood Experiences (ACEs).

Adverse Childhood Experiences

Adverse Childhood Experiences (ACEs) can be cumulative in their nature and fall within the broad categories of abuse (physical, sexual, emotional), neglect (physical, emotional, the absence of close relationships) and challenges linked to the home environment (familial violence, substance misuse, mental illness, parental separation or divorce, involvement with the criminal justice system) (Smith, 2018). There is a strong evidence base for the link between ACEs and longer-term negative outcomes for children, alongside increased rates of behaviour difficulties. This is explained by Reyneke (2020: 145) in his statement that 'when these children experience emotional pain, they tend to react with troubling behaviour and self-destructive acts'. Thinking about the iceberg metaphor introduced at the beginning of this chapter, the reason for the behaviour is due to their core needs of safety and security (knowing and trusting that adults can keep them safe and meet their basic needs) not being met.

Behaviour as a Form of Communication

As a teacher, you will come across a range of behaviours displayed by children in your classroom. Some of these behaviours may be helpful, such as following your instructions straight away or working constructively on a group activity. Others may be less helpful, such as ignoring your instructions or walking away from you when you are talking. Regardless of how positive or negative the behaviour is, as Hibbin and Warin (2020) argue, all behaviour is a form of communication and therefore needs to be understood before any adjustments are made. MacLeod et al. (2010) also emphasise the importance of understanding that some of the behaviours that we see in school may be linked to a child needing to functionally adapt to their environment and are therefore a coping strategy. An interesting illustration of the need of children, even as young as 18 months, to feel engaged with adults is demonstrated by the 'Still Face Experiment', which was initially conducted in 1975 by Edward Tronick and colleagues. In this experiment, the child's mother keeps a blank face for three minutes while the child is trying very hard to interact and gain the attention of their mother. As the time goes on, the child becomes increasingly withdrawn and distressed, pushing against their highchair and crying. The need for human interaction runs deeply in most children, even if they are not skilled at generating positive interactions.

Keeping Notes About a Child's Behaviour

Observing children carefully and keeping records over time can help you to establish the *function* of their behaviour, to consider why are they behaving in that way, what purpose is it serving for them and what they are trying to communicate through their behaviour. One way of doing this is through using the ABCC model:

- **Antecedents**: The context in which the behaviour occurs and what happened just before you saw the behaviour. You might consider who was near the child, what the learning task was, what the classroom environment was like (noisy, quiet, structured, unstructured, etc.).
- **Behaviour**: Clearly describe the behaviour in observable terms so that someone who wasn't there can picture it in their mind (avoid generic terms such as 'attention seeking' or 'aggressive').
- **Consequences**: What happened immediately after the behaviour? What did the teacher say/do? What did their peers say/do? What did the child do?
- **Communication**: What do you think was the message that the child was trying to convey through their behaviour?

When you have an understanding of the function of the behaviour, you can begin to consider where you might intervene to help with managing behaviour and this will be considered further in Chapters 3 and 4.

What Has Learning Got To Do With Behaviour?

Reflecting back to the Interactive Factors Framework, cognitive factors were highlighted as an important 'within-child' area that might influence how a child behaves and responds in your classroom. The link between behaviour in the classroom and academic attainment is widely recognised in research, and Zimmermann et al. (2013) argue that it is a cyclical relationship with both factors influencing each other. This link does not always relate to particular learning difficulties either. For example, in their work looking into the different causes of challenging behaviour in the classroom, MacLeod et al. (2010) found that these behaviours also arose from the work being too easy or not particularly interesting for the children.

Learning Differences

A more detailed exploration of children with special educational needs and disability (SEND) can be found in Chapter 18, but you will find in your teaching practice that a child's individual needs may not always have been formally identified, so a broad understanding of more general learning differences can be helpful. Many of you will have heard of dyslexia, for example, and indeed, some of you may well have been identified as having dyslexia yourself. Evidence shows us how dyslexic learners can be good at discussion-based activities, but as soon as they are faced with a pen-and-paper task their behaviour can change. The reason for this change in behaviour is often linked to their growing awareness of their difficulties in getting their ideas down onto paper. This then has a negative impact on their self-esteem and sometimes it is easier for them to disrupt in an attempt to avoid written tasks.

You are also likely to come across pupils with different neurodevelopmental conditions (such as autism, ADHD or dyspraxia) where they may struggle with understanding classroom expectations for a variety of reasons, which may make them anxious, thus impacting on their behaviour. It is also important to be aware that not all children will have a formal diagnosis such as those described above, but they still may experience similar difficulties. If we can begin to understand what it is that is causing their difficulties (not to diagnose, but to support), then we can take action to help them feel safe and secure and thus reduce the potential triggers for their behaviours.

Question Guide 2.1

Developing Safe and Secure Environments

The *CCF* states that 'a predictable and secure environment benefits all pupils, but is particularly valuable for pupils with special educational needs' (DfE, 2019: 26).

When you reflect on effective practice as part of your placement, you can use these questions as a basis for discussion with your teacher-mentor to explore how they keep the classroom environment predictable and secure. You can also find out why this is helpful for *all* pupils, but particularly those with special educational needs.

- How do you communicate your different expectations of the pupils without making them feel like they might not be as clever as some of the other pupils in the class?
- How do you share your attention and time with all pupils, including those with additional learning needs?
- How do you communicate to the pupils that you care about them?

Executive Functioning

A number of pupils with learning differences such as ADHD, autism and dyslexia also struggle with their 'executive functioning skills'. Executive functioning is about our ability to plan, organise and implement our response to various tasks and activities. It also includes our ability to self-regulate (i.e., manage our emotional responses) in order to be able to respond. Think about a time when you had more than one assignment due in and possibly also had a deadline in your personal life (a work or family event that you were involved in organising). At times like these, we use our executive functioning skills to help with prioritising and working out a plan of action so that we can complete everything in time. You may have experienced a bit of stress or anxiety about managing to get it all done, but you (hopefully) managed to calm yourself down so that you could start on your first priority. Some children can experience difficulties with executive functioning.

Case Study 2.3

Executive Functioning in the Classroom

In this example, Matt, an undergraduate student teacher, has asked his Year 5 class to write an account of what they did over the school holidays. Matt thought that starting with the children's experiences was a great way to encourage them to write and told them to turn to the next page in their books and just start writing. To Matt's surprise, within minutes of starting the task, Belle has thrown her pen across the classroom and is sitting with her head on her desk.

For the children in your classroom who experience difficulties with their executive functioning, just producing a piece of written work can present a range of challenges. They have to think about what they want to write, sequence it logically, think about the words and how to spell them, remember what it was that they wanted to write and then actually write it down, legibly and with accurate punctuation. They need to be able to do all of that while also regulating any emotional response to the task that they might be experiencing. Belle may not have enjoyed the school holidays and may even have experienced a traumatic event during this period. Understanding this helps us to realise *why* some children who have executive functioning difficulties might behave in a less helpful way when faced with a written task.

Chapter Summary

In this chapter, we considered some of the reasons why children may behave in different ways. We established that some of these reasons may be linked to their home background or learning differences, and that their brain may just be 'taking over' to protect themselves. We explored some ways of trying to work out why they are behaving in a particular way so that we can help them by understanding the root of the problem and therefore responding to their underlying needs, which are causing the behaviour in the first place.

You were asked at the beginning of the chapter to consider the one thing that you might do differently as a result of your reading: what would your answer be?

Further Reading

Bombèr, L. (2020) *Know me to teach me: Differentiated discipline for those recovering from Adverse Childhood Experiences.* Belper, UK: Worth Publishing.

This text helps to explain the importance of understanding the context in which children's behaviour has developed, and the importance of developing positive relationships which help to create an emotionally safe environment and thus reduce behavioural challenges in the classroom.

Faith, L., Bush, C.-A. and Dawson, P. (2022) *Executive functioning skills in the classroom: Overcoming barriers, building strategies.* London and New York: Guilford Press.

This book provides an accessible overview of the nature of executive functioning skills, alongside some practical strategies for supporting executive functioning within the classroom context. An inclusive approach is advocated, whereby the approaches are included in our day-to-day teaching practice, rather than through specific interventions.

Siegel, D. and Bryson, T. (2012) *The whole-brain child.* New York: Random House.

This book explains in a helpful and accessible manner the brain activity which underpins the different behaviours that we see in children. It provides some useful tips on the slight adjustments we can make in the language we use when working with children to respond to their current situation. Siegel has also produced a number of videos using a hand model to explain the structure and functioning of the brain in an accessible way. They can be easily found by searching on YouTube.

References

Bronfenbrenner, U. (2005) *Making human beings human: Bioecological perspectives on human development.* Thousand Oaks, CA: Sage.

Department for Education (DfE) (2019) *ITT core content framework.* London: DfE.

Dunlap, G., Strain, P.S., Fox, L., Carta, J.J., Conroy, M., Smith, B.J., Kern, L., Hemmeter, M.L., Timm, M.A., McCart, A. and Sailor, W. (2006) 'Prevention and intervention with young children's challenging behaviour: perspectives regarding current knowledge', *Behavioral Disorders*, 32(1), 29–45.

Frederickson, N. and Cline, T. (2015) *Special educational needs, inclusion and diversity: A textbook* (2nd edn). Buckingham and Philadelphia, PA: Open University Press.

Garvey, D. (2017) *Nurturing personal, social and emotional development in early childhood: A practical guide to understanding brain development and young children's behaviour.* London: Jessica Kingsley.

Hibbin, R. and Warin, J. (2020) 'A language focused approach to supporting children with social, emotional and behavioural difficulties (SEBD)', *Education 3–13*, 48(3), 316–331.

Krause, A., Goldberg, B., D'Agostino, B., Klan, A., Rogers, M., Smith, J.D., Whitley, J., Hone, M. and McBrearty, N. (2020) 'The association between problematic school behaviours and social and emotional development in children seeking mental health treatment', *Emotional and Behavioural Difficulties*, 25(3–4), 278–290.

MacLeod, G., MacAllister, J. and Pirrie, A. (2010) 'Emotional education as second language acquisition?', *International Journal of Emotional Education*, 2(1), 33–48.

Morris, P., Millenky, M., Raver, C.C. and Jones, S.M. (2013) 'Does a preschool social and emotional learning intervention pay off for classroom instruction and children's behavior and academic skills? Evidence from the foundations of learning project', *Early Education and Development*, 24(7), 1020–1042.

Ofsted (2021) *Guidance: Positive environments in which children can flourish.* London: Ofsted. Available at: www.gov.uk/government/publications/positive-environments-where-children-can-flourish/positive-environments-where-children-can-flourish (accessed 19 July 2022).

Powell, N.P., Boxmeyer, C.L., Baden, R., Stromeyer, S., Minney, J.A., Mushtaq, A. and Lochman, J.E. (2011) 'Assessing and treating aggression and conduct problems in schools: implications from the Coping Power program', *Psychology in the Schools*, 48(3), 233–242.

Reyneke, R. (2020) 'Increasing resilience, lowering risk: teachers' use of the Circle of Courage in the classroom', *Perspectives in Education*, 38(1), 144–162.

Schopler, E. (1994) 'Behavioral priorities for autism and related developmental disorders', in E. Schopler and G.B. Mesibov (eds.), *Behavioral issues in autism*. New York: Plenum Press, pp. 55–75.

Siegel, D. and Bryson, T. (2012) *The whole-brain child.* New York: Random House.

Smith, L. (2018) *ESSS outline Adverse Childhood Experiences (ACEs): Interventions in education.* Available at: www.iriss.org.uk/sites/default/files/2018-04/iriss-esss-outline-adverse-childhood-experiences-2018-4-23.pdf (accessed 20 July 2022).

Tronick, E., Adamson, L.B., Als, H. and Brazelton, T.B. (1975) 'Infant emotions in normal and perturbated interactions', *Biennial meeting of the Society for Research in Child Development.* Denver, CO.

Zimmermann, F., Schütte, K., Taskinen, P. and Köller, O. (2013) 'Reciprocal effects between adolescent externalizing problems and measures of achievement', *Journal of Educational Psychology*, 105(3), 747–761.

3
MANAGING BEHAVIOUR

Colin Forster

Chapter Objectives

- To consider the importance of a values-based approach to behaviour management.
- To explore the principles of effective classroom management.
- To consider the interconnected nature of behaviour management with all other aspects of good teaching.

In this chapter, we address an issue that worries many student teachers: how they will manage children's behaviour. Teaching is often stressful and one of the main stressors for many teachers is an anxiety about how to 'control' children's behaviour. The good news is that learning to manage children's behaviour is not a mystery art but a set of skills and ways of working that can be developed and improved with practice. In this chapter, we consider the key ideas that will support student teachers to develop effective approaches to managing children's behaviour and, in Chapter 4, we take this a stage further and consider how we can help children to learn to manage their own behaviour.

Managing Behaviour … But Whose Behaviour?

Bennett (2020: 29) states: 'Better behaviour improves every aim of school we can imagine'. He argues that, whatever you see as being the main purpose of education, this ambition will be achieved more effectively if children behave well in school. This is hard to argue with: if we want children to be successful in their learning in mathematics and English, it helps if they can learn in a calm and focused environment; if we want children to learn how to listen to and respect others, this is easier to achieve when the classroom reflects these values.

It is easy to see, therefore, why aiming for good behaviour from children is a laudable goal. However, there is an important (and in some ways challenging) principle that we have to accept: *it is impossible to control children's behaviour*. This may not seem like an encouraging statement to read so early in a chapter about behaviour management, but, unless we plan to rule by extreme fear, it is a principle that we need to accept. The good news is that there is one person in the classroom whose behaviour you can control: YOU! As O'Brien (2021: 53) notes: 'We need to critically examine our own conduct in our classrooms … as it is the vital ingredient in improving behaviour'.

Critical Task 3.1

Values

Have a look at the list of core values in Table 3.1 and identify how these values might impact on the ways in which you might manage children's behaviour. We've suggested four core values and you may like to add one or two more.

Table 3.1   Core values

My core values	How these might impact on my approach to managing children's behaviour
Equality	
Dignity	
Consistency	
Respect	

Manage Your Own Behaviour

It turns out that the key to learning to manage children's behaviour is learning to manage your own behaviour as a teacher. This relates to a whole range of your ways of behaving, ways of being and ways of thinking, and even small changes in your approach can make a big difference in how the children respond. Changing the ways in which we do things takes some effort, but every improvement takes us another step towards being a highly effective teacher.

One good example of how to manage yourself as a teacher is to think about the order in which words emerge from your mouth. In terms of how children respond, there is a huge difference between saying to a class, 'Are you ready?' and 'Show me you are ready': one invites children to call out to answer the question and the other does not. Similarly, in terms of how the children respond, there is a world of difference between saying, 'What's the capital city of Wales? Put your hand up!' and 'Put your hand up if you can tell me the capital city of Wales': one reacts to children calling out and the other pre-empts calling out.

Another example of controlling our own behaviour is ensuring that we always appear to be calm on the outside, regardless of how we feel on the inside. Teaching can be stressful at times and it can be easy for this stress to 'leak out'. One of the first ways that this can happen is through our voices, which can become louder and higher-pitched as we become more stressed or try to make ourselves heard over the noise of the classroom. At times like this, take a deep breath, keep your voice low-pitched and quiet. This is important because significant mirroring occurs between children and their teachers: the louder we are, the louder the children get; the calmer we are, the calmer the children become.

Some student teachers start their journey towards Qualified Teacher Status (QTS) with the idea that they should always be on the lookout for children misbehaving, so that they can 'tell the children off', and they gradually learn that it is much better to turn this on its head, and start looking for opportunities to 'catch children being good'. This is an important change in the way that we think as teachers, as it impacts on our approach to managing behaviour and on our relationships with children, which, in turn, leads to more positive behaviour.

Formation of positive habits as a teacher will increase the positive responses from children: welcoming the children into the classroom, smiling and having an individual chat with each child will all contribute to a positive classroom environment and better behaviour. A positive, proactive approach at the start of every day (and the start of every lesson) will make a huge difference to how the children respond to you and how they relate to each other.

Stay True to Your Values

Most student teachers choose to come into teaching because they hold certain values and are determined to have a positive impact on the world. As we identified in Critical Task 3.1, it can be helpful to think carefully about your values and what these might 'look like' in practice, and you should remain alert to any mismatch arising between your espoused values and how you are conducting yourself in relation to managing children's behaviour. For example, if you believe that all children should be treated equally and yet find yourself speaking quite differently to some individuals or groups of children, it is time to step back and remind yourself that you are able to make choices about your own conduct. Similarly, if you believe that children should be treated with dignity and respect and yet you find yourself speaking to children in an angry voice, it is time to take a deep breath and ask yourself what needs to change. As Dix (2017: 19) says, 'A simple shout to castigate a child emerges from a base instinct that is never the intelligent response to poor behaviour'.

In this section, we have established a key principle: the teacher is only able to control their own behaviour. This has profound implications for the way that we think about every aspect of our practice as we refine the skills required to manage behaviour both positively and effectively. In the next section, we'll explore this further through identifying some of the key building blocks of effective behaviour management.

The Big Ideas of Managing Behaviour

There are no 'off-the-peg' solutions to managing children's behaviour in school, because every child is different, every class is different, every day and even every lesson are different. While it is impossible to provide a guide for what to do in every possible situation, there are some general principles that underpin effective approaches to behaviour management that can be adapted to respond to changing circumstances.

Have High, Explicit Expectations

Good teachers have a clear idea about what kinds of behaviour they are hoping to see in their classrooms. They also have a clear notion of the line between what is acceptable and what is not.

— Critical Task 3.2 —

High Expectations

Imagine you are about to start teaching a lesson. Think of three or four things that you would like the children to be doing before you begin teaching. How might you communicate your expectations to children?

Great teachers communicate their high expectations to the children with reliable clarity: they get the expectations out of their own heads and into the children's heads. There are many good ways of doing this, from modelling expected behaviours to using effective phrases, such as 'Let me see who is...'.

The important thing is to hold high expectations of children, make these expectations explicit to them and ensure a good degree of consistency around these expectations, so that the children can be confident that what was acceptable yesterday is acceptable today and what was unacceptable yesterday is unacceptable today.

— Observation Guide 3.1 —

Communicating High Expectations

When observing how children's behaviour is managed in a school, there are important things to notice, related to the way in which teachers make their expectations explicit and how they support children to live up to these high ideals:

- Focus closely on how the teacher communicates their expectations to the children. Note the exact phrases the teacher uses to make expectations explicit.
- Note how expectations are followed up with praise or reprimand. Note the exact phrases the teacher uses.

The 'Magic Ratio' of Praise and Correction

The 'magic ratio' refers to the relationship between the number of positive and negative comments made by the teacher, and the resulting or likely impact on children's behaviour. A teacher who utters more negative than positive comments is likely to create a negative learning environment, in which children do not feel valued by the teacher and, as a result, behave poorly. However, a teacher who is largely more positive than negative is likely to create a positive environment, in which the children respond well to a teacher who they feel is 'on their side'. The magic ratio has sometimes been thought of as something in the region of 3:1 or 4:1 (i.e., three or four praise statements for every corrective statement). In reality, there is no 'magic ratio'. Caldarella et al. (2020: 3) explored the impact of what they call the 'praise-to-reprimand ratio' (PRR), and found that:

> Though no PRR threshold (e.g., 3:1, 4:1) was found where behaviour dramatically improved, a positive linear relationship was evident, showing that the higher the teachers' PRR, the higher the students' on-task behaviour percentage.

There are some important implications here: teachers who create classroom cultures based on positivity rather than negativity are more successful in maintaining a calm working environment in which good behaviour is promoted. This is not based on the use of the 'magic ratio' as a mathematical 'formula', but as a reflection of the positive relationship between the teacher and the children. If you like the children and let the children know that you enjoy working with them, they are more likely to respond positively to you. If you constantly nag children and are grumpy with them, don't be surprised if they do not fully get on board with you.

One important point to remember about the 'magic ratio' is that there is no suggestion that children should never be corrected or reprimanded: the '1' in the 3:1 or 4:1 ratio reminds us that it is fine to be clear with children if their behaviour is not acceptable.

— Critical Task 3.3 —

Choosing How to Respond to Low-level Disruption

Imagine you are teaching an excellent lesson when Alex interrupts your flow by absent-mindedly tapping their pen on the table. You have a choice of how to respond:

- Stop teaching and tell Alex to stop tapping their pen. Flare your nostrils and glare slightly if you like.
- Briefly identify and name a few children (preferably including one who is sitting very near Alex) who are listening well or keeping their hands still and then continue teaching.

What are the relative benefits and disbenefits of each option?

Active Ignoring of Low-level Disruption

One of the reasons why the magic ratio is effective is because the teacher is emphasising the kinds of behaviours that they want to see rather than emphasising or drawing attention to inappropriate behaviour. To take this a stage further, many expert teachers aim to actively ignore some low-level inappropriate behaviours. This seems counter-intuitive to begin with, but is fully consistent with a teacher recognising that they can only control their own behaviour, and must therefore make choices about how they do so. It is easy to spot children doing the wrong thing and reprimand them; the harder, and smarter, thing is to manage behaviour without being drawn into a negative approach.

— Response to Critical Task 3.3 —

Choosing How to Respond to Low-level Disruption

We asked you to consider the benefits and disbenefits of two ways of responding to Alex, who has interrupted your excellent teaching by absent-mindedly tapping their pen on the table.

- If you stop what you were saying to tell Alex to stop tapping their pen, you have interrupted your teaching and Alex has learnt a valuable lesson: in order to get this teacher's attention, I just have to do something a bit irritating. Worse still, Alex is not the only child in the class to learn this. The other 29 children have also learnt the same lesson. Pretty soon, you could enter a downward spiral of nagging children for relatively minor disruptions.
- If you briefly identify a few children who are listening well or keeping their hands still, Alex will almost certainly refocus and you can quickly continue teaching. You have avoided the downward spiral and maintained the sense of positivity in your relationship with the class.

Just to be clear, you should not ignore *all* inappropriate behaviour: some issues need addressing immediately and decisively. The important thing is to be in control of yourself and your own behaviour and responses ... and avoid being manipulated by the children. Actively ignoring low-level disruption that is designed to seek your attention, make you cross or interrupt the learning of other children is not easy and requires practice, but it enables you to stay in control and behave in ways that are aligned with your positive values and beliefs about teaching and learning.

Calm Use of Voice

One of the elements of managing your own behaviour that takes quite a bit of practice is learning to manage your voice. As identified earlier in the chapter, it is important to keep your voice calm at all times, regardless of whether you are feeling tired, stressed, grumpy or angry on the inside. It is particularly important to keep your voice calm when you are having a conversation with a child about an element of their behaviour. If you shout at a child, it is likely that all they will hear is the shouting. They are more likely to learn from the encounter if you calmly explain why their behaviour was inappropriate.

Non-verbal Communication

Watch any experienced teacher and you will see that they utilise a range of non-verbal approaches to manage children's behaviour. Perhaps the best known of all such non-verbal strategies is 'the look', the Paddington hard stare that subdues any unruly child. Of course, 'the look' may sometimes be needed, but it is the non-verbal equivalent of speaking harshly to a child, so other, more positive, non-verbal communications should be prioritised and utilised routinely.

Let's start with the smile! Welcome your class with a smile every morning and at the start of every new teaching session. It will communicate to them that you are happy to work with them. See if you can share a personal smile with each child during the day. Smiling is good for you and a smile is often reciprocated, building a connection between the smilers.

Rogers (2015: 95) notes that we should aim to utilise the 'least-intrusive' approach as much as possible, and non-verbal communication has the advantage of allowing you to continue your teaching without interruption. Making eye contact or including a brief pause in a sentence can refocus a child or alert them to the fact that you have noticed what they are doing (or not doing). Similarly, tactically positioning yourself in the classroom or moving, while teaching, to be next to a particular child can have a settling effect on the class. Hand gestures can also be used to communicate that children should wait or turn around, all without interrupting the flow of your teaching or your interaction with other children.

Observation Guide 3.2

Use of Voice and the Nature of Communication

When observing how children's behaviour is managed in a school, remember that positive relationships underpin great teaching:

- Notice how the teacher uses their voice: do they regulate their voice, using a range of volume and pitch? Do they use their voice in different ways, depending on whether they are engaging the children in learning or managing behaviour?
- Notice how the children respond to the teacher's use of voice: do they hang on the teacher's every word?
- Notice how the teacher uses their voice when making behavioural expectations explicit or when dealing with unwanted behaviour.
- Watch for non-verbal communication to manage behaviour: pauses, eye contact, gestures, modelling.

The Interconnected Nature of Behaviour Management and Good Teaching

When the children's behaviour has been challenging or fallen short of expectations in a particular lesson, it is easy for student teachers to think that they should evaluate and improve their 'behaviour management strategies' (e.g., making expectations more explicit, being stricter with sanctions or using more praise). However, Ellis and Tod (2018: 31) caution against thinking of 'behaviour management and the promotion of learning as distinct elements of the teacher's role'. There are many reasons why children might misbehave in a lesson and it is important to reflect on all aspects of our teaching, to see if we can identify any other elements that may have contributed to the children's less-than-brilliant behaviour. In this section, we will consider how all elements of good teaching can contribute to positive behaviour, or conversely, how children's disappointing behaviour may have its roots in an aspect of teaching that can be enhanced.

Assessment and Planning

The Education Endowment Foundation (EEF) (2019) identify a key element of effective behaviour management as being to 'know and understand your pupils and their influences'. Good teaching starts with knowing your pupils well: what are their strengths? What do they find hard? Who do they work well with? What makes them smile? What interests do they have outside school? Which approaches to learning seem most effective for them? Where is the best place for them to sit? The list is endless, but it is clear that knowing your pupils well will enable you to plan more engaging learning opportunities for them. If they are engaged with the learning, they are more likely to behave well.

Similarly, a secure understanding of each child's recent progress will enable you to match the learning to the children's current attainment and ensure that the work is neither too easy nor too hard. Work that is too easy can lead to boredom or frustration and work that is difficult for children to access or succeed with is likely to lead to disengagement.

Case Study 3.1

Adaptive Teaching and Behaviour

Amran, a postgraduate student teacher, is teaching a science lesson. To avoid too much disruption, he decides to leave the children sitting at their tables as they were for the previous lesson, which was literacy, in which the children were grouped by prior attainment. The task that he sets requires each group to read a short section of text about the conditions for germination of seeds and then to complete a worksheet to answer questions based on their reading. This lesson does not go well. Amran finds himself dealing with a number of children who are 'off task' and 'being silly'.

It is no surprise that this lesson is not a great success. Quite apart from the fact that Amran has chosen a deathly-dull task, many children find the work difficult to access: the text is too hard for them and, because they are working with children of similar attainment levels, there is no one on the table who might be able to help them.

Collaboration with Other Adults

It is important to remember that you do not have to handle every element of classroom practice yourself: you are part of a team. As we will explore further in Chapter 15, it is valuable to develop positive and collaborative approaches to working with Teaching Assistants (TAs) and other adults in the classroom, and it will have a positive impact on children's behaviour if you develop a consistent approach with your TAs and other adults, based on shared values.

Some children's behaviour may be related to other elements of their learning, so remember to seek advice and support from the school SENCo and specialist support staff. If you are able to work with others to find ways to make children's learning journey more enjoyable and successful, it is likely to have a positive impact on their behaviour.

Working with parents is an essential, but sometimes daunting, aspect of promoting positive behaviour. O'Brien (2021: 169) emphasises the need to see parents as equal partners, so that you can work together to promote the interests of the child, without blame on either side: 'Parents will respect you if you communicate well, communicate early and if they are convinced that you are genuinely trying to improve the situation'. This point about early communication is particularly important: don't delay arranging a conversation with a parent if an issue needs to be discussed, as it is much better to 'nip things in the bud' rather than store up a set of issues to be addressed.

Subject and Pedagogical Knowledge

As we will explore in Chapter 8, when it comes to teaching, it helps if you know what you're talking about. When you are confident of the subject content, you are able to teach in a confident and engaging way: you are more likely to sound enthusiastic about the content and more open to questions and comments from the children. Conversely, when you are not confident in the subject content, your teaching tends to be more stilted and hesitant, and questions from children are less welcome, as you worry you might not be able to answer them. When our teaching is less confident and less engaging, the children sense this and behaviour can begin to wobble. If you know that you are going to be teaching something tricky, aim to be confident about both the content itself and how you are going to explain it to the children.

In the course of your journey towards QTS, you will learn a great deal about how children learn and how to engage them in productive and valuable learning. It is important to apply this professional knowledge in your teaching. Don't be surprised if the children are fidgety if you have talked at them for 30 minutes. Don't be surprised if they are whispering to each other if you have not planned opportunities for legitimate talk. Don't be surprised if they are clamouring for your attention during independent work, if you have not explained the task clearly or if you have over-complicated things.

In summary, make sure you are well planned, well prepared and that the teaching and learning is an engaging and positive experience for the children.

Critical Task 3.4

The Interconnected Nature of Behaviour Management and Good Teaching

Reflect on a lesson that you have taught where the behaviour was not as good as you would have liked it to be. In addition to improving your skills in 'behaviour management', identify whether there was another aspect of your teaching that may have been improved to have a more positive impact on the children's behaviour.

Table 3.2 Behaviour and good teaching

Aspect of teaching	What might you have done differently to have had a more positive impact on the children's behaviour?
Knowledge of the children's abilities, interests or motivations	
Planning of the learning activities	
Preparation of the lesson resources, timings or transitions	
Collaboration with Teaching Assistants, SENCo or parents	
Subject knowledge	
Knowledge of how children learn	

Rewards, Sanctions and Intrinsic Motivation

There is now widespread acceptance that a Victorian-style behaviour management regime, based on punishments, is not the kind of humane approach to education that is desirable in the 21st century. The emphasis now is on taking a positive approach and building learning environments that are supportive and developmental, as supported by Dix (2017: 8): 'Why crush behaviours with punishment when you can grow them with love?'

The Limitations of Rewards

The use of rewards is now widespread in primary schools and they come in a wide variety, as outlined by the Department for Education (DfE) (2022) in their latest guidance:

Examples of rewards may include:

- verbal praise
- communicating praise to parents via phone call or written correspondence

- certificates, prize ceremonies or special assemblies
- positions of responsibility, such as prefect status or being entrusted with a particular decision or project
- whole-class or year group rewards, such as a popular activity.

Using rewards to encourage good behaviour may seem to be a bit like motherhood and apple pie: what could possibly be wrong with giving a child a sticker, a house point, a merit mark, or a certificate? According to Kohn (2018), potentially, quite a lot! Kohn argues that some of the limitations of rewards include:

- children can develop a dependence on rewards, which have to become bigger, better or more exciting over time to maintain their impact
- medium-term and long-term intrinsic motivation is negatively impacted through the use of extrinsic motivators (rewards)
- there are often hidden messages associated with rewards, for example, that no one would want to learn anything for the sheer joy or interest of it … and only if a reward is on offer.

Ultimately, it is worth us reminding ourselves that the purpose of education is to help children learn how to become the best version of themselves. In this context, behaviour management should be seen as an educative process, in which children learn to manage their own behaviour, rather than responding to the short-term stimulus of rewards.

Question Guide 3.1

Establishing and Reinforcing Routines

The *ITT Core Content Framework* (*CCF*) states that 'establishing and reinforcing routines, including through positive reinforcement, can help create an effective learning environment' (Department for Education, 2019: 26).

When reflecting on effective practice when on placement, here are some questions to ask your teacher-mentor or another member of the teaching team about how they manage behaviour in ways that promote good behaviour and pre-empt poor behaviour. Remember to frame your questions professionally and positively, to avoid any suggestion of implied criticism.

- Can you tell me about some classroom routines that you have that contribute to positive behaviour?
- How do you reinforce these routines so that they have maximum impact on positive behaviour?
- Do any routines have to be adapted for any individual children?

Sanctions and Their Impact

Sometimes, working within the school policy, it is necessary to use a sanction or consequence to respond to inappropriate behaviour. Consistency is key here, as sanctions should be applied fairly so that the same expectations apply each day. Children should know and understand how the 'system' works (e.g., how warnings are given) and understand that the sanction is not just being imposed on them, but is a consequence of the choices they have made about their behaviour.

It is worth reflecting on what we 'achieve' by utilising sanctions and how we can get the most out of them. For example, keeping a child in for five minutes at playtime does not, of itself, change the child's outlook on their behaviour, and may fuel any disaffection with school or negatively impact your relationship with the child. Remember that your job as a teacher is not just to ensure that children behave well but to help them learn about their own behaviour and become better at regulating and managing themselves (as we will discuss further in Chapter 4). Therefore, taking five minutes to invest in your relationship and to chat calmly about how their behaviour might be more appropriate in the next lesson might be a better use of time than just 'keeping them in'. This kind of approach will enable you to have a long-term, positive and life-enhancing impact on the children that you teach.

Question Guide 3.2

Building Effective Relationships

The *CCF* states that 'building effective relationships is easier when pupils believe that their feelings will be considered and understood' (DfE, 2019: 26).

When reflecting on effective practice when on placement, here are some questions to ask your teacher-mentor or another member of the teaching team about how they build effective relationships to promote good behaviour.

- Can you tell me about how you build positive relationships with all the children?
- Are some children 'harder to reach' than others? How do you respond to this?
- Do you agree that building effective relationships is easier when pupils believe that their feelings will be considered and understood?
- How do you encourage children to communicate their feelings?

Response to Critical Task 3.1

Values

In this task, we asked you to consider how your core values might impact on the ways in which you manage children's behaviour. Here, we have made some suggested responses. Remember that the important thing is to notice when your conduct as a teacher is out of alignment with your values. This is a sign that you need to take stock and reflect on how your approach might need to be developed.

Table 3.3 Core values revisited

My core values	How these might impact on my approach to managing children's behaviour
Equality	Be clear that you don't have favourites or non-favourites. Treat all children equally, including those who are less-well behaved.
Dignity	Speak to all children as though they are your equal in terms of their importance.
Consistency	Aim to communicate similar expectations every lesson and every day.
Respect	Use a calm voice at all times, particularly when discussing poor behaviour with children.

Response to Critical Task 3.2

High Expectations

In this task, we asked you to imagine that you are about to start teaching a lesson and to identify the three or four things that you would like the children to be doing before you begin teaching, and to consider how you might communicate your expectations to children.

There are no specific 'right' answers here, but you might want the children to be:

- sitting down
- sitting still
- looking towards the teacher or the board.

Having these expectations clear in your own mind is only the start. The next challenge is to get these expectations out of your head and into the children's heads. You will find your own form of words to use, but the use of 'Let me see who is…' is one clear approach:

- Let me see who is sitting down.
- Let me see who is sitting still.
- Let me see who is looking this way.

Chapter Summary

In this chapter, we have considered the importance of holding your values close when teaching and managing children's behaviour, so that all your interactions are based on the principles of treating children with dignity and respect. We have identified some key elements of effective practice in managing behaviour, such as making expectations explicit, being positive and avoiding being side-tracked by low-level disruption. We have considered the central importance of good teaching to promoting good behaviour and identified the need to be thoughtful and reflective in the deployment of both sanctions and rewards.

Further Reading

Bennett, T. (2020) *Running the room: The teacher's guide to behaviour*. Woodbridge, UK: John Catt Educational Ltd.

This book makes a compelling case for why teachers should focus on managing behaviour.

Kohn, A. (2018) *Punished by rewards: The trouble with gold stars, incentive plans, A's, praise, and other bribes* (25th anniversary edn). Boston, MA: Houghton Mifflin.

As ever, Alfie Kohn takes a research-informed approach to challenge widely-held assumptions about the potential power of rewards to promote good behaviour. This is a 'must-read' for every teacher.

Ockwell-Smith, S. (2017) *The gentle discipline book*. London: Piatkus/Little Brown.

Although aimed at parents, Ockwell-Smith's text offers some very valuable suggestions both for understanding children's behaviour and for managing it, through managing your own responses.

References

Bennett, T. (2020) *Running the room: The teacher's guide to behaviour*. Woodbridge, UK: John Catt Educational Ltd.

Caldarella, P., Larsen, R., Williams, L., Downs, K., Wills, H. and Wehby, J. (2020) 'Effects of teachers' praise-to-reprimand ratios on elementary students' on-task behaviour', *Educational Psychology*, 40(10), 1306–1322.

Department for Education (DfE) (2019) *ITT core content framework.* London: DfE.

Department for Education (DfE) (2022) *Behaviour in schools: Advice for headteachers and school staff.* London: DfE. Available at: https://assets.publishing.service.gov.uk/government/ uploads/system/uploads/attachment_data/file/1089687/Behaviour_in_Schools_guidance_ July_2022.pdf (accessed 9 February 2023).

Dix, P. (2017) *When the adults change, everything changes: Seismic shifts in school behaviour.* Bancyfelin, Carmarthen, Wales: Independent Thinking Press.

Education Endowment Foundation (EEF) (2019) *Improving behaviour in schools: Six recommendations for improving behaviour in schools. London: EEF.* Available at: https:// educationendowmentfoundation.org.uk/education-evidence/guidance-reports/behaviour (accessed 9 February 2023).

Ellis, S. and Tod, J. (2018) *Behaviour for learning: Promoting positive relationships in the classroom* (2nd edn). London: Routledge.

Kohn, A. (2018) *Punished by rewards: The trouble with gold stars, incentive plans, A's, praise, and other bribes* (25th anniversary edn). Boston, MA: Houghton Mifflin.

O'Brien, J. (2021) *Better behaviour: A guide for teachers* (2nd edn). Los Angeles, CA: Sage (Corwin Press).

Rogers, B. (2015) *Classroom behaviour: A practice guide to effective teaching, behaviour management and colleague support.* (4th edn). Los Angeles, CA: Sage.

4
CHILDREN MANAGING THEIR OWN BEHAVIOUR: SELF-REGULATION

Chantel Yeates, Kevin Day and Colin Forster

Chapter Objectives

- To consider the importance of children understanding their emotions.
- To explore how to support children to regulate their emotions and behaviour.
- To reflect on the role of restorative practice in helping children to reflect on the impact of their behaviour and how they might choose different actions.

In the previous chapter, we considered the teacher's role in managing children's behaviour. In this chapter, we go a stage further and consider how children can learn to manage their own behaviour. We explore what is meant by self-regulation and some of the factors that might make this difficult for children, before exploring the key approaches teachers can take to support children in learning to self-regulate, based on positive relationships, the development of emotional intelligence and the use of restorative practice.

Rather than seeing poor behaviour as something that 'gets in the way of learning', helping children to learn about their emotional responses and how they can regulate their own behaviour is potentially life-changing, and some of the most profound and meaningful teaching you are ever likely to undertake.

Introduction to Self-regulation

Self-regulation is the ability to recognise and manage your own emotions, behaviours and responses to things that are happening around you, that may impact on you directly or indirectly (Robson and Zachariou, 2022). It is an essential aspect of emotional development; if you are able to regulate and control your emotions, you can therefore focus more effectively, problem-solve more logically, approach tasks calmly, work with others more collaboratively (Cowley, 2021). Having the ability to self-regulate during challenging situations also builds confidence, independence and resilience.

Within the *Statutory Framework for the Early Years Foundation Stage* (Department for Education (DfE), 2021), one of the 17 Early Learning Goals relates to self-regulation. It forms part of the personal, social and emotional development area of learning and development, which is identified as a prime area. The *ITT Core Content Framework* (*CCF*) identifies that 'the ability to self-regulate one's emotions affects pupils' ability to learn, success in school and future lives' (DfE, 2019: 26), further signifying its importance for children, and therefore its importance for you as a student teacher.

Self-regulation develops over many years, starting from birth and often continuing into adulthood, and how easy this journey is depends on a number of factors, including the capacity and needs of the individual child and their experiences at home and in school as they develop and mature. As children develop their 'understanding of their own feelings and those of others' (DfE, 2021: 12), they can begin to find ways to regulate, including when something has provoked or upset them. Children often develop self-regulation through connection with others and positive relationships and will learn, over time, from others that model self-regulated behaviour. As children become more familiar with the process of self-regulation, the time taken to return from a dysregulated state to a regulated state may decrease.

Critical Task 4.1

The Value of Self-regulation

Can you think of an example where you have had to rely on self-regulation? Something, or someone, must have triggered some kind of emotion within you. Perhaps someone 'cut you up' in traffic, or someone lost their temper and began to shout at you. Maybe someone said something unkind or thoughtless.

How did this make you feel? What was your immediate response? What emotion was this? Were you able to self-regulate? What higher-order thinking was needed to self-regulate? What processes were needed? What was the outcome of this self-regulation? What do you think would have been an alternative outcome if you were unable to self-regulate?

Co-regulation

At times, due to developmental stage, emotional immaturity or other needs (such as special educational needs, disability or trauma), children can be unable to self-regulate. In this case, co-regulation is needed. Murray et al. (2015, quoted in Conkbayir, 2022: 40) define co-regulation as 'warm and responsive interactions that provide the support, coaching, and modelling children need to understand, express and modulate their thoughts, feelings and behaviours'. Supportive adults will be needed to help the dysregulated child to understand their emotions and how to self-regulate.

Conkbayir (2022) suggests that self-regulation can only develop effectively if children have first experienced co-regulation, so co-regulation is seen as essential. However, over time, it is crucial that co-regulation allows the child to learn strategies to develop self-regulation. The aim is that this becomes an independent practice that they are able to draw on when they are dysregulated.

Trauma-informed Teaching

Children who have experienced trauma are likely to find regulation of their emotions even more challenging on a daily basis. It could be due to the fact that they have never had a trusted adult, or emotionally available adult, to help them identify their emotions and co-regulate in their formative years, or due to their trauma, their brain may be constantly on high alert. Their amygdala, the region of the brain that is primarily responsible for processing emotions, may react to situations extremely quickly in an attempt to keep them safe from 'perceived harm'. In this case, children can react with fight, flight, freeze or other stress responses.

Supporting children who have experienced trauma to regulate their emotions requires a high level of patience, understanding and emotional intelligence. As explored in Chapter 2, we would encourage all teachers to be curious about the behaviour a child may be exhibiting and to try to understand what may be triggering these emotions and the reaction to certain situations.

> Ultimately, what determines how children survive trauma, physically, emotionally or psychologically, is whether the people around them – particularly the adults they should be able to trust and reply upon – stand by them with love, support, and encouragement. Fire can warm or consume, wind can caress or cut. And so, it is true with human relationships: we can both create and destroy, nurture and terrorize, traumatise and heal each other. (Perry and Szalavitz, 2017: xxviii)

Adverse Childhood Experiences

Studies into Adverse Childhood Experiences (ACEs) started in the mid-1990s when the American Centers for Disease Control worked with health insurance provider Kaiser Permanente. The work was led by Dr Vincent J. Felitti, who coordinated research with over 17,000 participants. The results were profound, highlighting significant health issues (mental and physical) for adults who had a high number of traumatic experiences in childhood (Felitti, 2002).

Developments in neuroscience and studies into the outcomes of children who have experienced ACEs highlight physical differences in brain development resulting from excessive activation of the stress response system. A high number of ACEs causes reduced impulse control for the child, leading to significant challenges around emotional regulation and managing relationships. There is also a recognised impact on physical health and development into adulthood. In addition to direct early interventions to help families and reduce abuse, harm or neglect, other 'protective factors' can improve outcomes for children who have experienced ACEs. Teachers and trusted educational professionals who have regular contact with children are in a privileged position to be the trusted, safe and emotionally available adults that the child might not have at home. If teachers with knowledge of ACEs and trauma-informed approaches can offer a child a high level of empathy, recognise that behaviour is communication, and keep building trusting relationships within a safe environment, progress towards co-regulation and then self-regulation can occur. These skilled, emotionally available adults offering a trauma-informed approach can become 'educational champions' to children, making an immeasurable positive impact on their future education and development towards adult life.

Solving the Puzzle and Changing Lives

It is worth beginning to look at behaviour as you would when beginning to do a jigsaw puzzle. Take each piece of the behaviour and see it in isolation. Be curious as to what the behaviour is telling you. Be patient as you explore and work out what is occurring and the possible reasons why. Don't lose sight of the whole puzzle while focusing on individual pieces. Step back and look at the bigger picture regularly. As you begin to understand each puzzle piece, the whole picture will become clearer. At first, you may be overwhelmed by what you are seeing, so take time to understand each puzzle piece as you link them together. You may, or may not, enjoy completing jigsaw puzzles as a pastime or hobby, but the patience and skills needed for such a task may be useful when working with children! In the next section, we'll begin to think about the role of the teacher in supporting children as they begin to learn how to regulate their own behaviour.

Relationships are Fundamental

In education, good relationships are the key to everything: they should underpin all elements of the teacher's work and form the foundation for every interaction with every child.

This might sound easy, but it takes skill, patience and resilience to establish, develop and main-tain relationships, particularly with children whose early life experience has made it difficult for them to relate to or trust adults. To be a great teacher for these children, we need to have a good understanding of our own emotions and how we relate to others.

It is a basic human need for us to feel we belong in a place and are visible. Children need to feel seen, heard and understood, and this can only be accomplished through genuine human connection. Teachers utilise a range of relational skills to recognise and respond appropri-ately to each child's emotional needs. Dix (2017: 52) notes that, 'positive rapport and great relationships cannot be fast tracked. Little and often, slow and steady wins the race. Let them know you care in the most subtle and discreet ways possible'. This may take time, energy and patience but the impact for the teacher and the child can be priceless.

Children who have experienced trauma have a higher level of distrust in adults, and there-fore forming relationships may take longer and be more challenging for the teacher on an emotional level. Through curiosity, creating a safe environment and building relationships, you will help these children to feel more regulated and ultimately this should enable effective learning. Perry and Szalavitz (2017: 258) put it like this: 'the more healthy relationships a child has, the more likely they will be able to recover from trauma and thrive. Relationships are the agents of change and the most powerful therapy is human love.'

Critical Task 4.2

Reflect On Your Own Relationships With Teachers

Reflecting on our own relationships and educational experiences can be helpful in developing our own practice and how we develop relationships with children. Reflect on the following questions:

- Who was the teacher you believed you had the best relationship with at school?
- What skills or qualities did this teacher have? Why did you feel connected to them?
- What was the impact on your learning?

Building Relationships

It takes time to build relationships with children, but the impact can be life-changing. Often it is daily conscious thoughts, and effort, that are required to build relationships with the chil-dren in your care. Relationships can be built by showing a genuine interest in a child and their hobbies, interests, likes and dislikes. Children need to be seen and feel valued, and having a common interest with an adult helps establish these connections.

When working with children, be curious about their thoughts and behaviours. Find out what they enjoy doing and try to create that connection with them through their interests. Children are very good at knowing if adults are authentic in their approaches, so ensure you use positive language, positive tone of voice and positive body language as you interact and build relationships. A child needs to know that you really do care and have an interest in them, and you are not just 'ticking a box'. Hughes (no date) advocates using a PACE approach: Playfulness, Acceptance, Curiosity and Empathy. Being genuinely interested in the child's ideas, interests and feelings helps build safe, trusting and meaningful relationships.

Building relationships takes time and yet damaging them can happen in almost no time. Think of the analogy of putting money in a savings account. Every positive action to build relationships is a small contribution to your savings. When a conflict occurs in a relationship, a large 'withdrawal' from the savings account occurs. However, if you had a well-established relationship before the moment of conflict, there will be enough in the 'bank' for you to begin restoring the relationship once more.

— Question Guide 4.1 —

Building Positive Relationships

The *CCF* states that 'building effective relationships is easier when pupils believe that their feelings will be considered and understood' (DfE, 2019: 26).

When reflecting on effective practice while on placement, here are some questions to ask your teacher-mentor or another member of the teaching team about how they build relationships to help children regulate their own behaviour. Remember to frame your questions professionally and positively, to avoid any suggestion of implied criticism.

- How have you approached building relationships quickly with a new class or group at the start of the year or when you are new to them?
- Can you recommend techniques or approaches to help me establish a relationship with a shy or withdrawn child?
- If I am finding it difficult to build a positive relationship with a child who displays challenging behaviour and needs guidance and boundaries, what are the things I should consider?

Emotional Intelligence

The term 'emotional intelligence' was first coined by Goleman (1995), who recognised that success in life depends on so much more than just having a high IQ (Intelligence Quotient), and that having the ability to understand one's own emotions and those of others equips humans to relate positively to each other and work together to achieve great things.

According to Corrie (2003: 3):

> Emotional Intelligence (EI) is a way of understanding and shaping how we think, feel and act. Our personality or ego is made up of our emotional, physical and mental bodies and everyone has a unique combination of these.

Understanding, recognising and regulating emotions is learnt through observing and working alongside others who model these attributes. Many children need support with understanding their own emotions and those of others. Some children are quickly able to interpret encounters that trigger emotions, while others need a longer period of time to identify, process and manage their own emotions. Having emotionally intelligent adults around allows children to learn from them as they model self-regulation and appropriate behaviour. As adults, we need to help children recognise the variety of emotions that they may feel in different situations and then how their behaviour may be altered due to the triggering of various emotions. It requires that the adult is emotionally aware and in tune with their own emotions and responses, in order for them to react appropriately and with empathy when the child needs it the most.

The adults need to be able to express emotions, often those that they are seeing in the child, by using appropriate words and modelling for the child. Time needs to be taken for the child to understand emotions and feelings and why they might be experiencing these. Adults need to validate the emotions and reinforce that the feelings are real and appropriate for the experience the child is having. Asquith (2020: 68) suggests that children's emotions can 'quickly overwhelm them, as they do not yet fully understand what these emotions are or how to cope with them'.

Naming the emotion, recognising the feeling and the impact it may have on our wellbeing is a starting point for children to be able to understand emotional intelligence. Over time, with the emotionally available adult and the modelling of co-regulation, the child will become more in tune with their own emotions, will begin to understand themselves better and begin to see how their emotional state impacts on their behaviour.

— Case Study 4.1 —

Building a Connection

At the start of term, Mrs Jones observes Sarah looking anxious as she walks towards the classroom. She notes Sarah's bright pink and fluffy school bag and decides to connect with a brief chat. 'Whoa! Look at that. Can I hold that bag? That fluffy texture looks too good to miss!' She strokes it and asks Sarah where she got it.

A casual observer might wonder why Mrs Jones appears so excited about a bag. Of course, this interaction is not really about the bag. Mrs Jones is making a connection with Sarah to reduce her anxiety and improve her confidence.

Restorative Practice

'Restorative practice' is a term used to describe behaviours, interactions and approaches which help to build and maintain positive, healthy relationships, resolve difficulties and repair harm where there has been conflict (Finnis, 2021). It is based on an intervention approach, known as 'restorative justice', which has been used within the criminal justice system to make perpetrators accountable for their own actions and to encourage positive behaviour. According to Restorative Justice 4 Schools (no date), restorative justice is based on the four key principles of 'respect, responsibility, repair and re-integration'. The approach provides schools with a positive and developmental alternative to simply 'punishing' children when they have done something 'wrong'. It aims to take an educative approach to help children reflect on their behaviour, understand its impact on others and on themselves, and identify ways to improve future outcomes.

Traditional sanctions and consequences are often ineffective with vulnerable children who need to develop their self-regulation skills. Many sanctions merely isolate the child from their peers and project shame (a destructive emotion) onto a child, thus eroding the potential positive relationship between the adult and the child.

Restorative practices enable those who work with children to focus on building relationships that create and inspire positive change (which sometimes requires challenge as well as support). Many schools use restorative practices to enable school staff to communicate effectively with children and families and, in a study by McCluskey et al. (2008), it was found that some staff identified significant improvements in classroom climate. Taking time to repair and reflect on the harm and impact of behaviour on others can reap much longer-term rewards and build stronger and more sustainable relationships than simply 'keeping a child in at playtime' (Hansberry, 2016).

Restorative practice processes for conflict resolution in schools often involve:

- Creating and promoting a sense of community, social responsibility and shared accountability through building strong relationships.
- Ensuring all staff, pupils and parents are aware of the principles of restorative practice.
- Restorative meetings with a trained staff member, in which all parties talk about their part in the conflict and how it affected them.
- Work on repairing the relationship and reflection on how issues or hurt could be avoided in the future.

Restorative practice is not a quick fix. However, Gregory et al. (2016) discovered that the more teachers immersed themselves in restorative approaches, the better students rated their relationships with their teachers, leading to a greater sense of respect between teachers and students. Practising a restorative approach, in a climate which is focused on positive relationships, can become a way of being. Over time, this can develop into a natural approach for all who want to resolve conflict and rebuild relationships after conflict.

Teaching in a restorative way also helps us develop our own emotional intelligence. By working through conflicts in a restorative way, we will gain a better understanding of our own emotions and those of others. We will also begin to understand the impact of our actions on others. Being able to process our emotions and understanding what triggers our responses develops our emotional intelligence over time. The more understanding we gain around our own emotions, the better our self-regulation skills will become, enabling us to more effectively support children in developing their own.

— Critical Task 4.3 —

Preparing for Co-regulation

Rania has just moved near your school as she has been placed with new foster carers, and she is going to join your class. Her school files identify that she has had some temporary exclusions from her previous school and friendship issues. She has a diagnosis of ADHD but no further learning difficulties. What actions might you take to prepare her for joining your class in one week's time?

— Question Guide 4.2 —

Creating a Secure Environment

The *CCF* states that 'a predictable and secure environment benefits all pupils, but is particularly valuable for pupils with special educational needs' (DfE, 2019: 26).

When reflecting on effective practice when on placement, here are some questions to ask your teacher-mentor or another member of the teaching team about how they manage behaviour in ways that promote good behaviour and pre-empt dysregulation, often deemed as poor behaviour. Remember to frame your questions professionally and positively, to avoid any suggestion of implied criticism.

- What have you considered about the room layout and the daily routines that have helped support children with additional needs or vulnerabilities?
- How do you know how the children are feeling throughout the day?
- How do you support a child who impacts on the learning and wellbeing of others?

From Co-regulation to Self-regulation

Teachers who model emotional intelligence and self-regulation help children to become aware of their own emotions and the emotions of others. Children learn from the adults around them, especially those with whom they have a positive relationship and who are emotionally available to them. An adult who is attuned to their needs and their responses can help them process and understand their own feelings when they have been triggered emotionally. At these times, it is important for teachers to demonstrate emotional control and appropriate reactions themselves, and to help children 'unpick' situations, to help the children understand their emotions and then be aware of appropriate responses.

Adults should avoid expressing anger or frustration in a negative manner, such as shouting, being aggressive or by the knee-jerk issuing of sanctions. Instead, it is best to respond in an understanding and relational manner, implementing restorative approaches to resolve conflicts. For the children, this is highly valuable learning that teaches them essential life skills.

> Regulation is essential for laying down firm, secure 'foundations' when we're working generally with traumatised children and young people, and especially at times of crisis. We need to give them regular, relational experiences with us day by day which are regulating, in order to teach pupils in our care who have experienced toxic stress, ways to soothe and quieten the lower parts of their brains. They need the experience first through co-regulation, and then, over time, they will learn how to self-regulate. (Bombèr, 2020: 6)

Observation Guide 4.1

Co-Regulation

When observing how children are supported to regulate their own behaviour, remember that the teacher's role in co-regulation is vital.

Specific things to observe:

- Notice how the teacher builds connection with individual children and the class as a whole.
- Notice how the teacher uses non-verbal communication (e.g., eye contact, thumbs up, smiling).
- Notice how the teacher models appropriate behaviour (calm voice, good listening), particularly when managing unwanted behaviour.
- Notice how the teacher gives children choices when discussing their behaviour with them, to promote their self-regulation.

This approach is particularly important for children that have experienced ACEs as their ability to control their emotions will be more limited. Children who have experienced trauma may not be able to self-regulate; they may need additional empathy and compassion from the adults around them. It is essential that these adults connect with the child before trying to resolve an issue. As Golding et al. (2015) suggest, *connection* needs to be established before *correction* can be effective.

Case Study 4.2

Connection Before Correction

Jamie is in the corridor after running from the lesson. Mr Griffin approaches and sits on the floor next to him. 'Before we talk about the lesson today, I have been waiting to ask whether you saw the Liverpool match last night. I was thinking of you during the match as I know it's your team. What did you think of that goal?' Jamie manages a half-smile and Mr Griffin continues: 'Now, what happened in class just now?'

In this example, we see the importance of 'connection' to the child and how this impacts positively. Mr Griffin could have chosen to sanction Jamie for leaving the class without permission, or shout at him for sitting in the corridor unsupervised or demand an instant explanation about his behaviour. If this is forced when Jamie is still angry or anxious, it is likely to lead to an escalation rather than an improvement in behaviour. In this case, Mr Griffin delays rushing for an instant resolution and helps Jamie connect and feel safe, and prepares him emotionally to explore why he is sad, angry or anxious.

Response to Critical Task 4.3

Preparing for Co-regulation

In this task, we asked you to consider how you would prepare to support Rania in joining your class. Here are our thoughts:

Rania would benefit from a phased transition, if possible. Transitions are very difficult for all children, so allowing some time to build familiarity with the school building during a visit after the end of the school day will reduce anxiety and build confidence before Rania's first proper day in class.

It would also be good if she could begin to form a relationship with the class teaching assistant, ideally before she begins attending school. They could then check on her throughout the days during her first full week.

We all feel anxious when we are not sure what is going to happen, so giving Rania an idea of the timetable, including information about what happens at lunchtime, would help to reduce her anxiety levels.

Finally, it would be great for Rania to have an opportunity to have her voice heard about what would work well for her in this new setting and to be able to discuss what she can do when she feels anxious or unsure about something.

Chapter Summary

In this chapter, we have considered the importance of building relationships and understanding our own emotions when working with children, especially those that have experienced trauma and may not be able to regulate their emotions. It is essential that we support children to develop their emotional intelligence through modelling our responses and co-regulation with the children. We have looked at how emotionally available adults can work alongside children to support with the transition from co-regulation to self-regulation during situations that may trigger them emotionally. We explored how the principles of restorative practice can be used to resolve conflict when it arises and further build relationship and emotional intelligence. Ultimately, we have identified that the teacher is highly significant in the lives of children and that helping children learn to manage their own behaviour will be some of the most life-changing teaching we can do.

Further Reading

Bombèr, L.M. (2020) *Know me to teach me: Differentiated discipline for those recovering from adverse childhood experiences*. Belper, UK: Worth Publishing.

This is an extremely helpful book to gain an understanding of the effects of trauma on children and how we can differentiate our approaches to support these pupils and help them understand and regulate their emotions.

www.traumainformedschools.co.uk

This is the website for Trauma Informed Schools UK and it provides valuable guidance and advice about how to support children who have had Adverse Childhood Experiences.

References

Asquith, S. (2020) *Self-regulation skills in young children: Activities and strategies for practitioners and parents*. London: Jessica Kingsley.

Bombèr, L.M. (2020) *Know me to teach me: Differentiated discipline for those recovering from adverse childhood experiences*. Belper, UK: Worth Publishing.

Conkbayir, M. (2022) *The neuroscience of the developing child: Self-regulation for wellbeing and a sustainable future*. Abingdon, UK: Routledge.

Corrie, C. (2003) *Becoming emotionally intelligent*. London: Network Educational Press.

Cowley, S. (2021) *Learning behaviours: A practical guide to self-regulation in the early years*. Woodbridge, UK: John Catt Educational Ltd.

Department for Education (DfE) (2019) *ITT core content framework*. London: DfE.

Department for Education (DfE) (2021) *Statutory framework for the early years foundation stage: Setting the standards for learning, development and care for children from birth to five*. London: DfE.

Dix, P. (2017) *When the adults change, everything changes: Seismic shifts in school behaviour*. Bancyfelin, Carmarthen, Wales: Independent Thinking Press.

Felitti, V.J. (2002) 'The relation between adverse childhood experiences and adult health: turning gold into lead', *The Permanente Journal*, 6(1), 44–47.

Finnis, M. (2021) *Restorative practice*. Bancyfelin, Carmarthen, Wales: Independent Thinking Press.

Golding, K.S., Tucci, J. and Mitchell, J. (2015) 'Connection before correction: supporting parents to meet the challenges of parenting children who have been traumatised within their early parenting environments', *Children Australia*, 40(2), 152–159.

Goleman, D. (1995) *Emotional intelligence*. London: Bantam Books.

Gregory, A., Clawson, K., Davis, A. and Gerewitz, J. (2016) 'The promise of restorative practices to transform teacher–student relationships and achieve equity in school discipline', *Journal of Educational and Psychological Consultation*, 26(4), 325–353.

Hansberry, B. (2016) *A practical introduction to restorative practice in schools: Theory, skills and guidance*. London: Jessica Kingsley.

Hughes, D. (no date) *The attitude: Playfulness, acceptance, curiosity, empathy.* Available at: www.danielhughes.org/p.a.c.e.html (accessed 16 February 2023).

McCluskey, G., Lloyd, G., Kane, J., Riddell, S., Stead, J. and Weedon, E. (2008) 'Can restorative practices in schools make a difference?', *Educational Review*, 60(4), 405–417.

Perry, B. and Szalavitz, M. (2017) *The boy who was raised as a dog and other stories from a child psychiatrist's notebook: What traumatised children can teach us about loss, love and healing* (3rd edn). New York: Basic Books.

Restorative Justice 4 Schools (no date) Available at: www.restorativejustice4schools.co.uk/wp/?page_id=45 (accessed 16 February 2023).

Robson, S. and Zachariou, A. (2022) *Self-regulation in the early years.* London: Learning Matters.

SECTION 2
PEDAGOGY

5
HOW PUPILS LEARN

Jackie McNeil

Chapter Objectives

- To explore some theoretical perspectives about how children learn.
- To consider how we can ensure that children develop and sustain deep knowledge and understanding in the longer term.
- To reflect on how teachers can use their understanding of how children learn to inform their practice.

In this chapter, we explore what learning is and why it is important for student teachers to understand how children learn. We explore a range of different theories about how learning occurs and identify the 'common threads' that run between them. We consider how our understanding of how children learn has implications for our practice as teachers.

What we know about learning mainly stems from theories developed during the mid-20th century in the world of psychology and, more recently, developments in neuroscience and an understanding of the behaviour of the brain. Work in these fields has led people to consider what works effectively, in terms of pedagogy (the practice of teaching), to ensure that children learn. The *ITT Core Content Framework (CCF)* (Department for Education (DfE), 2019: 11), specifically Standard 2, explicitly links 'knowing about how children learn' to supporting good progress. As an intending teacher, it is therefore essential that you develop an understanding of how children learn and some key theories which have influenced thinking about this topic.

What Do We Mean by Learning?

In the *CCF* (DfE, 2019: 11), learning is defined as 'involving a lasting change in pupils' capabilities and understanding', and so we can see that learning is a process of change. This can be a change in what we know and understand, or a change in what we do or believe. Learning is not necessarily related to chronological age but is about previous experiences and building on what has been previously learnt. It starts from birth, as babies begin to make sense of the world around them. Brain development means that they have innate cognitive skills for remembering, reasoning and developing language.

While children learn at different rates, they all have the capacity to learn, and this is a fundamental principle that all teachers should hold on to. When a child fails to learn something, it is not because they cannot learn; it is because they have not been taught effectively. Holt (1982: 2) suggests that he held himself responsible: 'If my students weren't learning what I was teaching, it was my job to find out why.'

Why Do You Need to Know About How Children Learn?

Put simply, your understanding of how children learn will inform the decisions you make about how to teach. As a student teacher, it is important to understand that all children are capable of learning, even if they don't appear to all learn in the same way. As we will go on to explore in the next chapter, teaching is a problem-solving activity: you will seek to solve the problem of how your teaching can enable children to learn all that they need to. Practice in the classroom has developed over time and has been informed by a wealth of rich, evidence-based research. Hattie (2012) suggests that teachers should carefully consider the impact that their teaching has on student learning and use this to evaluate the effectiveness of their teaching skills and approaches.

Established Theories About Learning

Macblain (2022: 59) suggests that 'no single theory can fully explain how children learn'. With this in mind, in this section, we consider some key theories which have been influential on thinking and practice in primary education and we explore the areas of common ground between them.

Constructivism

In the mid-20th century, a theory of learning called 'constructivism' was developed. This theory centres on the notion that learners actively build their own understanding, based on the experiences that they have. The constructivist view moved away from earlier ideas about children and learners being passive in the development of understanding, and it became generally more accepted that building on prior knowledge and understanding is fundamental to new learning (Aubrey and Riley, 2022). This is explicitly reflected in the *CCF* (DfE, 2019: 11), which states that 'prior knowledge plays an important role in how pupils learn'. We will consider this further as we explore the concept of planning for progression in the next chapter.

Piaget, sometimes described as the 'grandfather' of constructivism, explored this theory with his own children and, although his work was criticised for the limitations in research design, his findings led people to consider the idea that children 'construct' their own knowledge and understanding through interaction with their environments. A key principle of Piaget's theory (Piaget and Inhelder, 1969) was the idea that learners develop *schemata* (organised 'chunks' of knowledge and/or understanding), which are built on and developed to enable new learning to happen (Wray, 2018). Schemata is the plural of *schema*; each 'chunk' is a separate schema. As people encounter something new, they interpret the experience and adjust what they already know and understand about the world around them. Piaget described this process as *adaptation*, identifying that it causes people to change their schemata in response to the new information. Initially, concrete experiences support the development of schemata and, later, learners are able to relate to more abstract ideas.

Piaget suggested that there are two processes involved in adaptation. One is called *assimilation*, which tends to be less challenging for learners, as new information tends to fit comfortably alongside what is already known and understood, and there is little disruption to an existing schema. The other process is *accommodation*, which can be more challenging or even uncomfortable for learners, as the new information does not fit comfortably with what the learner already knows and understands. The schema may need significant adaptation, or may even be replaced with a new schema entirely, in order to accommodate the new information (Bates, 2019). To exemplify these processes, let's consider a toddler whose schema relating to dogs has been built on their interactions with a grandparent's yellow labrador. Imagine that the toddler meets a black labrador belonging to their new neighbour, who asks if the toddler would like to stroke 'the dog'. The toddler alters their dog schema, assimilating that dogs can be different colours, but largely look the same, based on meeting two dogs. Now imagine that, while in the park, the toddler encounters another dog, with the toddler's parent saying, 'Look at the dog', while pointing to a brown chihuahua. This is much more likely to require the process of accommodation, as this 'dog' looks nothing like the toddler's knowledge of 'dog', other than having fur, a tail and four legs (all of which are also true of cats, rabbits, and so on). The schema needs significant adaptation to accommodate this new knowledge. If you think of schemata as being like folders, the 'dog' folder now needs a set of dividers, as the toddler comes to understand that there are different types of dog. With every new experience or learning situation, children's schemata will be adapting.

Despite the limitations of Piaget's research, and the time that has elapsed since it was published (Piaget and Inhelder, 1969), the notion of schemata remains embedded in our understanding of how pupils learn today, with the DfE (2019: 14) stating that 'in all subject areas, pupils learn new ideas by linking those ideas to existing knowledge, organising this knowledge into increasingly complex mental models (or "schemata")'. However, other aspects of his theories about how children learn have been subsequently disputed. For example, Piaget proposed that stages of development are related purely to the chronological age of the child, and that their age is therefore a crucial factor in when they can move towards interpreting abstract ideas. However, this model was criticised for underestimating the abilities of very young children and their potential, as well as ignoring environmental factors, such as motivation and culture, and the influence of others.

Social-constructivism and Scaffolding

Vygotsky was a Russian theorist who placed great importance on the role of language as a vital cultural tool involved in learning. Vygotsky developed the notion of the *zone of proximal development* (ZPD) as the 'place' where learning can happen, suggesting that the ZPD is the space between what a child can do independently and what a child can do with the support of a *'more knowledgeable other'* (MKO) (Vygotsky, 1978). Language provides the medium through which the child and the MKO can work together on learning, working within the child's ZPD. The importance of language and talk is also firmly situated within the *CCF* (DfE, 2019: 18), which notes that 'high-quality classroom talk can support pupils to articulate key ideas, consolidate understanding and extend their vocabulary'.

Bruner then built on Vygotsky's ideas. Although he concurred with some of Piaget's views, Bruner recognised the importance of the teacher in actively supporting learners as they encounter new concepts, enabling them to move through the stages from concrete to abstract understanding, working within Vygotsky's ZPD. This process, which he called *scaffolding*, could be gradually reduced as the learner became more independent in thinking and acquired new skills, just as the scaffolding on a building can be removed when the building is safe to stand unaided (Bruner, 1966). Throughout your placements, you will learn from expert colleagues about how much scaffolding might be needed for particular pupils, what types of scaffolding to provide and how to identify when to reduce/remove the scaffolding in place.

Knowing More, Remembering More: What Part Does Memory Play in Learning?

What we mean by 'learning', and the role that memory plays in learning, has been the subject of much debate. Willingham (2009: 88) describes learning as 'memory in disguise'. Kirschner et al. (2006: 75–77) also talk about learning as a 'change in long-term memory', stating that 'if nothing has changed in long-term memory, nothing has been learned', which suggests that learning, retention and remembering go hand in hand. You might relate to this, having come through an education system where much of what you had 'learned' was assessed through what you could remember in an exam. Exams are a test of your 'long-term memory' (what was stored in your brain) and your revision strategies will have ensured that you were able to recall the learning when it was needed most. Consider what you can remember now: have you retained it all?

Critical Task 5.1

Reflecting on Your Own Retention of Learning

Think about something you learned in school and consider why you still remember it now. Why has this knowledge, understanding or skill remained with you? For example, is there a connection to the way you were taught?

I gave up geography after Key Stage 3, but can still describe an ox-bow lake and why they form. I am sure this is because of the teaching strategies my geography teacher adopted, which included modelling, diagrams and explanations. I don't often need this information, but it is an example of how teachers adopt a range of strategies which help us to know more and to remember in the long term, not just in the short term.

What are the Implications for Teaching?

If memory is a key aspect of learning, then we need to make learning memorable, and this will be explored more fully in Chapter 9. It goes without saying that children will remember the original and creative lessons, rather than those which are mundane. However, this comes with a word of warning. There is a danger for teachers to focus on activity, rather than learning, and the emphasis on 'making learning fun' can often be distracting. While we recognise that motivation is a key aspect of whether children learn, good teaching does not necessarily equal 'fun'.

Knowing and understanding what your children know and can do is vital so that you can pitch the teaching appropriately, with just the right level of challenge, allowing children to work within their ZPD. Wiliam (2016), a respected expert in education (particularly in relation to assessment), suggests that if students do not have to work hard to make sense of what they are learning, they are less likely to remember it in six weeks' time. This statement is supported by numerous studies, suggesting that working hard and being challenged are conducive to learning. For example, Dweck (2006) argues that the learning environment and a challenge mindset can help to develop resilient learners, and a study by Lin-Siegler et al. (2016) found that if pupils recognise that sometimes learning involves a 'struggle', they will be more successful. Therefore, it is important that teachers match the level of challenge to the individual.

Challenges to Learning: Cognitive Load and Overload

The *CCF* (DfE, 2019: 11) identifies that 'an important factor in learning is memory, which can be thought of as comprising two elements: working memory and long-term memory'. It states that teachers need to learn how to identify and avoid 'overloading working memory'. Working memory 'is where information that is being actively processed is held, but its capacity is limited and can be overloaded', while long-term memory can be thought of 'as a store of knowledge that changes as pupils learn by integrating new ideas with existing knowledge' (DfE, 2019: 11). Knowledge from this store can be drawn upon or 'retrieved' when needed and used within the working memory. Cognitive Load Theory, a term coined in 1988 by John Sweller, suggests that because the working memory can only hold a small amount of information at any one time, the teaching approaches we choose should avoid 'overloading' it to maximise learning. In other words, if the cognitive load is too large for children to process, they will struggle to make progress in their learning.

Supporting children to improve their ability to retrieve prior learning from their long-term memory effectively and efficiently is important. If children are better at retrieval, this will free up working memory, allowing them to concentrate on new learning. If you are a driver, consider your progress from novice to expert. Remember that first lesson and the fear you probably felt: how would you remember to do all the right things in the right order? As a more experienced driver, it is likely you now arrive in a place with little recall of the journey, because everything came 'naturally'. That is because, after much practice and the ability to retrieve information about driving skills from your long-term memory, you have developed automaticity.

Sweller's (1988) theory identifies three different forms of cognitive load: intrinsic, extraneous and germane. *Intrinsic load* refers to the actual difficulty of what is being learned and this will be dependent on prior learning and the complexity of the topic; while we can seek to work within pupils' ZPD, we also need to ensure that we meet curriculum requirements. *Extraneous load* relates to how any new material is presented and the environment in which it is presented; this is the aspect that teachers have the most control over. *Germane load* is the cognitive effort that learners must put in to process and retain the latest information; it is influenced by the intrinsic and the extraneous loads.

In seeking to manage the intrinsic load, to try to avoid overload, we need to consider the importance of challenge again. Hattie and Hamilton (2020: 23) refer to 'the Goldilocks principle' of getting the level of challenge 'just right'. This is not necessarily easy to begin with. The DfE (2019: 11) recommends working alongside expert colleagues to learn how to break 'complex material into smaller steps', using information about prior knowledge to identify how small the steps need to be, and to learn how to support pupils in linking new learning to what they already know.

Managing the extraneous load requires teachers to carefully consider the classroom environment (and how conducive it is to learning) and the way in which we present material, so that we 'reduce distractions that take attention away from what is being taught' (DfE, 2019: 11). Chandler and Sweller (1992) found evidence of the split-attention effect, which occurs 'when different sources of information discussing the same topic are separated by time or space, such as a diagram with a key that corresponds to separate text next to it' (Shibli and West, 2018: no page), suggesting that this increases extraneous load as the learner needs to use their working memory to make connections between the different sources. Another example might be displaying a PowerPoint slide which is packed with words and expecting the children to read it while you are saying different words: there is conflict involved here.

Split-attention effect should not be confused with dual coding theory, which was first developed by Paivio in the 1970s (Sadoski and Paivio, 2013) and has been extensively tested since then. Paivio theorised that learners can process verbal and visual information during explanations separately, but at the same time. He found that this can later aid retrieval from long-term memory, as there are two potential 'memories' for the same information which can be retrieved. While split-attention effect increases extraneous load, and therefore increases the chance of cognitive overload, dual coding has been demonstrated to reduce extraneous load and therefore support learning (Sadoski and Paivio, 2013). Indeed, the DfE (2019: 17–18) identifies that student teachers should learn how to 'make good use of expositions' by 'combining a verbal explanation with a relevant graphical representation of the same concept or process, where appropriate'.

Case Study 5.1

Cognitive Overload

Lottie, a postgraduate student teacher on her second school placement, is teaching her first maths lesson to a Year 2 class. The focus of the lesson is fractions. Lottie has discussed the children's prior learning in Year 1 with the class teacher, so she knows that they have previously covered halves and quarters.

To begin the lesson, Lottie shows the children some pictorial representations of a new fractional amount, thirds, as outlined in the National Curriculum programme of study (DfE, 2013: 109). She has chosen to show a mix of shapes divided into parts and some written fractions; these are bunched together on one slide, and are thus quite small for the children to see. After a quick recap about what a fraction is, Lottie shows a 'fraction fun' video, which she hopes will help the children to remember some of the important vocabulary. After a brief and somewhat rushed explanation of how to colour in the fractional amounts, she sends the children to their tables with a worksheet to complete. The first task is to label the fraction shaded in a range of pictures. The second task is to shade in the parts of shapes that represent the given fractions. There are lots of words on the worksheet.

Soon after sending the children to their tables, Lottie finds that there are lots of hands in the air because children are unsure about what to do. The responses on the worksheets indicate that many of the children are confused and are guessing how many parts to colour in.

In her lesson evaluation, Lottie writes: 'the children did not get this today', but in discussion with her mentor, Lottie finds it quite difficult to unpick what had been unsuccessful about her teaching. Here is the advice she was given by her mentor:

> It's really important to make clear connections to prior learning: don't expect the children to just remember what they were taught and what they learnt last time. Start the lesson with a recap to reactivate that prior knowledge, and check that they are secure with that before moving on to the next step in the learning.
> Keep things simple:

Continued

- It's fine to have high expectations that they should use the right vocabulary, but think about how this is introduced. Help them to understand and remember those new or difficult words. Write them on the board, with pictorial prompts, and refer to them as you say them, or have flash cards or a word bank for them to use.
- Think about the presentation of information. Avoid cluttered, wordy PowerPoints. The children need to make sense of the information, so be aware of sensory overload. Make sure you don't confuse fun with learning: you thought the video might help them to remember but it actually added to the extraneous load.
- Consider the tasks you ask children to do: keep them simple and focused on the intended learning, making sure this is built around a sequence of small steps. Guide the children through a few examples together, but make sure you do most of the work in the first couple (modelling) and then encourage the children to do them more independently (guided practice). This should then prepare them for independent practice.

There is plenty of important feedback here for Lottie to consider; the mentor has really focused on the impact of Lottie's teaching on children's learning. Lottie needs to work on reducing intrinsic and extraneous load for children. It would be useful for Lottie to discuss with her mentor some practical and generic suggestions about the presentation of material and task design, so that she can adapt the suggestions to different lessons. Lottie would benefit from observing a subsequent maths lesson led by her teacher-mentor and noting carefully how the teacher builds on prior learning, breaks the learning into small steps and scaffolds the learning to support the children to make progress.

A key thing for all student teachers to learn, through working with expert colleagues, is how to reduce intrinsic and extraneous cognitive load. Shibli and West (2018: no page) suggest that there are three principles to remember to avoid cognitive overload:

- Break down subject content when introducing new topics and pause regularly to check understanding.
- Present instructions clearly without using too many sources of information at the same time.
- Be wary of reducing cognitive load too much: the learning process should be manageable, but not overly fragmented.

Question Guide 5.1

Reducing Cognitive Load

The *CCF* states that student teachers should:

> learn how to … avoid overloading working memory by … discussing and analysing with expert colleagues how to reduce distractions that take attention away from what is being

taught (e.g. keeping the complexity of a task to a minimum, so that attention is focused
on the content). (DfE, 2019: 11)

To help you to understand how teachers can reduce cognitive load, use some of these questions
to guide your discussions with an expert colleague:

- How do you ensure that lessons build on previous learning?
- How do you break down new material into smaller chunks?
- How do you ensure the learning environment helps children focus?
- What are your priorities when designing teaching resources?
- How do you ensure you do not aim to cover too much in the lesson?

Applying Knowledge of How Children Learn to Your Teaching

Having established some key ideas in terms of how pupils learn, we can now consider the
implications for teaching, some of which will be explored further in the next chapter.

Purposeful Practice

The DfE (2019: 12) suggests that 'regular purposeful practice of what has previously been
taught can help consolidate material and help pupils remember what they have learned',
which should therefore help children to store this learning in their long-term memory. The
more we practise something, the more automatic it becomes, as we established earlier. Howard-
Jones (2018: 132) suggests that practice 'paves the way for us to learn more'.

Drawing upon multiple bodies of research, Rosenshine (2012) developed ten principles of
instruction, which are intended to increase the effectiveness of teaching. One of these principles relates to guided practice. Rosenshine suggested that more effective teachers present new
learning in small chunks, following each with guided practice, where the teacher works with
pupils to complete further examples together, initially through modelling and then giving
increasing responsibility to the learners. This guided practice might be described as a sort of
'supported rehearsal' before children undertake independent practice.

Another principle (Rosenshine, 2012: 18) is to 'require and monitor independent practice',
which should follow guided practice. Again, the intention is that this should lead to automaticity and free up space in the working memory for new learning or to apply what has been
learnt in new contexts. Note the use of the word 'monitor' here. Just requiring significant independent practice is not enough: the teacher needs to monitor independent practice to check
for 'a high success rate', which is another of Rosenshine's principles (2012: 17). If you notice
that children are struggling during independent practice, then they need to be brought back
together for more guided practice.

Retrieval

If the information stored in long-term memory is going to be useful to children, they need to be able to retrieve it quickly and easily so that they can use it alongside new information in their working memory. There is now an understanding that the capacity to retrieve can be improved through practice, with the DfE (2019: 12) suggesting that 'requiring pupils to retrieve information from memory, and spacing practice so that pupils revisit ideas after a gap, are also likely to strengthen recall'.

The value of rapid retrieval from long-term memory can be exemplified through considering the process of early reading. You may have worked with a young child who is reading a new book to you, and you may have noticed what they do when decoding a new word. If they can retrieve the grapheme–phoneme correspondences, such as 'sh', quickly from the long-term memory, they are likely to be able to decode the new word sh-i-p fairly quickly, as their working memory is free to undertake the task of blending the phonemes together. However, if they struggle to match the graphemes with their corresponding phonemes, perhaps needing to refer to a classroom display or action as a prompt, there is less room in the working memory to blend the phonemes.

Observation Guide 5.1

Embedding Key Concepts

The *CCF* states that student teachers should 'learn how to … increase likelihood of material being retained, by … observing how expert colleagues plan regular review and practice of key ideas and concepts over time' (DfE, 2019: 12).

Observe how your teacher-mentor uses practice and retrieval to support children's learning. In particular, you should look out for the following:

- Is modelling used when new material is introduced?
- Is there an opportunity for guided practice, with the teacher working alongside the children on examples and gradually transferring responsibility over to the children?
- Do children then have the opportunity to undertake plenty of independent practice?
- How does the teacher-mentor respond if a child struggles during independent practice? Does the response change if there are multiple children struggling?
- When ideas are revisited, how is this done? How long is left between teaching and revisiting? Is the spacing always the same or does it differ?

Worked Examples

Guided practice, as discussed above, tends to be most effective when it is preceded by the use of modelling and worked examples, so that you take an 'I do it' (modelling and worked examples), 'we do it' (guided practice), 'you do it' (independent practice) approach to teaching.

The *CCF* (DfE, 2019: 12) notes that 'worked examples that take pupils through each step of a new process are also likely to support pupils to learn'. Rosenshine (2012: 15) concurs, suggesting that 'providing students with models and worked examples can help them learn to solve problems faster'.

It is important to recognise that this is not showing children 'what a good one looks like', with the emphasis on the product, but rather focuses on the process itself. As Eperjesi and Parkin (2020: 16) explain, children need to see *'how* you are working, rather than *what* you have done'. It follows, therefore, that you will need to articulate your thought process as you are working through an example.

Case Study 5.2

Applying Theory to Practice

Faye is the Assistant Headteacher of a large primary school. Below, she explains how developing her staff team's understanding of how children learn has been key to raising standards across the school:

> The Senior Leadership Team at school were familiar with the work of Rosenshine (2012) and Sherrington (2019) from our independent research. The Principles of Instruction particularly resonated with us, as this aligns with our own evidence-informed practice approach. We facilitated whole-school CPD [continuous professional development] about how children learn, with an emphasis on cognitive science and the brain, particularly the working and long-term memory. We explored how this translates into classroom practice, and staff began applying cognitive load theory in the classroom, as well as considering how and when to scaffold learning, and use retrieval strategies with maximum success.
>
> One key learning outcome for us as a staff team was reducing extraneous load. We had previously focused on ensuring worksheets and PowerPoints looked aesthetically pleasing, with images and colourful text, rather than considering the clarity of the information being presented for children. This was our first adaptation and is particularly evident in maths. We now have an agreed structure for PowerPoints, with agreed slide design and sequence across the whole school. This has reduced extraneous cognitive load and allows familiarity for the pupils, which has reduced learning anxiety; children know the routine and 'what comes next'.
>
> We created an action plan to incrementally embed the principles of instruction, focusing on each of Sherrington's (2019) four strands in turn: reviewing material, questioning, sequencing concepts and modelling, and stages of practice. This has involved staff exploring the research and evidence behind each 'big idea'. Staff worked in 'coaching pairs' to observe one another implementing each idea in the classroom and have shared examples of good practice with each other. We reviewed our Teaching and

Continued

Learning policy in line with the research, and staff in school are feeling more confident in implementing the strategies. There has been a positive impact on engagement for all pupils and an increasing number of pupils are able to 'remember more over time', with staff focusing on effective retrieval, building working and long-term memory and sequencing a progressive curriculum to develop schemata. On reflection, many of the strategies were already being used by some of our teachers; sharing this evidence and research base means that all staff are now acutely aware of the rationale informing their classroom pedagogy.

We can see from this account that there are two key aspects that have led to school improvement. First, there was a willingness of the staff to take on board the pedagogical ideas because they were research-based and supported by evidence. Second, teachers worked collaboratively to support each other's professional development, recognising that this would ultimately have an impact on children's learning.

Brain Science and Neuromyths

We now know more about the developing brain and cognitive processes than we have ever known before because of scientific and technological advances. However, teachers should be selective and cautious about the validity of information presented to us. Weisberg et al. (2008: 470) refer to the 'seductive allure of neuroscience explanations' and warn against believing anything which is not based on robust evidence or research.

Deans for Impact (2015: no page) states that 'Teachers should be able to recognise common misconceptions of cognitive science that relate to teaching and learning'. These particular misconceptions might also be known as 'neuromyths'.

━ Critical Task 5.2 ━

Neuromyths: True or False?

Consider the statements in Table 5.1. Are they based on scientific fact and research or are they neuromyths? Think about what influenced your answer.

Table 5.1 Neuromyths

Playing brain games makes you more intelligent.	Children can have different learning styles; these are visual, kinaesthetic and auditory.	We only ever use 10% of our brain.
Individuals are either left-brain or right-brain thinkers and this has an impact on their cognition and personalities.	Intelligence is fixed.	Most learning happens in the first three years of life.

When you have decided which ones you think are true, undertake some reading to find out if you were correct or not, and establish how and why these statements are now commonplace.

What Do You Know and Believe About the Brain?

The media, including social media, play a considerable part in convincing us about how the brain behaves and how we might use this knowledge to increase brain activity and improve learning. The challenge here is to separate truths, which are usually supported by rigorous research and study, from fiction.

One common neuromyth is the idea that people have particular learning styles, suggesting that understanding learning styles will enable the teacher to match learning activities appropriately. The *CCF* (DfE, 2019: 20–21) states: it is 'a common misconception that pupils have distinct and identifiable learning styles. This is not supported by evidence and attempting to tailor lessons to learning styles is unlikely to be beneficial.' A US review into all available research concluded that there was not one single study which could prove that using learning styles to inform teaching led to children achieving better results (Pashler et al., 2008). Unfortunately, despite this, the myth about learning styles still exists.

Chapter Summary

In this chapter, we have established that learning is about change, where children build their understanding of the world by making connections with their previous knowledge. We have considered a number of theories about how children learn, and why it is important for teachers to understand these theories. We have explored the role that memory can play in learning and that teachers need to be mindful about avoiding cognitive overload, and we have offered some strategies for doing so. We have considered some important implications for our teaching, as well as recognising that, while understanding brain science is important, teachers need to be certain about what is supported by evidence and what is not.

Further Reading

Aubrey, K. and Riley, A. (2022) *Understanding and using educational theories* (3rd edn). London: Sage.
This is a good starting point to help you find out more about the educational theories discussed here, along with the ideas of a range of influential thinkers whose work has helped shape what we know about learning today.

Willingham, D.T. (2009) *Why don't students like school?* San Francisco, CA: Jossey-Bass.
This is an easy-to-read, interesting and thought-provoking text about cognition and learning, and what it means for the classroom and you as a student teacher.

References

Aubrey, K. and Riley, A. (2022) *Understanding and using educational theories* (3rd edn). London: Sage.

Bates, B. (2019) *Learning theories simplified* (2nd edn). London: Sage.

Bruner, J. (1966) *Toward a theory of instruction.* Cambridge, MA: Harvard University Press.

Chandler, P. and Sweller, J. (1992) 'The split-attention effect as a factor in the design of instruction', *British Journal of Educational Psychology*, 62, 233–246.

Deans for Impact (2015) *The science of learning.* Austin, TX: Deans for Impact.

Department for Education (DfE) (2013) *The national curriculum in England: Key stages 1 and 2 framework document.* London: DfE.

Department for Education (DfE) (2019) *ITT core content framework.* London: DfE.

Dweck, C.S. (2006) *Mindset: The new psychology of success.* New York: Random House.

Eperjesi, R. with Parkin, A. (2020) 'Art and design: modelling to promote creativity', in C. Forster and R. Eperjesi (eds.), *Teaching the primary curriculum.* London: Sage, pp. 11–27.

Hattie, J. (2012) *Visible learning for teachers: Maximizing impact on learning.* London: Routledge.

Hattie, J. and Hamilton, A. (2020) 'Real gold vs. fool's gold: the visible learning™ methodology for finding what works best in education'. Available at: www.visiblelearning.com/sites/default/files/Real%20Gold%20vs.%20Fools%20Gold_FINAL_app.pdf (accessed 11 February 2023).

Holt, J.C. (1982) *How children fail.* New York: Delta/Seymour Lawrence.

Howard-Jones, P. (2018) *Evolution of the learning brain.* Abingdon, UK: Routledge.

Kirschner, P.A., Sweller, J. and Clark, R.E. (2006) 'Why minimal guidance during instruction does not work: an analysis of the failure of constructivist, discovery, problem-based, experiential, and inquiry-based teaching', *Educational Psychologist*, 41(2), 75–86.

Lin-Siegler, X., Ahn, J.N., Chen, J., Fang, F. and Luna-Lucero, M. (2016) 'Even Einstein struggled: effects of learning about great scientists' struggles on high school students' motivation to learn science', *Journal of Educational Psychology*, 108(3), 314–328.

Macblain, S. (2022) 'How do children learn?', in C. Carden (ed.), *Primary teaching: Learning and teaching in primary schools today* (2nd edn). London: Sage/Learning Matters, pp. 59–80.

Pashler, H., McDaniel, M., Rohrer, D. and Bjork, R. (2008) 'Learning styles: concepts and evidence', *Psychological Science in the Public Interest*, 9(3), 105–119.

Piaget, J. and Inhelder, B. (1969) *The psychology of the child.* New York: Basic Books.

Rosenshine, B. (2012) 'Principles of Instruction: research-based strategies that all teachers should know', *American Educator*, Spring, 12–20.

Sadoski, M. and Paivio, A. (2013) *Imagery and text: A dual coding theory of reading and writing.* Oxford: Taylor & Francis.

Sherrington, T. (2019) *Rosenshine's principles in action.* Woodbridge, UK: John Catt Educational Ltd.

Shibli, D. and West, R. (2018) *Cognitive load theory and its application in the classroom.* Available at: https://my.chartered.college/impact_article/cognitive-load-theory-and-its-application-in-the-classroom/ (accessed 11 February 2023).

Sweller, J. (1988) 'Cognitive load during problem solving: effects on learning', *Cognitive Science*, 12(2), 257–285.

Vygotsky, L.S. (1978) *Mind in society: The development of higher psychological processes.* Cambridge, MA: Harvard University Press.

Weisberg, D.S., Keil, F.C., Goodstein, J., Rawson, E. and Gray, J.R. (2008) 'The seductive allure of neuroscience explanations', *Journal of Cognitive Neuroscience*, 20(3), 470–477.

Wiliam, D. (2016) *Learning styles: What does the research say?* Available at: https://deansforimpact. org/learning-styles-what-does-the-research-say/ (accessed 11 February 2023).

Willingham, D.T. (2009) *Why don't students like school?* San Francisco, CA: Jossey-Bass.

Wray, D. (2018) 'Looking at learning', in T. Cremin and C. Burnett (eds.), *Learning to teach in the primary school* (4th edn). London: Sage/Learning Matters, pp. 66–76.

6
PLANNING AND TEACHING FOR MEANINGFUL LEARNING

Kate Thomson

--- Chapter Objectives ---

- To explore the factors that might influence planning decisions.
- To consider the importance of using research to inform planning and teaching.
- To reflect on the most impactful aspects of planning and teaching for meaningful learning.

In this chapter, we explore the importance of planning and reflect on the planning and teaching strategies that are likely to have most impact on pupils' learning. We establish that careful thinking about learning outcomes, the role of the teacher and the sequence of learning experiences are particularly important in securing pupils' progress.

Why is Planning Important?

Most student teachers start their training with aspirations to become 'great' teachers, and to 'make a difference'. It is surprisingly challenging to define what constitutes 'great' teaching. Coe et al. (2014: 9) recognise that 'it makes sense to judge the effectiveness of teaching from its impact on assessed learning'. Our goal, therefore, should be to implement strategies that enable us to make a difference, by maximising the impact that we have on children's learning. A focus on careful and considered planning is a mechanism for doing this.

Classroom life is fast paced and busy; there is a lot for teachers to think about when they are in the heart of the action. It makes sense, then, to make some decisions before the lesson starts and to have a coherent plan for learning in the short, medium and long term.

Planning is a problem-solving activity; it is the place where logical, reasoned thinking about teaching and learning meets creativity. It is through planning that teachers can construct an engaging learning adventure for the children they teach and ensure all children make progress.

Critical Task 6.1

Teacher Decision-making

Think about a lesson you have observed recently. Take a ten-minute period of that lesson and make a list of all the decisions you think the teacher had to make. Now reflect on that decision-making process.

- Which decisions had to be made in the moment?
- Which decisions could have been made in advance, when planning?
- Which decisions had most impact on pupils' learning and so need more careful thought?

Planning at Different Levels

In recent years, there has been increased emphasis on curriculum design and planning. Ofsted (2019) has emphasised that the curriculum lies at the heart of education. Most schools will produce curriculum plans at a range of levels. These reflect the school's 'intent' and show how the curriculum will be 'implemented' in the classroom:

- **Whole school plans**: show what will be taught and when it will be taught, across the school and across the year.
- **Medium-term plans**: show the sequence of lessons, within a unit of work.
- **Weekly or other short-term planning**: show the detail of the planned teaching, including how it will be informed by assessment.

When training, student teachers are also usually required to write lesson plans. These enable them to learn how to interpret the curriculum requirements, devise learning objectives and pupil activities, and plan their teaching role. The process also allows student teachers to engage in mental rehearsal of the lesson and perhaps identify any potential issues or challenges in advance.

A Word About Workload

Planning is important because it means that teachers approach their practice in a thoughtful and well-focused way and make best use of the teaching time available. The planning process helps teachers to focus on learning and encourages them to think carefully about their role in securing pupils' progress.

However, research on workload shows that some schools have, in the past, made excessive demands on teachers in terms of paperwork and planning (Independent Teacher Workload Review Group, 2016). Excessive paperwork can distract teachers from the core business of thinking carefully about how they will implement the curriculum and meet the needs of the children in their care. Kathryn Greenhalgh, Chair of the Review Group, concluded that 'teachers want to spend their time on the things that will make the biggest difference to pupils' learning and progress' (Independent Teacher Workload Review Group, 2016: 3). This means thinking carefully about what to write in plans at all levels, and only writing those things that are likely to make a difference to the quality of the teaching and the impact on learning.

Identifying a Clear and Explicit Focus for Learning

As we have established, careful planning enables teachers to implement lessons that are focused and purposeful. Some aspects of planning seem to be more important than others because they allow us to maximise the impact we have on the learners. It is vital that teachers are clear about *what* they want children to learn in a particular lesson and can communicate this clearly to pupils. Hay McBer (2000: 11) noted that 'in classes run by effective teachers, pupils are clear about what they are doing and why they are doing it'.

The process of writing learning objectives begins with interpretation of the curriculum. Teachers should select aspects of the *National curriculum* (Department for Education (DfE), 2013) that they intend to address in a particular lesson or series of lessons. This enables the teacher to establish what will be taught. As you will see in Chapter 11, it is important to use assessment to 'pitch your teaching', so that any learning episode you plan builds on the learning that has gone before and is appropriately challenging. Knowledge of the curriculum and the needs of the children you are teaching will enable you to identify appropriate expectations. It is helpful to ask yourself:

- What do I want children to *know*?
- What do I want children to *understand*?
- What do I want children to *be able to do* by the end of this lesson or series of lessons?

In this way, learning objectives will usually provide a clear statement of the knowledge, concepts and skills you want children to learn. Fautley and Savage (2013) stress the importance of focusing on learning, rather than doing, when writing learning objectives. The learning objectives are statements describing what you want children to *learn* by the end of the lesson, rather than what you are going to ask them to *do*.

In a Key Stage 2 history lesson, in a unit of work on the Stone Age to the Iron Age, we might decide the learning objectives are:

- To know the features of the houses in the Neolithic settlement of Skara Brae (knowledge).
- To understand why the houses were built in this way (conceptual understanding).
- To use photographs and archaeologists' drawings to ask and answer questions about the past (skills).

Critical Task 6.2

Focused Lesson Objectives

These objectives for the same lesson would be less successful. Can you explain why?

- To know about Skara Brae.
- To understand the work of archaeologists.
- To annotate a picture of Skara Brae.

When considering the objectives in Critical Task 6.2, it is likely that you have identified the following:

- Objective 1 is too broad. It would not make the lesson tightly focused. The teacher would not be clear about the specific knowledge that needs to be taught.
- Objective 2 uses the wording 'understand', when 'know about' would be more appropriate. This objective does not have a focus on conceptual understanding.
- Objective 3 describes the teaching and learning *activity* rather than the skills-based *learning*.

It is important to be realistic about what can be achieved in a particular lesson. Most lessons will have two or three learning objectives. Your aim will be to support all children to reach these objectives by the end of the lesson. As a rule, it is better to 'do less, better' and recognise that deep learning will come from explicit, well-focused and well-paced teaching. It is better to focus on a few learning objectives and teach them well than teach many issues superficially.

Other strategies can also be used to ensure there is an explicit focus for learning in your plans. An enquiry-led approach, where children work to answer an overarching question, is useful in motivating children and establishing a focus for learning. For example, in a geography lesson, a Year 6 class might explore physical processes by investigating the question: 'Why does the River Severn flood?'. The question is posed at the beginning of the lesson, pupils undertake investigations using a variety of sources and draw conclusions based on 'evidence and rigorous thinking' (Catling and Willy, 2018: 10). In a later lesson, pupils might be asked, 'How might we prevent flooding in the future?'. This emphasis on enquiry ensures that geography teaching is purposeful and problem-oriented, and that there is a focus on higher-order thinking skills, such as investigating, analysing, evaluating and proposing solutions (Catling and Willy, 2018).

By devising clear learning objectives and using questions as a planning tool, you can ensure that your teaching is aligned with the curriculum requirements and is well focused.

Planning Your Role as a Teacher

Planning involves thinking critically about the deployment of resources in a lesson. The most important resource in the room is you, the teacher. You have the potential to make a real difference to pupil outcomes if you think carefully about your role within a lesson. Hay McBer's (2000: 6) research into teacher effectiveness found that there are three 'distinctive and complementary' factors within teachers' control that significantly influence pupil progress:

- teaching skills
- professional characteristics
- classroom climate.

The focus on teaching skills here is important. Hay McBer (2000: 11) found that effective teachers 'were very actively involved with their pupils at all times'. Effective teachers create a purposeful learning environment by deploying a range of carefully selected teaching skills and techniques. They make the most of every opportunity to teach and to scaffold and support children's learning.

This is a significant point: what we have learnt is that effective teachers *teach*. This should not come as a surprise, but it is all too easy to focus on planning pupil activities rather than thinking about the teaching process. Effective teachers do not simply set tasks and then sit back and watch while the pupils complete them: they engage in direct and explicit teaching which moves children on in their learning.

The quality of teaching matters. What a teacher says and does in a lesson matters. It is therefore important that these aspects of practice are given due attention during the planning process.

More recent thinking about teacher effectiveness has been influenced by research into children's learning. As we have seen in Chapter 5, work in the field of cognitive science, particularly that related to working memory and long-term memory, seems to suggest that some approaches to teaching and learning are more effective than others (Deans for Impact, 2015). Pupils are likely to need explicit teaching of knowledge and skills, and planned opportunities to revisit and practise what they have learned (Rosenshine, 2012). It is important that teachers engage in whole-class teaching, but also intervene in purposeful ways with groups and individuals to move their learning on.

Teaching strategies such as direct instruction, modelling and questioning are particularly important in developing pupils' knowledge, conceptual understanding and skills. Deans for Impact (2015: 3) note that 'making content explicit through carefully paced explanation, modelling, and examples can help ensure that students are not overwhelmed'.

Direct instruction: This is 'a teaching style in which the teacher is actively engaged in bringing the content of the lesson to pupils by teaching the whole class directly' (Muijs and Reynolds, 2018: 36). Periods of direct instruction should be well structured, so pupils can make links with what they already know (Rosenshine, 2012). Learning objectives should be shared explicitly with pupils (Muijs and Reynolds, 2018) and material should be broken down into small steps. There should be time built in for practice before moving on to the next step (Rosenshine, 2012; Muijs and Reynolds, 2018).

Modelling: 'Modelling is the process of making new learning explicit to pupils' (Glazzard and Stones, 2021: 47). Modelling can take a variety of forms but is likely to involve periods of demonstration. Teachers can support learning by modelling each step in the learning process systematically and by providing opportunities for 'guided practice' (Glazzard and Stones, 2021: 48). Effective teaching also involves modelling metacognitive strategies, such as checking and editing work, and 'thinking aloud': this means modelling the thought processes that accompany a process, such as 'narrating' use of the index in a non-fiction book.

Questioning: Teachers employ a variety of questioning strategies for different reasons. Questions can be used to assess pupils' understanding, but also to help them to practise 'new material' and connect new information to their prior learning (Rosenshine, 2012: 14). Questions can also be used to prompt higher-order thinking skills, such as inference, analysis and evaluation.

Teachers need to think carefully about how and when these strategies are implemented, so that learning is broken down into small steps, teaching is explicit and pupils can make good progress.

Observation Guide 6.1

Teaching Strategies

The *ITT Core Content Framework* (CCF) states that student teachers should learn to plan effective lessons by:

- Using modelling, explanations and scaffolds, acknowledging that novices need more structure early on in a domain.

- Including a range of types of questions in class discussions to extend and challenge pupils (e.g., by modelling new vocabulary or asking pupils to justify answers).
- Providing appropriate wait time between question and response where more developed responses are required. (DfE, 2019: 17–18)

On placement, watch your class teacher as they are teaching and, using Table 6.1, record all the instances when they carry out the following teaching strategies:

Table 6.1 Teaching strategies

Teaching strategies	The example I observed	The impact that this strategy had on children's learning (knowledge, understanding and skills)
Tell		
Explain		
Model		
Ask		
Demonstrate		

At which point(s) in the lesson did you observe these strategies? For example, did you observe them during a whole-class teaching episode at the beginning of the lesson, or while children were working in groups or independently?

Did you notice any other ways in which the teacher supported or extended the children's learning?

Since these strategies are so important in terms of their impact on learning, they must be carefully planned. It can be helpful to make explicit use of 'teaching verbs' in a lesson plan. These might even be written in a different colour, so they stand out:

- tell
- explain
- model
- ask
- demonstrate.

It is often helpful to plan what you will do and say while employing these strategies. For example, in an English lesson, a teacher may decide to use shared writing to model the writing process. In this case, it will be helpful for them to plan what they will *write* on the whiteboard in the demonstration phase of the lesson, but it will also be helpful for them to plan what they will *say*. This might involve narrating the thinking process, explaining word choices or modelling reading aloud to check the text makes sense. By modelling metacognitive strategies and 'thinking aloud', teachers can draw attention to strategies that are not always intuitive (Glazzard and Stones, 2021: 50). Of course, it is likely that the modelling process will also include some elements of telling (e.g., punctuation rules, word meaning) and questioning. Questioning may be rhetorical, such as when thinking aloud a teacher may ask themselves: 'Which word works best here?'. Alternatively, as advised by Glazzard and Stones (2021), questioning may be used to check understanding, as part of the modelling process: 'Now I have shown you, can you tell the person next to you what makes a good piece of persuasive writing?'.

It is worth investing time in planning the detail of the teaching strategies you will employ because research identifies a correlation between the quality of instruction and pupils' learning (Coe et al., 2014). This may mean mentally rehearsing what you will say and do or making brief notes in a weekly plan or lesson plan. It is not always necessary to write at length, but it is important to think through what you will say and do, and record the things that may be difficult to remember.

Case Study 6.1

Planning for Teaching

Josh, an undergraduate student teacher, has just taught a history lesson. The start of the lesson seemed to have gone well. The Year 2 class was engaged by Josh's animated retelling of the story of the Great Fire of London. He asked some good questions, which helped the children to reflect on what had happened during this event.

The children then began some independent work, labelling contemporary pictures of the fire. This part of the lesson was less successful; some children could not describe what they could see in the picture, while others struggled to write. Josh moved around the room, responding to individual children when they asked for help. He often simply restated the task.

In their feedback, Josh's mentor suggests that his teaching in this phase was not well focused and that the issue lay with his planning. This is Josh's plan for this part of the lesson:

> Hand out the pictures. Tell the children to label the picture. Circulate and help children who get stuck.

Josh emphasised planning the parts of the lesson where he was working with the whole class, and perhaps failed to recognise that he had an opportunity to have an impact on children's learning throughout the whole lesson. His focus on simply 'helping' during the independent phase of the lesson led him to underestimate his role in supporting pupils' progress.

It might have been helpful for Josh to replace the word 'help' with the word 'teach' and to ask himself, when planning, what he might teach and how he might teach, as he works with groups and individuals. In this instance, Josh might have:

- asked some questions to check and extend pupils' understanding

- explicitly taught some subject-specific vocabulary, to help children name features in the pictures
- modelled the skill of labelling.

By thinking carefully about his teaching role in the main part of the lesson, Josh could have extended the impact he had on pupils' learning.

Critical Task 6.3

Planning for Impact

In Case Study 6.1, we considered Josh's planning for his teaching, which included this phrase:

> *Hand out the pictures. Tell the children to label the picture. Circulate and help children who get stuck.*

Can you rewrite this part of Josh's plan for him? What could he do to support children who were labelling pictures of the Great Fire of London? Think about how he might deploy some of the teaching strategies we have discussed previously, such as direct instruction, modelling and questioning.

Constructing the Learning Journey: Planning for Progression in Learning

It is helpful to consider learning as a journey. The journey begins with an understanding of children's existing levels of knowledge and understanding and finishes when the children meet the new learning objectives. Many researchers have recognised the importance of breaking learning down into small steps, with opportunities for direct instruction and guided practice along the way (Hay McBer, 2000; Rosenshine, 2012). Rosenshine (2012) identifies this as one of six key instructional behaviours employed by effective teachers. This strategy is likely to be effective because it breaks the material into manageable 'bite-sized' pieces. Research on learning theory suggests that it is important to avoid cognitive overload and stresses the importance of considering the capacity of young children's working memories when planning for progression (Deans for Impact, 2015). By taking small steps, learning can build incrementally and sequentially.

It is likely that you will need to plan small steps within a lesson. This might involve, for instance, direct instruction and teacher-led modelling, followed by guided practice and, ultimately, independent work. The learning is broken down into its constituent parts and scaffolded at every stage of the lesson (Glazzard and Stones, 2021). For example, when teaching a Year 4 class about volcanoes, a teacher might use diagrams to explain how volcanoes are formed and what happens when they erupt. This might involve some explicit teaching of geographical language, such as magma, crater, vent, lava and ash clouds, and an explanation of the physical processes involved. Later in the lesson, pupils might be asked to use and apply this new knowledge when labelling photographs of a real volcano and perhaps explain what is happening while watching film footage of a specific eruption. In this example, the period of direct instruction has given children the knowledge and understanding they need to be able to engage fully with the independent task. Direct instruction has been followed by guided practice (Muijs and Reynolds, 2018).

The focus on sequencing is equally important when planning a series of lessons within a unit of work. In the past, teachers were often encouraged to begin the planning process by brainstorming ideas for activities and producing a topic web. The problem with this approach was that it did not give due attention to sequence. To maximise impact, teachers need to break learning into small steps and think carefully about the order of lessons (Rosenshine, 2012).

Let us take the step analogy a little bit further: let us imagine a staircase. We can use the staircase in Figure 6.1 as a framework for planning a sequence of lessons within a unit of work. Each step on the staircase represents one activity or lesson.

The staircase analogy reminds us that we should have high expectations, and that children should make progress as they work through the sequence of lessons. The analogy also reminds us that every step on the staircase rests upon, and is supported by, the step below. Early lessons give children the knowledge that they need to develop conceptual understanding later in the unit of work. This ensures 'that students have the prior knowledge they need to master new

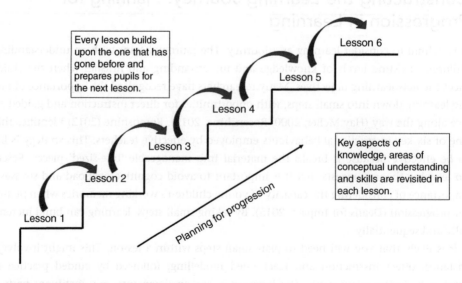

Figure 6.1 Annotated staircase diagram

ideas' (Deans for Impact, 2015). Early lessons in the sequence provide the firm foundations for the more challenging work that follows.

The planning process might begin by drawing a staircase and plotting out a sequence of lessons, writing an idea for a lesson on each step. Alternatively, a 'staircase' might be constructed on a table-top, using sequenced sticky notes. Teachers might plan by writing an idea for each activity on each separate note and then explore different ways of sequencing them, so that learning builds step by step. It can be helpful to 'think aloud' when exploring the rationale for a sequence: 'This lesson has to come first because ...', 'This lesson builds on the one before by ...', 'This lesson needs to come near the end of the sequence because ...'.

It is often helpful to plan the last lesson in the sequence first. Ask yourself: What do you want children to be able to do by the end of the unit of work? What can I plan in the last lesson that will challenge and extend learning? Once this final lesson is planned, you can then identify the steps to learning that need to precede it. This can be done by identifying what children need to know, understand and be able to do in order to engage fully with the last task and meet the learning objectives for the unit of work.

Some lessons are better taught at the beginning of the sequence, whereas others are better placed towards the end of the unit. A common error that many inexperienced teachers make when planning for the foundation subjects is to plan extended writing tasks too early in the sequence of lessons. It is important to remember that children need to know and understand a great deal to be able to produce pieces of high-quality, non-fiction writing. They also need plenty of opportunities to talk about the content they are going to write about (Palmer, 2011).

Critical Task 6.4

Critiquing Planning

Consider this scenario where a teacher wants children to learn about the sinking of the *Titanic*, as part of a history unit on significant events in the past, at Key Stage 1.

> In lesson 1, the teacher starts by telling the children the story of this event.
> The children are then asked to write a recount of the event in their own words.

This lesson is unlikely to go well. Year 2 children are unlikely to know or understand enough about this event, at this point in the sequence, to produce a high-quality piece of writing. Sometimes teachers explain underachievement by focusing on problems the child may have. In fact, it is the teacher who has created the problem here. They have not broken the learning down into enough steps (Rosenshine, 2012). They have not understood that new knowledge needs to be introduced and then revisited and reinforced, before young children are able to retrieve this information with ease and use it in new ways. They have not understood that children need to talk about the event, before they can be expected to write about it (Palmer, 2011).

Continued

This scenario might be better:

Lesson one: The teacher uses contemporary pictures to tell the story of the voyage of the *Titanic*. The children talk about what happened and write a caption for a photograph of the ship in the dock.

Lesson two: The teacher helps children to remember what they learned about in the last lesson. The teacher reads a picture book version of the story. The children are guided to listen out for new information. They record three things they now know about the *Titanic*.

Lesson three: The teacher explains what a timeline is and models working from left to right, sequencing pictures of the event on a washing line. The teacher explains that the spacing between the pictures is important, because it shows how much time has passed between each event. The children work in groups to sequence a larger set of pictures to create a table-top timeline.

Lesson four: The teacher explains the features of a recount, making links to previous learning in English. They model the writing process for children, by recounting an event that all the class have participated in. The children write a simple recount, with some receiving additional support through engaging in guided writing.

Lesson five: The class watches a video about the *Titanic*. With the teacher's help, the children use the pictures from lesson 1 as prompts to retell the story, adding detail by drawing upon the knowledge they have gained in lessons 1–4. The children use a writing frame and a word bank to write their own recount of the voyage of the *Titanic*.

Consider what makes the second plan better. How has the teacher broken the learning down into steps? How have they prepared children for the challenging writing task at the end of the unit? How does each lesson build upon the one that has gone before?
   Now consider whether the learning objectives for this sequence of lessons have been met.

Learning objectives:

- To know what happened to the *Titanic* on its first voyage.
- To understand the sequence of events within the story.
- To use stories and picture sources to find out about the *Titanic*.

See if you can identify where each of these objectives was explicitly taught within the unit.

In the second example explored in Critical Task 6.4, you should notice that the teacher has planned opportunities for pupils to revisit and build upon prior knowledge and understanding. The teacher recognises that this knowledge is new to these young children and that they will have to work hard to make this new knowledge 'stick' in the pupils' long-term memory. Once knowledge is secure, pupils are then asked to use and apply what they have learnt in a new context.

Through the careful sequencing of small steps, the teacher has planned for progression in historical knowledge. The children know much more at the end of the sequence than they did at the beginning. This knowledge has, in turn, enabled the pupils to develop an understanding of the chronology of the event.

In every lesson, there is explicit teaching: direct instruction, modelling and scaffolding and, over time, the children are supported in moving from dependence to independence. They are given the knowledge, understanding and skills to enable them to do this.

Sometimes, teachers worry that this process is time-consuming, and that planning opportunities for revisiting means that less material can be covered in a unit of work as a whole. It is worth remembering that the *National curriculum* (DfE, 2013) sets out the minimum statutory requirements: the *what* of the curriculum. It is up to individual teachers to determine *how* this will be taught. On balance, it seems better to recognise that effective teaching takes time, and to do less, better. As we have seen, careful sequencing, and planned opportunities for revisiting and practising, promote deep learning and ensure pupil progress (Deans for Impact, 2015).

Question Guide 6.1

Teaching for Long-term Learning

The *CCF* states that student teachers should:

> Learn how to … model effectively by … discussing and analysing with expert colleagues how to make the steps in a process memorable and ensuring pupils can recall them (e.g., naming them, developing mnemonics, or linking to memorable stories). (DfE, 2019: 18)

When reflecting on effective practice while on placement, here are some questions to ask your teacher-mentor or another member of the teaching team about how they teach for long-term learning. Remember to frame your questions professionally and positively, to avoid any suggestion of implied criticism.

- What do children in this class find difficult to remember?
- How do you help children commit new knowledge to their long-term memory?
- How important is repetition? Do you think it is possible to repeat too often?

Continued

- How important is it to revisit new knowledge and ideas throughout a unit of work or across a term or year?
- How do you create 'hooks' for remembering using resources or storytelling?
- Can you give me an example where you have used a mnemonic to help children remember?
- Do you use different strategies for helping children remember a process rather than a set of facts?
- Do you use different strategies with different groups and individuals?
- How do you know whether children have remembered the things you have taught them?

Chapter Summary

In this chapter, we have discussed the importance of careful and considered thinking about planning and teaching to ensure meaningful learning. Planning enables the teacher to construct a learning journey that has a significant impact on learning. It encourages teachers to think critically about their own practice in the classroom and their own role at each stage of the lesson. We have identified some key elements of effective practice, such as the need to be clear about learning outcomes and to engage in clear and explicit teaching in every lesson. We have also considered the central importance of breaking learning down into small steps, doing less better, and thinking carefully about the sequence of learning opportunities when planning. It is by employing strategies such as these, that we can have a significant impact on pupils' learning.

Further Reading

The following online materials and text may be helpful in further developing your knowledge and understanding of planning and teaching for meaningful learning:

Education Endowment Foundation (EEF) (2023) *Teaching and learning toolkit*. Available at: https://educationendowmentfoundation.org.uk/education-evidence/teaching-learning-toolkit (accessed 11 April 2023).

This resource is an accessible summary of a wide range of approaches to improving teaching and learning. It is based on research evidence and aims to support teachers in making decisions about how they might improve learning outcomes for children.

Muijs, D. and Reynolds, D. (2017) *Effective teaching: Evidence and practice* (4th edn). London: Sage.

This book provides a useful overview of the characteristics of effective teaching, including chapters on direct instruction, interactive teaching, collaborative group work and metacognition, and self-regulated learning.

References

Catling, S. and Willy, T. (2018) *Understanding and teaching primary geography* (2nd edn). London: Sage.

Coe, R., Aloisi, C., Higgins, S. and Major, L.E. (2014) *What makes great teaching? Review of the underpinning research. Project report for the Sutton Trust, London.* Durham: Centre for Evaluation and Monitoring, Durham University.

Deans for Impact (2015) *The science of learning.* Austin, TX: Deans for Impact.

Department for Education (DfE) (2013) *The national curriculum in England: Key stages 1 and 2 framework document.* London: DfE.

Department for Education (DfE) (2019) *ITT core content framework.* London: DfE.

Fautley, M. and Savage, J. (2013) *Lesson planning for effective learning.* Maidenhead: Open University Press.

Glazzard, J. and Stones, S. (2021) *Evidence based primary teaching.* London: Learning Matters/Sage.

Hay McBer (2000) *Research into teacher effectiveness: A model of teacher effectiveness. Research Report No. 216.* Norwich: Department for Education and Employment.

Independent Teacher Workload Review Group (2016) *Eliminating unnecessary workload around planning and teaching resources: Report of the Independent Teacher Workload Review Group.* London: Department for Education.

Muijs, D. and Reynolds, D. (2018) *Effective teaching: evidence and practice* (4th edn). London: Sage.

Ofsted (2019) *Education inspection framework: overview of research.* London: Ofsted.

Palmer, S. (2011) *How to teach writing across the curriculum: Ages 6–8.* London: Routledge.

Rosenshine, B. (2012) 'Principles of Instruction: research-based strategies that all teachers should know', *American Educator,* Spring, 12–20.

7
ADAPTIVE TEACHING

Rachel Eperjesi

┌─ **Chapter Objectives** ───┐

- To consider what adaptive teaching is and its importance.
- To explore some approaches to adaptive teaching.
- To identify links between adaptive teaching and other aspects of effective teaching.

└──┘

In this chapter, we define 'adaptive teaching' and consider why it is an important aspect of effective teaching. Throughout, we recognise and value all learners as individuals, while also acknowledging the importance of setting 'high expectations for all pupils' (Department for Education (DfE), 2013: 8). We explore some approaches to adaptive teaching. We reflect on links between effective adaptive teaching and other aspects of teaching, such as planning, assessment and working collaboratively.

What is Adaptive Teaching and Why is it Important?

In the *Teachers' standards* (DfE, 2011: 11), adaptive teaching is defined as when teachers 'adapt teaching to respond to the strengths and needs of all pupils'. The *ITT Core Content Framework (CCF)* (DfE, 2019) incorporates a series of 'Learn that...' and 'Learn how to...' statements in section 5 (Adaptive teaching) as a framework for student teachers' learning in this key area of pedagogy.

The PISA 2015 results (Organisation for Economic Co-operation and Development (OECD), 2016) found that academic attainment was significantly higher for pupils whose teachers always or regularly adapted teaching to the needs of the pupils, than for pupils whose teachers did that rarely or never. As an international study, PISA results are highly regarded and influential in shaping educational policy. It is important to recognise that the 2015 results focused particularly on teaching and attainment in science for 15-year-olds, but are also likely to apply across the primary age range and across the curriculum.

To successfully engage in adaptive teaching, student teachers first need to accept the fundamental principle that 'pupils are likely to learn at different rates and to require different levels and types of support from teachers to succeed' (DfE, 2019: 20). If you have spent some time in a primary classroom, or indeed in any learning environment with multiple learners, you are likely to have noticed this already. I have vivid memories from my childhood of undertaking summer school swimming lessons and remaining in the beginners' group all week, while others who were with me on Monday had advanced through multiple groups by the end of the week. You can probably think of examples from your own childhood, or perhaps as an adult, such as finding learning to drive much easier or much more difficult than a friend.

The notion of adaptive teaching, therefore, is simply that as children will learn at different rates and need different support to learn, our teaching needs to recognise that by adapting to ensure that all children's progress is maximised and to avoid a 'one-size-fits-all' model. If we applied that principle to clothes or shoes, we would quickly see how ridiculous a 'one-size-fits-all' model is. The same is true of teaching.

— Critical Task 7.1 —

Which Children May Need Adaptive Teaching?

Spend some time considering the sorts of situations and scenarios which might lead to a child needing adaptive teaching to maximise their progress.

Which Children May Need Adaptive Teaching?

When completing Critical Task 7.1, you may have identified that children with special educational needs and/or disability (SEND) and children learning English as an Additional Language (EAL) are likely to need adaptive teaching, and you are quite right. However, it goes beyond that. Every child is a unique learner, with their own individual and diverse learning needs. A child may need very little additional support to succeed in one subject but need far more support in another. One child's capacity to learn may be consistently or permanently impacted by a particular situation, whereas another child may need additional support on a temporary basis.

What is Differentiation and How is it Related to Adaptive Teaching?

One of the points within the adaptive teaching section of the *Teachers' standards* (DfE, 2011: 11) indicates that teachers need to 'know how and when to differentiate appropriately, using approaches which enable pupils to be taught effectively'. More recent publications, such as the *CCF* (DfE, 2019), do not use the term 'differentiation' at all, and the shift in language appears to be deliberate. Mould (2021: no page) suggests that, while differentiation remains an important element of adaptive teaching, it is difficult to define. She suggests that we need to consider differentiated support and differentiated outcomes as very different from each other, noting that while 'providing focused support to children who are not making progress is recommended, creating a multitude of differentiated resources is not' (Mould, 2021: no page).

Bromley (2021: no page) supports Mould's view, arguing that more traditional forms of differentiation can be time-consuming for teachers and 'perpetuate attainment gaps' by lowering our expectations and placing an artificial 'cap' on the learning of some pupils. This argument aligns with the point made in the *CCF* (DfE, 2019: 20) that 'adaptive teaching is less likely to be valuable if it causes the teacher to artificially create distinct tasks for different groups of pupils or to set lower expectations for particular pupils'.

Deunk et al. (2018) analysed findings from a range of research reports on the impact of differentiation practices on learning in primary schools. While this kind of meta-analysis can be helpful in identifying trends and agreement across multiple pieces of research, there can also be challenges, in that 'the details and fine-grained insights [of the original studies] can be lost' (Forster and Eperjesi, 2021: 50). Deunk et al. (2018: 42) found that differentiation had a 'small overall positive effect on students' academic performance', but that the effect differed according to the nature of the differentiation. In particular, they found that grouping pupils by attainment does not, on its own, have a positive impact on learning and may have a 'small negative effect' for lower-attaining students. Their conclusion does not align with the Education Endowment Foundation's findings in their *Teaching and learning toolkit* (EEF, 2023), which argued that within-class attainment grouping can have a small positive impact on pupil progress. It should be noted, however, that the EEF recognises that their findings were based on weak evidence and that results varied significantly between studies. Deunk et al. (2018) also found significant variation in results between studies and suggest that a possible reason for the discrepancy is that results depended on what teachers then did with those groups, rather than the grouping itself. We will consider effective grouping later in the chapter.

High Expectations for all Pupils

High expectations are crucial. The *CCF* (DfE, 2019: 9) states that all student teachers should learn that high expectations 'can affect pupil outcomes; setting goals that stretch and challenge pupils is essential'. However, as we have established, children will learn at different rates and need different types of support to learn. Some student teachers can find this challenging, as they may perceive that there is a tension between the notion of 'unique learners' and having high expectations for all learners.

Unique Learners

All our learners will be unique. Even in the case of identical twins, there will be many differences in terms of their preferences, personalities and learning strengths and needs. The classroom would be a much less interesting place if children were all the same.

Recognising each child as a unique learner should always be your starting point in adaptive teaching. As identified in the *CCF* (DfE, 2019: 20), 'seeking to understand pupils' differences, including their different levels of prior knowledge and potential barriers to learning, is an essential part of teaching'. Remember that differences will include pupils' strengths, interests, hobbies and skills, as well as their areas of difficulty or need.

Closing 'The Gap'

In any given topic area, in any curriculum subject, there will always be some children who are likely to find it harder to learn and make progress than others. Children's starting points will vary significantly. Some more traditional forms of differentiation, such as setting different tasks for different children, can lead to a lowering of expectations for some children, which may extend the attainment 'gap' within the class rather than narrow it.

Instead, adaptive teaching aims for the same or very similar high expectations for all children, 'teaching the same lesson to all 30 students, and doing so by "teaching to the top" while providing scaffolds to those who need additional initial support in order to access the same ambitious curriculum and meet our high expectations' (Bromley, 2021: no page). In adaptive teaching, it is the scaffolding that is 'differentiated'. We will consider what some of those scaffolds might look like, to support all learners to make progress while, maintaining high expectations for all.

Approaches to Adaptive Teaching

In this section, we consider some adaptive teaching approaches. Some aspects are discussed in less detail than others, particularly those that are explored in other chapters (e.g., meeting the needs of pupils with SEND in Chapter 18). Before discussing how we might make adaptations for particular children, we identify some simple things that can make your classroom and teaching more inclusive and accessible for all children.

Consider the positioning of things like your whiteboard, your carpet area, children's tables and chairs, to ensure children have as clear a view as possible. Try sitting in different places yourself, noting the 'better' and 'more challenging' positions (and improving these, if possible). Think carefully about who sits where; for example, avoid seating a child with a hearing impairment, who relies on lip-reading, in a position where they cannot see your face. A central position is best in this case, but not right in front of you so that they have to crane their neck to look at you.

Ensure that it is easy for children to hear you and each other speaking (and for you to hear them) in whole-class situations. Consider how you might improve the acoustics, perhaps by adding more soft furnishings to reduce the echo in the room.

Think carefully about where you position children who are left-handed. In a class of 30, you are likely to have three or four children who are left-handed. If you position a left-handed child next to a right-handed child, the left-handed child should sit on the left to avoid their arms knocking into each other as they write.

Children who have a colour vision deficiency (CVD) tend to have more difficulty reading red or green text, so, on your whiteboard, use colours with more contrast, such as black and blue. While the colour-coding of resources can be very supportive for some children, it can be challenging for those with CVD, so aim to also use words and/or pictures. It is likely that at least one child in your classroom will have some form of CVD, even if you (and possibly they) are not aware of it.

This is not an exhaustive list, but offers some examples to get you thinking of some straight-forward things that you can easily control or adapt to make your classroom and teaching more accessible.

Approaches for Individuals and Groups

In Chapter 6, we explored some of the factors that are involved in high-quality teaching. If we can ensure that our teaching is of consistently high quality and that our expectations are appropriately high, we are very likely to have a significant impact on children's progress and, by extension, their 'life chances' (DfE, 2019: 9). In this section, we explore some ways in which you can adapt your teaching to promote the progress of children who may need more support.

Really get to know the children in your class as individuals. In addition to finding out about their areas of need and their strengths, find out what they enjoy and what they dislike. Try to identify which types of situations and activities they seem to do best in, and, conversely, which they find more challenging.

In addition to finding out what children might be struggling with, Mould (2021: no page) advocates trying to 'identify reasons' for those struggles. If you can resolve whatever is causing the struggles, it goes without saying that you should.

Children with SEND are likely to need adaptive teaching. The Education Endowment Foundation (2020) identifies five key recommendations designed to narrow the attainment gap between children with SEND and children without:

- Create a positive and supportive environment for all pupils without exception.
- Aim to understand individual pupils' learning needs using the graduated approach of 'assess, plan, do, review'.

- Ensure all pupils have access to high-quality teaching; good teaching for pupils with SEND is good teaching for all.
- Complement high-quality teaching with carefully selected small-group and one-to-one interventions.
- Work effectively with teaching assistants.

These recommendations can be valuable for all children, not just those with SEND. For example, assessment as part of the assess–plan–do–review cycle will enable us to identify which children may require some adaptation to be successful in the next lesson and which children seem to be struggling 'in the moment'. We can then quickly adapt our teaching to be responsive to their needs.

Most of the time, you may find it useful to group children in 'mixed attainment' groups so that children might learn from and support each other collaboratively. At other times, you may find it helpful to group children by attainment (remembering that attainment can vary in different subjects) so that you can make specific adaptations to suit those children. In doing so, remember that this tends not to be effective if you are setting particular groups very different tasks or have very different expectations for them. Instead, it is more effective to have the same/similar expectations and task for all children, and to vary the type and level of support to ensure all are successful. The DfE (2019: 20) note that 'flexibly grouping pupils within a class to provide more tailored support can be effective, but care should be taken to monitor its impact on engagement and motivation, particularly for low attaining pupils'. Flexible grouping is a strategy that the EEF (2020) also suggests can be employed to ensure high-quality teaching, particularly for pupils with SEND.

Another strategy suggested by the EEF (2020) is scaffolding, which involves providing pupils with 'temporary supports that are gradually removed or "faded out" as they become increasingly independent' (Mould, 2021: no page). Research has shown that scaffolding can have a very positive impact on children's progress in learning, but it depends on the quality of the scaffolding, the extent of the scaffolding and how it changes over time (van de Pol et al., 2015).

— Critical Task 7.2 —

Forms of Scaffolding

Consider what types of 'temporary support' might be beneficial for the scenarios presented in Table 7.1.

Table 7.1 Temporary supports for learning

Scenario	Possible 'temporary supports'
History, Year 2: you are using a newspaper article from the period you are studying to find out about a key event. Some of the language may be unfamiliar. There are a few children in the class with poor reading comprehension.	
PSHE, Year 6: you are using role-play in groups to explore scenarios relating to drugs, e.g., being offered some marijuana. There is one child with social anxiety and two children with expressive language difficulties.	
PE, Year 4: you are focusing on refining throwing and catching skills, ahead of applying these in a modified version of rounders. There is one child with a physical impairment, which affects their mobility, coordination, and arm and hand strength.	

English as an Additional Language

Having EAL can be a challenge for learners: not only are they learning English, but they are also learning *through* English across the curriculum (Solomon and Wilson, no date). It is important to recognise that learners with EAL are not a homogeneous group. Learning to speak a second (or subsequent) language is a journey, and different pupils learning EAL will be at different points on that journey. Getting to know your pupils as individuals is crucial, as factors such as how long they have been learning English, whether their parents/carers speak English (and how often and how well), when, how and why they arrived in the UK, and how literate they are (and how much education they have had) in their first language can all impact on the approaches required to meet their needs. The Bell Foundation (no date, a) suggests that three principles should guide you when teaching pupils with EAL:

- Being bilingual or multilingual is an asset, not a deficit (if you were teaching a child whose first language is English and they were learning another language, you would view that positively; it should be the same for children learning EAL).
- High expectations should be maintained in terms of cognitive challenge.
- Proficiency in English is closely linked with academic success.

Teachers, therefore, have a dual focus: developing pupils' use of English and ensuring that the language does not create a barrier to accessing the curriculum. We must work on both aspects concurrently. Below are some potentially useful strategies for teaching pupils with EAL, many of which are likely to be helpful for other pupils too.

Use an assessment framework, such as the one provided by The Bell Foundation, to assess language proficiency. Ensure you consider all four strands – speaking, listening, reading, writing – as most children will be at different stages in each of the strands.

When planning, consider the language demands for the lesson and plan to teach language (vocabulary and language structures) alongside the lesson's content. For learners with EAL, this may go beyond the subject-specific vocabulary as they may also need to learn basic vocabulary and functional vocabulary (e.g., sort, compare). This approach may also benefit other children in your class.

Pupils learning EAL tend to make progress more quickly when they are integrated with their class as much as possible, rather than being withdrawn and taught separately (Sharples, 2021). That is not to say that pupils learning EAL should never receive separate input; in some instances, carefully planned and targeted intervention can be beneficial, such as pre-teaching particular vocabulary prior to a lesson.

For all children, activating prior learning is important. For pupils learning EAL, particularly those who have had some education in their first language, it may reveal that they already have the content knowledge and understanding, so they can focus their attention more fully on the language in that lesson. In addition, activating prior knowledge can help pupils make connections between different aspects of their learning, helping to reinforce the learning and any associated language.

Providing models of language, such as the use of sentence stems or repeating back in a rephrased manner, is recommended. In turn-taking situations, pupils with EAL might take their turn last, so that they are aware of the expectations and have had time to mentally rehearse their response. Where all pupils are using the same sentence stem, the repetition can reinforce the language for pupils with EAL. The pupil learning EAL may opt to copy another pupil's answer or to select one of their own. You might even offer a simple choice, for example, asking them to pick between apple and banana to complete the sentence stem 'My favourite fruit is…'.

The use of visuals, such as objects and pictures, helps to make sense of the language, particularly if the child already knows the associated word/phrase in their first language. The Bell Foundation (no date, b) suggests that graphic organisers, such as tables, Venn diagrams, flow charts, concept maps, provide a means of visually presenting information. Such tools can be helpful for pupils learning EAL as they can contain all the relevant information, but place fewer demands on their reading and writing skills than full texts.

Adding labels to displays in multiple languages can also be supportive, both for translation purposes and to remind all children that there are many different languages beyond their own first language (Bower, 2018).

Modelling and guided practice (which have been explored more fully in Chapters 5 and 6) are part of good practice for all children, but are particularly helpful for pupils learning EAL, allowing them to see, as well as hear, what is expected.

Consider your grouping strategies carefully. In many situations, you will want to group pupils learning EAL with other pupils who will provide a good model of English and will be encouraging and supportive of contributions made by pupils learning EAL. If using talk partners, it is often helpful to include a pupil learning EAL in a group of three (a 'talk triangle') as the other two pupils can model the two-way dialogue, with the pupil learning EAL contributing when and if they feel comfortable to do so.

If there are multiple pupils learning EAL who have the same first language, you may wish to group them together occasionally, particularly if the content of the lesson is challenging, so that they can discuss in their first language to secure their understanding first. This approach also provides another opportunity to demonstrate that all languages are valued. It is important, though, to ensure that same-language groupings are not used too often, as it limits exposure to, and use of, English.

For all pupils, contextualising learning can be very helpful, as it tends to be more memorable and relatable to children's lives. For pupils learning EAL, contextualising learning can be particularly beneficial because new vocabulary can be connected to something meaningful, rather than an abstract concept.

Dual-language texts can be valuable, both to support learning within the classroom and to allow pupils learning EAL to share these with other pupils and with parents/carers. While these texts are becoming more easily accessible, it is also straightforward to create dual-language materials, such as knowledge organisers and word banks (Bruce, 2021). Knowledge organisers are defined as a single page which 'sets out the important, useful and powerful knowledge on a topic' (Miller, 2018: no page). You can use a translating tool, a language dictionary or seek support from someone else who speaks the pupil's first language to create such materials.

There is now a wealth of technology that can be used to support pupils learning EAL, such as translation tools for oral language and 'talking pens' for written language. Ensure that you select with care, based on the pupil's level of English and the intended learning outcomes for each lesson.

When learning any language, oral language tends to develop before written language. Before expecting a pupil learning EAL to write in English, they need to have opportunities to say out loud what they intend to write. They may use technology to record what they say, or they may say it to a partner or adult. Both techniques provide an opportunity to reflect on what they have said and to correct any errors before adding the challenge of transcription. Talking before writing is good practice for many pupils as they are developing their writing skills, not just those learning EAL.

In this section, we have focused particularly on adaptive teaching strategies for pupils learning EAL. Where pupils (and their families) are newly arrived, it is also crucial to ensure that they feel welcomed and valued as part of the school community, which is explored more fully in Chapter 17.

Case Study 7.1

Interventions

May-Ling, a postgraduate student teacher, has just started a placement in a new school. Having noticed some intervention slots on the timetable, she is keen to understand more about how the school organises interventions. Her teacher-mentor explains the school's approach:

> Over the last two years, we have used guidance from the Education Endowment
> Foundation, particularly their reports on making best use of teaching assistants and on

Continued

special educational needs in mainstream schools, to refine our approach to intervention. Before, there were lots of interventions going on, with children frequently going in and out of lessons, and, honestly, it was chaotic at times.

Now, we are much more targeted. We use diagnostic assessment to identify which children are likely to benefit and to identify exactly what they need support with. We use intervention programmes that have been proven to have impact and teachers work with teaching assistants to ensure they are fully trained to deliver the programme. Sometimes, slight adaptations to the programme are planned, to ensure it meets the specific needs of the children. Sometimes, teachers will plan very specific things for teaching assistants to focus on within the intervention, for example, pre-teaching some key vocabulary to children with EAL before a new science topic.

Sessions are relatively brief (about 30 minutes), usually occurring three times per week, for a limited time period. The timing of these interventions has been carefully considered so that the children miss as little of the whole-class teaching as possible. Otherwise, as we seek to close one gap, we open up another. We also know how important it is, for example, for our learners with EAL to be immersed in English within the classroom. Communication between the teacher and teaching assistant is crucial, so that the teacher can keep track of the impact the intervention is having as well as making explicit connections between the intervention and the classroom teaching and learning.

It is clear that May-Ling's placement school is taking a research-informed approach to intervention to complement high-quality teaching, rather than replace it. Clear intentions, careful selection and thoughtful planning have all ensured that intervention has the maximum impact.

— Observation Guide 7.1 —

Adaptive Teaching

The *CCF* states that student teachers should 'learn how to … provide opportunity for all pupils to achieve success' (DfE, 2019: 20).

Observe how your teacher-mentor adapts lessons, while maintaining high expectations for all, so that all pupils have the opportunity to meet those expectations. In particular, look out for the following:

- Do all children receive the same input at the start of the lesson?
- How are additional adults deployed at different points during the lesson?
- How are resources used?
- How have children been grouped?
- Do all children complete the same or a similar task?

- What role does the teacher take while children are completing the task?
- Are children aware of the adaptations that are made? How?
- Do the approaches taken differ depending on the subject being taught?

Connections with Other Aspects of Your Practice

Honing your skills in adaptive practice will not exist in a vacuum: many other aspects of your practice will be intertwined with your adaptive teaching and you can read more about these in other chapters. For example, effective adaptive teaching depends on accurate assessment (Chapter 11), which then informs careful planning. As explored in Chapter 6, teaching, and therefore planning, is a problem-solving activity. How you can support and enable specific children to meet the same high expectations as their peers is part of the problem to be solved.

Your capacity to adapt your teaching will also rely on your subject knowledge (Chapter 8). Knowing your subject well allows you to predict which aspects particular children may find difficult so you can identify the foundational knowledge that children will need to secure first, before they can build upon it. You will also need to draw on your knowledge of how children learn (Chapter 5) to guide your planning and teaching.

Effective adaptive teaching is also closely related to your skills in working collaboratively with others, which will be explored in Chapters 15 and 18. You will need to deploy teaching assistants and other adults working in your classroom skilfully to maximise the impact on learning for all pupils. You will need to communicate with parents and carers to help you to understand your unique learners and provide feedback on their progress. You will need to liaise with expert colleagues, such as the SENCo or EAL lead, to help you to understand barriers to learning and extend your knowledge of supportive strategies.

Question Guide 7.1

Grouping for Impact on Learning

The *CCF* states that student teachers should:

> Learn how to ... group pupils effectively by ... discussing and analysing with expert colleagues how the placement school changes groups regularly, avoiding the perception that groups are fixed. (DfE, 2019: 21)

To help you understand how schools group pupils effectively, use these questions to guide your discussions with an expert colleague:

- How are children grouped in this class?
- When they are grouped by attainment, does this differ depending on the subject?

Continued

- When they are in mixed attainment groups, how do you decide who should work together?
- How do you organise talk partners?
- How often do you change groups?
- Do you ever move a pupil for just one lesson, then move them back to their usual group?
- Do the children ever choose their own partners or groups?

What to Avoid in Adaptive Teaching

Adaptive teaching is a complex aspect of teaching, not least because you will have 30 individuals in your class. What works for one child or in one situation may not work for the next child or in another situation, so there is no 'magic' set of strategies to be applied. However, there are some things that can be very unhelpful and should therefore be avoided:

- Low expectations: we need to find ways of adapting our teaching to help all children meet our high expectations. Having low expectations of some will only serve to increase the attainment gap.
- 'Artificially creating distinct tasks for different groups of pupils' (DfE, 2019: 20): this links to the previous point, as it can create a 'cap' on learning. As far as possible, pupils should all access the same learning and complete the same task, even if the task needs to be adapted or additional support put in place for some pupils.
- Assumptions: just because a previous pupil needed support in maths does not mean that their sibling will. Just because a pupil needs more support with reading does not mean that they will need support with all aspects of the curriculum (but you will need to consider the reading demands placed on them in other subjects). Just because a particular strategy was effective for a child with dyslexia in your last class does not mean that it will be effective for a different child with dyslexia in your current class.
- Stereotypes: remember that every pupil is a unique learner and it is your job to get to know each child and to use that knowledge to ensure that they make as much progress as possible while in your class.
- Fixed groupings: not only are all pupils unique when they enter your class, they will also make progress at different rates in different subjects. You will need to make professional decisions about which is the most appropriate way to group children in any particular situation, but you should also be prepared to be flexible over time, moving pupils between groups to best meet their learning needs.
- Neuromyths: for example, 'there is a common misconception that pupils have distinct and identifiable learning styles. This is not supported by evidence and attempting to tailor lessons to learning styles is unlikely to be beneficial' (DfE, 2019: 20–21). Neuromyths are explored in more depth in Chapter 5.

Response to Critical Task 7.2

Forms of Scaffolding

In Critical Task 7.2, we asked you to consider what types of 'temporary support' might be beneficial in the scenarios set out in Table 7.1. We have made some suggestions in Table 7.2, but there will be others and you should use your knowledge of specific children to help you to decide what is likely to be most beneficial.

Table 7.2 Suggested temporary supports for learning

Scenario	Possible 'temporary supports'
History, Year 2: you are using a newspaper article from the period you are studying to find out about a key event. Some of the language may be unfamiliar. There are a few children in the class with poor reading comprehension.	• Reading the article aloud, either to the whole class or to particular children • Explicitly teaching the unfamiliar vocabulary and/or providing a glossary • Providing a simplified version of the article which covers the main points in a more accessible format • Taking a layered approach to sources with some children, perhaps by using a picture source first before introducing the article • Using pairs or groups, so that children can work together on understanding the article
PSHE, Year 6: you are using role-play in groups to explore scenarios relating to drugs, e.g., being offered some marijuana. There is one child with social anxiety and two children with expressive language difficulties.	• Modelling the scenario yourself or using a video is likely to support all children • Working alongside specific children as they role-play • Providing a bank of actions and phrases that could be used or providing a skeleton script for some pupils • Allowing time for children to plan with a partner first • Allocating roles to specific children, e.g., it might be easier to be the person offering the drugs than the person deciding how to respond • Considering groupings carefully
PE, Year 4: you are focusing on refining throwing and catching skills, ahead of applying these in a modified version of rounders. There is one child with a physical impairment, which affects their mobility, coordination, and arm and hand strength.	• Modelling, using the 'thinking aloud' approach to focus on body position and body movements • Pairing the child with a physical impairment with an adult (or a child who is skilful at throwing and catching) • Reducing the distance between the child and their partner • Allowing a bounce before the child attempts to catch initially • Changing the ball to one that is larger and lighter (or substituting it for something like a balloon or rolled up towel)

Chapter Summary

In this chapter, we considered the importance of recognising that all pupils are unique, and each child will have individual and diverse learning needs. We emphasised the need to set high expectations for all learners. We explored the meaning of adaptive teaching and discussed some approaches for adapting teaching to meet the needs of learners who require additional support to meet our high expectations, including those learning EAL. We also considered how adaptive teaching links to other aspects of our practice and what we need to avoid doing when adapting our teaching practice.

No one is suggesting that adaptive teaching is easy, but, as Brien (2012: 133) identifies, it 'is more about teacher attitude than specific techniques'. You will need to be resourceful and willing to try different things, reflecting honestly on their impact. You will not always get it right, but you will keep trying to ensure that all children in your class make as much progress as possible. As a result, you will change their lives.

Further Reading

The following sources might be helpful to you in further developing your adaptive teaching:

Bromley, M. (2021) 'Adaptive teaching explained: what, why and how?', *SecEd: The Voice for Secondary Education*. Available at: www.sec-ed.co.uk/best-practice/adaptive-teaching-explained-what-why-and-how-pedagogy-classroom-teachers-curriculum-differentiation-teachers-standards-pisa/ (accessed 9 May 2023).

This accessible article explores what adaptive teaching is and the importance of scaffolding. It includes real examples from the author as to how he embedded adaptive teaching methods in his own teaching.

Mansworth, M. (2021) *Teach to the top: Aiming high for every learner.* Woodbridge, UK: John Catt Educational Ltd.

This helpful book focuses on what it means to 'teach to the top' and how all learners can be supported to meet high expectations.

The Bell Foundation. Available at: www.bell-foundation.org.uk/

National Association for Language Development in the Curriculum (NALDIC). Available at: https://naldic.org.uk/

Both websites include a wealth of information and materials for teachers working with pupils who are learning EAL.

References

Bower, V. (2018) 'Responding to linguistic diversity', in T. Cremin and C. Burnett (eds.), *Learning to teach in the primary school.* Abingdon, UK: Routledge, pp. 363–376.

Brien, J. (2012) *Teaching primary English.* London: Sage.

Bromley, M. (2021) 'Adaptive teaching explained: what, why and how?', *SecEd: The Voice for Secondary Education*. Available at: www.sec-ed.co.uk/best-practice/adaptive-teaching-explained-what-why-and-how-pedagogy-classroom-teachers-curriculum-differentiation-teachers-standards-pisa/ (accessed 28 August 2022).

Bruce, C. (2021) 'Adaptive teaching for EAL students in language-heavy subjects', *SecEd: The Voice for Secondary Education*. Available at: www.sec-ed.co.uk/best-practice/adaptive-teaching-for-eal-students-in-language-heavy-subjects-history-geography-english-literature-religious-studies-english-as-an-additional-language/ (accessed 28 August 2022).

Department for Education (DfE) (2011) *Teachers' standards*. London: DfE.

Department for Education (DfE) (2013) *The national curriculum in England: Key stages 1 and 2 framework document*. London: DfE.

Department for Education (DfE) (2019) *ITT core content framework*. London: DfE.

Deunk, M.I., Smale-Jacobse, A.E., de Boer, H., Doolaard, S. and Bosker, R.J. (2018) 'Effective differentiation practices: a systematic review and meta-analysis of studies on the cognitive effects of differentiation practices in primary education', *Educational Research Review*, 24, 31–54.

Education Endowment Foundation (EEF) (2020) *Guidance report: Special educational needs in mainstream schools*. London: EEF.

Education Endowment Foundation (EEF) (2023) *Teaching and learning toolkit*. Available at: https://educationendowmentfoundation.org.uk/education-evidence/teaching-learning-toolkit (accessed 11 April 2023).

Forster, C. and Eperjesi, R. (2021) *Action research for student teachers* (2nd edn.). London: Sage.

Miller, M. (2018) *Organising knowledge: The purpose and pedagogy of knowledge organisers*. Available at: https://my.chartered.college/impact_article/organising-knowledge-the-purpose-and-pedagogy-of-knowledge-organisers/ (accessed 14 February 2023).

Mould, K. (2021) *EEF blog: Assess, adjust, adapt – what does adaptive teaching mean to you?* London: Education Endowment Foundation. Available at: https://educationendowment foundation.org.uk/news/eef-blog-assess-adjust-adapt-what-does-adaptive-teaching-mean-to-you (accessed 28 August 2022).

Organisation for Economic Co-operation and Development (OECD) (2016) *PISA 2015 results (volume II): Policies and practices for successful schools*. Paris: PISA, OECD Publishing.

Sharples, R. (2021) *Teaching EAL: Evidence-based strategies for the classroom and school*. Bristol: Multilingual Matters.

Solomon, K. and Wilson, R. (no date) *Supporting learners who use English as an additional language*. Available at: https://my.chartered.college/early-career-hub/supporting-learners-who-use-english-as-an-additional-language/ (Accessed: 28 August 2022).

The Bell Foundation (no date, a) *Effective teaching of EAL*. Available at: www.bell-foundation.org.uk/eal-programme/guidance/effective-teaching-of-eal-learners/ (accessed 28 August 2022).

The Bell Foundation (no date, b) *Great idea: Graphic organisers*. Available at: www.bell-foundation.org.uk/eal-programme/guidance/effective-teaching-of-eal-learners/great-ideas/graphic-organisers/ (accessed 14 February 2023).

van de Pol, J., Volman, M., Oort, F. and Beishuizen, J. (2015) 'The effects of scaffolding in the classroom: support contingency and student independent working time in relation to student achievement, task effort and appreciation of support', *Instructional Science*, 43, 615–641.

SECTION 3
CURRICULUM

8
KNOW WHAT YOU'RE TALKING ABOUT: SUBJECT KNOWLEDGE FOR TEACHING

Tracey Wire

┌─ **Chapter Objectives** ─

- To explore what we mean by 'subject knowledge'.
- To consider how secure subject knowledge underpins effective planning and teaching.
- To reflect on how teachers might identify and address 'gaps' in their subject knowledge.

In this chapter, we discuss some of the ways in which knowledge has been described and defined within different subjects, and how different categories of knowledge are inextricably linked. We consider why teacher subject knowledge is important and discuss some of the ways that student teachers might identify areas for development and address gaps in subject knowledge.

Subject Knowledge and the Curriculum

Since the publication of the current *National Curriculum* (Department for Education (DfE), 2013), subject knowledge has been increasingly emphasised within guidance to schools and teacher education institutions (DfE, 2019; Ofsted, 2019). This represented a shift from a curriculum that emphasised developing conceptual understanding ('big ideas', such as faith, change or measurement) and skills to a 'knowledge based' curriculum (sometimes called a 'knowledge-led' or 'knowledge-rich' curriculum). Michael Gove (in his role as Conservative Minister for Education) and Nick Gibb (as Schools Minister) eagerly drew on the work of American educationalist E.D. Hirsch when designing the curriculum (DfE, 2013) and formulating policy. In 2015, Gibb explained that they had been persuaded by Hirsch's argument that what is needed is 'decisive leadership that will define what every adult should know so the information can be taught' mainly because, they claim, he presents a 'compelling social justice case' for his ideas (Gibb, 2015: 14).

For Hirsch (1984), the link between knowledge and social justice lay in his work related to the teaching of literacy in a community college in the USA, and the idea that teaching the 'right' knowledge would enable people from all backgrounds to develop a 'cultural literacy'. Students should, he argued, learn a body of foundational knowledge that is generally assumed in society and that would give individuals a basic level of access to everyday but significant documents, such as newspaper articles. Gove's and Gibb's commitment to these ideas led to the production of a national curriculum that set out clearly the 'base' knowledge to be taught in all maintained schools in England, across a range of core and foundation subjects. We will reflect on why this can present challenges for primary teachers later in the chapter.

What is Subject Knowledge?

In order to teach effectively, it is essential for us to get to grips with a number of different types of knowledge. You will also see a range of labels used to identify types of knowledge. This can be confusing, as the same type of knowledge can be given different names in different contexts, or might be overlapping or nested within one another (Pope, 2019). Of course, there are a number of different types of knowledge that student teachers need to develop; for example, they need to have knowledge of how children learn (see Chapter 5) and how to manage behaviour effectively (see Chapter 3). For the purpose of this chapter, however, we mainly focus on two types of knowledge: substantive knowledge and disciplinary or syntactic knowledge.

Counsell (2018: paras 8–9) presents a view of these two types of knowledge and why children need to learn them. She explains that *substantive knowledge* is what is taught as 'established facts', or the content of the curriculum, *including* concepts. For example, it is an established fact (substantive knowledge) that the River Seine is in Paris, which is the capital of France, which lies to the south of the UK. If you teach children these established facts, you should also be developing their growing understanding of the geographical concept of location. *Disciplinary knowledge*, on the other hand, is knowledge of how a particular discipline or subject 'works' in practice: the nature of the discipline. Teachers need to know and be able to teach children what it is like to be a scientist, a mathematician or a historian, for example. They need to know how knowledge is constructed within each subject area. To continue with the geography example, we need to know how to make and read a map so that we can teach children how to do this. However, as Husbands (2015: 47) points out, 'knowing how is not the same as having the skill'. For example, if you are a fan of *Strictly Come Dancing*, you might know the steps that make up a tango and know what constitutes good technique, but this knowledge does not make you a marvellous dancer of the tango; it does not mean you have the skill. The knowledge of 'how' needs to be applied and practised to develop the skill. Disciplinary knowledge is knowledge of how ideas and 'facts' are formulated, uncovered and evolve within a particular subject. For teachers, secure disciplinary knowledge is vital as it impacts the way they view the subject, make sense of what they read and make decisions about what and how they teach (Slekar and Haefner, 2010; Pope, 2019).

You will also almost certainly hear expert colleagues talk about prior knowledge and, perhaps, tacit knowledge. Prior knowledge is just what it sounds like: the explicit facts and concepts that we already know or about which we are developing an understanding. Tacit or 'unspoken' knowledge, however, is a little more difficult to pin down, to express or even to identify. It is what we know from experience and is developed through all aspects of our lives. For example, we might know how someone feels by looking at the expression on their face or have a sense of whether something is overcooked because of the smell of burning in the kitchen. Both prior and tacit knowledge have an impact on the acquisition of new substantive and disciplinary knowledge. You might be thinking this all sounds quite complicated but please bear with me as we go on to unpick it.

The emphasis on knowledge has led to a particular way of thinking about learning: children need to 'know more' and 'remember more' of a defined body of knowledge (Ofsted, 2019: 9). Children are only judged to have learnt something once it is lodged in their long-term memory (see Chapter 5). This, in turn, influences not only *what* but *how* we teach. Rightly or wrongly, for example, it has led to a rise in classroom practices, such as the use of knowledge organisers, spaced retrieval practice and low stakes testing.

While the move from skills to knowledge in the curriculum, along with some of the theories that underpin this shift, has been welcomed by many in educational research and teaching communities (e.g., researchED, 2022), it is not without its detractors and challengers. The theoretical foundations of this approach to teaching have been criticised for being incomplete, erroneous, vague and/or misapplied (e.g., see Ellerton, 2022). Author and academic Michael Rosen (2016) associates the move to a prescribed, knowledge-based curriculum with a decline in the teaching of the creative arts. Meanwhile, the question of which knowledge is privileged to become part of the curriculum has become a particular focus in the last few years, with moves to decolonise the curriculum. Organisations such as The Black Curriculum (2021), established in 2019, challenge the white, Eurocentric nature of the curriculum and advocate a reconceptualising of history content to include Black history. Their aim is for the curriculum to be inclusive and to reflect the multicultural nature of Britain's history and the diverse nature of current society, for the benefit of all.

Regardless of whether or not we have a skills-based or knowledge-based curriculum (or something in between), for a primary school teacher the issue of subject knowledge presents a number of potential challenges. The primary curriculum covers a diverse range of subjects. Inevitably, therefore, primary school teachers will begin from a non-specialist position in most, if not all, of the subjects they are required to teach. They simply do not begin with all the knowledge they need to teach all the subjects they must. Once they have realised this, they need to decide what it is they do not know. They then need to work out how they can fill the gaps to 'top up' their knowledge, before, finally, working to fill those gaps in order that they might effectively plan and teach.

Why Should You Develop Your Subject Knowledge?

In this section, we consider the importance of developing your subject knowledge so that you can make well-informed decisions about what and how you should teach. Among other things, it will help you to:

- assess pupil progress
- produce well-sequenced plans
- help children develop subject-specific and generic skills
- teach with confidence and enthusiasm.

So, as outlined in the *ITT Core Content Framework* (*CCF*): 'Secure subject knowledge helps teachers to motivate pupils and teach effectively' (DfE, 2019: 13).

How Does Your Subject Knowledge Impact the Choices You Make About What and How You Teach?

Let us imagine that you have been given the opportunity to plan a unit of work in history from scratch. If you are working in a maintained school, you must meet the statutory requirements of the *National curriculum* (DfE, 2013: 188–192) (those elements that are a legal requirement). Beyond that, teachers are free to make lots of choices about what and how they teach. If you are working in an academy or free school, strictly speaking your freedom to choose what to teach may be potentially even wider. This is where your subject knowledge (both your substantive knowledge and your disciplinary knowledge) begins to play a role.

Let us imagine further. You are in a Year 3 class and you have been asked to teach the class about 'the Roman Empire and its impact on Britain' (DfE, 2013: 189). The *National Curriculum* provides some suggestions of what you might cover within the unit of work; these are the non-statutory elements of the curriculum that appear in text boxes throughout the document. You do not have to address all or any of these. Your subject knowledge should help you to make good decisions about what you choose to cover.

Critical Task 8.1

Knowledge for Teaching

Before you read on, pause and consider what you need to know before you can begin to plan your unit of work. Identify both the substantive and disciplinary knowledge you require even to make a choice about the focus of the unit of work.

Of course, if you know very little about this period of history, or about how historians work, the task might seem a bit overwhelming. A good first step is to gain a solid overview of the period. This will help you develop your breadth of knowledge and help you to identify potentially interesting or significant aspects of the period to focus on. You will also want to develop your disciplinary knowledge through your research. When you are reading about the Romans in Britain, you also need to pay attention to how historians have reached their conclusions about the period. Ask yourself: 'what have they done to develop this knowledge?'. This is a two-way street in as much as your disciplinary knowledge will help you to make sense of the substantive knowledge and how it was developed, and vice versa. Once you have some promising ideas, it is time to start going into depth to develop your subject knowledge and to make further informed decisions. Remember to check back with the curriculum while making these decisions. This unit is about *impact*: what changed and what stayed the same following the Roman invasion and presence in Britain. You may, therefore, want to explore how the 'Britons' responded to the Roman advance, how successful the Romans were at occupying territory, and/or to examine the growth of towns and how they were organised.

Your disciplinary knowledge is important in helping you make decisions about what and how you teach. If you come to understand how historians work, it will help you to identify those 'topics' that are rich in learning potential, to weigh up your options. For example, recognising that historians use a range of artefacts to find out about the past is important. If you identify a focus that has lots of available artefacts, such as coins, pottery or letters, then it is likely to be significant, interesting and practical to teach because you will be able to resource it. You also need to understand what historians do with the artefacts: you will need to model how to handle, assess and interrogate your selected artefacts and enable children to engage with them in a similar way, taking into account that they are new to these sorts of activities and this type of thinking.

If you decide to focus part of your unit on Claudius' successful invasion, good subject knowledge will help you to identify the 'established facts' that it is most important to teach, to explore any uncertainties, contradictions or ambiguities with your class, and to identify the most appropriate resources to support the development of children's substantive and disciplinary knowledge. Good subject knowledge will help you to decide what and how to teach in a well-informed and principled way. It should not open the door to endless lessons of telling children historical (or any other) facts. It should enable you to plan for children to work like historians to develop their knowledge, understanding and skills through enquiry, and crucially, with your support.

These same principles apply whatever the subject and whatever the particular focus of a unit of work, be that 'states of matter' in science or the 'use of pitch and dynamics in composition' in music, for example.

Pupil Progress and Assessment

Strong subject knowledge and, potentially, the processes of your research should enable you to effectively sequence learning to ensure children progress in their learning. Intrinsically linked to effective sequencing of learning is ongoing formative assessment.

To plan for progression across and within units of work, primary teachers need an awareness of what has come before in children's learning (see Chapter 6 for a discussion of effective and meaningful planning for progression). So, to go back to the Romans, if you are going to teach children about impact, then you, and the children, need to know what Britain was like before the Romans arrived, during the Iron Age, so that you can make the comparison required to assess impact. Furthermore, it is not enough to know that the children have been taught about the Iron Age. You will need to check that they have retained the significant information: have they remembered what they learnt? Their prior knowledge provides your starting point for teaching and learning.

Jenner (Ofstednews, 2021) notes that, in subjects like history, knowledge is not built hierarchically in the same way as in, for example, maths, and that gaps in pupils' knowledge about concepts need to be addressed through multiple examples and contexts. Don't imagine that learning and knowing about the events of the Great Fire of London will prepare children to learn and know about the Romans. However, an awareness of what has come before in children's learning journeys and careful planning should mean that children can begin to develop an understanding of concepts like similarity and difference, cause and consequence, and chronology through a unit on the Great Fire of London, which can then be visited and further developed through a unit on the Romans a year later.

Within a unit of work, your secure subject knowledge will help you to be clear about what you want children to learn (your learning objectives) from one lesson to the next, to build towards the learning outcomes at the end of the sequence of lessons. Clarity about what learning 'looks like' means that assessment should be relatively straightforward. You should also be able to provide meaningful opportunities for children to show you what they have learnt and be able to judge the effectiveness of your teaching. Good subject knowledge should enable you to recognise where children have misconceptions, and sometimes to anticipate them and even plan how you might challenge them.

What About Skills?

Ofsted's Chief Inspector, Amanda Spielman, explains the link, as she sees it, between skills and knowledge within the curriculum in schools that have taken a 'knowledge-led' approach to the design of their curriculum:

> Knowledge and skill are intrinsically linked: skill is a performance built on what a person knows. That performance might be physical or cognitive, but skills matter and they cannot be separated from knowledge. They are, if you like, the 'know-how' in applying the 'known'. Knowledge and the capacity it provides to apply skills and deepen understanding are, therefore, essential ingredients of successful curriculum design. (Ofsted and Spielman, 2018: para 35)

This extract might lead you to think that children will spontaneously acquire skills if you have a knowledge-rich curriculum. Beware of this idea. Student teachers need to develop their own disciplinary and generic skills in a purposeful way alongside their knowledge so that they can plan to introduce both in purposeful and meaningful ways to children. Some of your knowledge and the children's knowledge should be developed through the application of these skills.

▬ Observation Guide 8.1 ▬

Application of Subject Knowledge in Teaching

The *CCF* states that student teachers should 'learn how to provide opportunity for all pupils to master essentials concepts, knowledge, skills and principles of the subject' (DfE, 2019: 13).

Discuss with your teacher-mentor how the development of their own knowledge and skills within a subject have informed their planning and teaching. Observe how they introduce subject knowledge to the class, building on prior knowledge. Remember that it is important to avoid being judgemental and to be sensitive when observing and discussing this aspect of teachers' professional practice. In particular, you should look out for the following:

- How does your teacher-mentor share their knowledge with the children?
- What impact do their disciplinary knowledge and skills have on the way they teach?
- What impact does this have on children's attitude to learning and their progress?

Identifying the 'Gaps' in Your Subject Knowledge

Sometimes it can be hard to know where to start in identifying gaps in your subject knowledge. It can even be hard to identify exactly what it is that we do not know. You might even have some misconceptions that you are unaware of. This can be tricky and sometimes you just won't know that you don't know something until a child asks you a question that you can't answer. Try not to worry about it and respond positively. You might, for example, say something like: 'That's a really good question. I'm not sure I know the answer to that. How could we find out?'. This could be a chance for everyone to learn. You might have studied something a long time ago, seen something on television, or read something on social media, for example, that leads you to believe you have some knowledge. Be careful and check that your memory is not faulty and your sources are not flawed.

There are lots of ways to begin to identify what you might need to work on. Exploring the curriculum and identifying areas where you feel less confident is a good place to start.

In maths and English, you might decide that it is a good idea to undertake the phonics screening check and SATs tests in the same way as the children. Past papers and practice materials can be easily found on the GOV.UK website. Just put the details of what you're looking for into your usual search engine. It might be helpful to do this with a friend or colleague. Choose an old paper, work through and mark it, and identify very specifically what it is that you do not know or are unsure about. You should then set yourself clear targets for the development of your subject knowledge and work to address them. Be careful, though. Do not be tempted to think that all you need to teach well, in terms of subject knowledge, is to be able to answer the questions on a test. There is so much more to these subjects than that. For example, in English, we might also think about 'knowing' or being familiar with a good range of high-quality fiction, non-fiction and poetry from a range of genres as good subject knowledge. Going back to the curriculum will help you to identify the less obvious aspects of a subject where you need to develop your subject knowledge.

As a student teacher, you will have been asked to assess and develop fundamental proficiencies in English and maths (Hollis, 2020). These are skills that you need in your wider professional role as a teacher. Using the assessment of these skills can also help you to identify gaps in your subject knowledge. For example, if you find it difficult to 'demonstrate a range of sentence constructions and punctuation' in your writing, it might be because you lack the underpinning knowledge of grammar and punctuation to do so.

Your teacher training institution might also ask you to undertake subject knowledge audits to help you to identify areas for development. There are also similar audits available online, produced by organisations such as the National Centre for Excellence in the Teaching of Mathematics (NCETM), a range of teacher training institutions and local authorities. It might be the case that while on placement you receive feedback about aspects of your subject knowledge or that you recognise, through reflection and self-evaluation, that there are things you need to work on. Again, set clear targets for yourself that will help you to focus your development where it is needed most.

Depending on where and how you are training, you are likely to receive feedback during taught sessions and on your assignments that might highlight subject knowledge issues that you need to address. Being reflective, self-evaluative and proactive are key to identifying your areas for development, and then effectively addressing them.

Case Study 8.1

Subject Knowledge Preparation for Teaching

Jamelia, an undergraduate student teacher in her second year of training, has been given responsibility for teaching a PSHE unit of work on drugs and alcohol while placed in a Year 5/6 class. She is observed teaching a lesson that focuses on the use of legal drugs. Jamelia begins by assessing the children's prior knowledge using a collaborative concept mapping activity, creating a diagram showing what they know and exploring links between different parts of that knowledge. The class is lively and engaged, the children are sharing what they know, and some misconceptions are emerging. One of the children puts their hand up, wanting Jamelia to settle an argument about e-cigarettes and whether or not they are addictive. Jamelia immediately responds that they are not. She then pauses and says they are, and then follows this statement with 'sometimes'. Another child repeats the question, stating emphatically that they are not, and demanding to know why they would be. Jamelia is now flustered and tries to move away from the subject. Behaviour in the class deteriorates, so Jamelia has to try to deal with low-level disruption throughout the lesson and the quality of teaching and learning is negatively impacted.

After the lesson, Jamelia reflects with her teacher-mentor, who asks her to consider why the children lacked focus for much of the lesson. Jamelia is able to identify that things started to go wrong when she was unable to respond confidently to the question about e-cigarettes. She did not have sufficient subject knowledge and lost faith in her capacity to effectively teach the lesson. Consequently, the children engaged in their own, rather disgruntled, debate that rumbled on throughout the lesson, having lost confidence in Jamelia. Jamelia realised that she had assumed that she had better subject knowledge than was actually the case because she regarded what she was teaching about as just part of everyday life. She recognised that she always needs to consider more carefully what she actually knows and what children will need to learn, and to take active steps to address these issues, and that subject knowledge has an impact beyond the content of a lesson.

More careful planning might have helped Jamelia to avoid this situation as it might have helped her to recognise that she did not have good enough subject knowledge to teach the lesson well. Jamelia might also have used this experience as a learning opportunity for herself and the children, as described above, by being honest about her own uncertainty and discussing with the children how they might go about settling the argument for themselves, thereby keeping the lesson on-track and providing a life lesson about learning itself as well as finding an answer to the question.

What to Do and Where to Go to Develop Your Subject Knowledge

First, you need to make sure you allocate some time to developing your subject knowledge, not just as a student or early career teacher but throughout your career. You will need to think about subject areas where you are less confident and then drill down.

— Critical Task 8.2 —

Beginning to Identify your Strengths and Areas for Development

First, make a list of those subjects where you feel confident in your subject knowledge and make another list of those where you know you need to develop. Now have a look at the

Continued

National curriculum (DfE, 2013), choose a year group(s), preferably one(s) that you have had little or no experience of teaching, and look at what you actually need to teach for each subject. It might change the list you have already made. You might need to move some subjects from one category to the other. Now identify just one area of knowledge that you need to work on within one subject. For example, you might have realised that you need to develop your subject knowledge of upper Key Stage 2 grammar in English, about plants in science, or the Vikings in history. Now consider what you might do to address the gaps in your knowledge.

As a general rule, begin to develop your breadth of knowledge and then delve deeply into particularly important aspects of subject knowledge.

While resources like Wikipedia, social media (where you can find experienced teachers and subject groups), podcasts, television programmes and so on are unlikely to be the end point of your subject knowledge development, these sorts of resources can often be a good starting point and can give you ideas about the direction you might take. They can also help you delve a little more deeply into specific aspects of a subject. Approach these critically, in just the same way as you would any publication: consider who produced the materials and if they are in some way an expert, and identify when and why they were produced, to assess their usefulness.

Subject associations can be really useful for developing subject knowledge and for directing you to what you might do to develop it further. Often, parts of associations' websites are free to everyone, although frequently much of what they offer is hidden for members only. Your teacher education institution might subscribe and give you access to some associations, as might your placement schools. Some associations offer membership to students and early career teachers at reduced rates. Either way, they are usually a reliable place to start to build your subject knowledge.

Reading is likely to be a necessary part of your subject knowledge development journey. Often, this means reading texts aimed at adults rather than children, as children's texts tend to be rather limited and are produced to use within the classroom context with the support of a teacher. Developing your subject knowledge therefore means a visit to the library, be that in person or online.

Sometimes it can be useful and enjoyable to take a 'field trip'. You might, for example, visit a museum or exhibition, or attend a lecture or webinar focused on a particular aspect of subject knowledge. Usually, but not always, this would be at the point where you are really focusing on developing the depth of your subject knowledge rather than its breadth. Remember to be 'brave' when you do this. Ask questions and engage in conversations; you never know, you might actually enjoy it once you get started!

Take advantage of the resources around you. Look out for subject-specific Teachmeets in your area, where teachers come together to share practice. Your university will have subject experts, your schools will have subject leaders, and you will have a teacher-mentor: they are there to help you. They cannot develop your subject knowledge for you, but they can support you to develop the skill of identifying what you need to know and understanding how to go about it.

How the 'Act' of Teaching Can Help You to Develop Your Subject Knowledge

The very act of teaching and of considering what and how to teach is likely to support the development of your subject knowledge and to develop empathy with the learners in your class. It is unlikely that you will be 'full of all knowledge' on the first occasion you begin to teach a unit of work.

While the research is limited, there is some evidence to suggest that the processes of preparing to teach, thinking about how you organise the teaching and learning, and how you will develop children's subject knowledge all help teachers to develop their own subject knowledge (Duran, 2016; Kobyashi, 2019). It has certainly been my personal experience and that of many of my colleagues, past and present. The mode of teaching can also have an impact on the development of knowledge. For example, using explicit instruction in a lesson might require and develop different levels and types of knowledge than a collaborative, enquiry-based approach, for both the teacher and children. The emphasis on subject knowledge development within the curriculum might lead you to think that the most straightforward way to teach is by 'telling' children the subject knowledge. In the real world, this is not how disciplines work. For example, among other things, scientists undertake investigations and experiments, historians explore primary and secondary sources, geographers take part in fieldwork. This is how experts develop their knowledge and we need to enable children to do the same. Working collaboratively with children in these ways should provide the structure necessary for teachers and children to develop their disciplinary knowledge and skills, while expanding their content knowledge. However, it is important to be aware that children are not experts but novices. 'Novices and experts cannot think in all the same ways' (Glasser and Chi, 1988, quoted in Deans for Impact, 2015: no page). So, your role as the teacher is vital. You will need to provide a range of appropriate scaffolds to support the learning process and promote good progress.

—— **Question Guide 8.1** ——————————————————————

Developing Subject Knowledge

The *CCF* states that student teachers should 'learn how to develop as a professional by: learning to extend subject and pedagogic knowledge as part of the lesson preparation process' (DfE, 2019: 29).

To help you to understand how teachers and schools manage the development of subject knowledge for teaching, use some of these questions to guide your discussions with an expert colleague:

- What opportunities are there, both formal and informal, for teachers to develop their subject knowledge as part of the school community?

Continued

- What is the role of the subject leader in supporting the development of colleagues' subject knowledge?
- How do teachers independently develop their own subject knowledge and are there resources they would recommend?

Chapter Summary

In this chapter, we have considered what is meant by the term 'subject knowledge' and how different ways of defining the term have influenced the development of the curriculum and the ways we teach in the classroom. We have identified the importance of secure subject knowledge in underpinning effective teaching, and identified how you can begin to identify gaps in your subject knowledge. For example, you can systematically review the curriculum and undertake subject knowledge audits, identify the resources you can draw on to develop your subject knowledge, and ensure that you are well prepared and confident to teach.

Further Reading

Council for Subject Associations (no date) *Subject association directory: Practical help for teaching subjects in your school* (2nd edn). Available at: www.subjectassociations.org.uk/the-cfsa-directory/ (accessed 7 November 2022).

If you want to find an association for a particular subject, it should be listed in this publication.

Pope, D. (ed.) (2019) *Understanding subject knowledge for primary teaching*. London: Sage/ Learning Matters.

This helpful book has some general advice about how to develop your subject knowledge, but also a chapter devoted to each curriculum subject.

TES magazine. Available at: www.tes.com/magazine

This publication will help you to develop an understanding of the ongoing debates surrounding the knowledge-based curriculum and other important current issues in education.

References

Counsell, C. (2018) 'Taking curriculum seriously', *Impact*, 12 September, no page. Available at: https://my.chartered.college/impact_article/taking-curriculum-seriously/ (accessed 3 May 2023).

Deans for Impact (2015) *The science of learning*. Austin, TX: Deans for Impact.

Department for Education (DfE) (2013) *The national curriculum in England: Key stages 1 and 2 framework document*. London: DfE.

Department for Education (DfE) (2019) *ITT core content framework*. London: DfE.

Duran, D. (2016) 'Learning-by-teaching: evidence and implications as a pedagogical mechanism', *Innovations in Education and Teaching International*, 54(5), 476–484.

Ellerton, P. (2022) 'On critical thinking and content knowledge: a critique of the assumptions of cognitive load theory', *Thinking Skills and Creativity*, 43, 100975.

Gibb, N. (2015) 'How E.D. Hirsch came to shape UK government policy', in J. Simons and N. Porter (eds.), *Knowledge and the curriculum*. London: Policy Exchange. Available at: https://policyexchange.org.uk/wp-content/uploads/2016/09/knowledge-and-the-curriculum.pdf (accessed 28 February 2022).

Hirsch, E.D. (1984) 'Cultural literacy'. Paper presented at the National Adult Literacy Conference, Washington, DC, 19–20 January. Available at: https://files.eric.ed.gov/fulltext/ED241697.pdf (accessed 28 February 2022).

Hollis, E. (2020) 'Fundamental proficiencies: what should ITT providers be doing in response?', *National Association of School-Based Trainers*, 10 March. Available at: www.nasbtt.org.uk/fundamental-proficiencies-what-should-itt-providers-be-doing-in-response/ (accessed 29 November 2022).

Husbands, C. (2015) 'Which knowledge matters most', in J. Simons and N. Porter (eds.), *Knowledge and the curriculum: A collection of essays to accompany E.D. Hirsch's lecture at Policy Exchange*. London: Policy Exchange, pp. 43–50. Available at: https://policyexchange.org.uk/wp-content/uploads/2016/09/knowledge-and-the-curriculum.pdf (accessed 20 July 2022).

Kobyashi, K. (2019) 'Learning by preparing-to-teach and teaching: a meta-analysis', *Japanese Psychological Research*, 61(3), 192–203.

Ofsted (2019) *Inspecting the curriculum*. London: Ofsted. Available at: https://assets.publishing.service.gov.uk/government/uploads/system/uploads/attachment_data/file/814685/Inspecting_the_cturriculum.pdf (accessed 19 July 2022).

Ofstednews (2021) 'Tim Jenner on what it means to get better at history', *Ofstednews*. Available at: www.youtube.com/watch?v=L5GeAsg8nZ4 (accessed 7 November 2022).

Ofsted and Spielman, A. (2018) 'HMCI commentary: curriculum and the new education inspection framework', *GOV.UK*. Available at: www.gov.uk/government/speeches/hmci-commentary-curriculum-and-the-new-education-inspection-framework (accessed 20 June 2022).

Pope, D. (2019) 'Introduction', in D. Pope (ed.), *Understanding subject knowledge for primary teaching*. London: Sage/Learning Matters, pp. 1–15.

researchED (2022) 'Bringing researchers, teachers and policy makers together', *researchED*. Available at: https://researched.org.uk/ (accessed 16 November 2022).

Rosen, M. (2016) 'Dear Justine Greening, Michael Gove attacked school arts openly. You do it on the QT', *The Guardian*, 6 December, no page. Available at: www.theguardian.com/education/2016/dec/06/justine-greening-michael-gove-school-arts-michael-rosen (accessed 3 May 2023).

Slekar, T.D. and Haefner, L.A. (2010) 'Syntactic knowledge in history and science education', *Journal of Thought*, 45(1–2), 7–16.

The Black Curriculum (2021) *The Black Curriculum* [website]. Available at: https://theblackcurriculum.com/ (accessed 28 February 2022).

9
RICH LEARNING ACROSS THE CURRICULUM

Rachel Eperjesi

Chapter Objectives

- To consider the term 'the curriculum' in its broadest sense, and how it relates to our aspirations for primary education.
- To explore some approaches for enriching children's learning experiences.
- To reflect on some potential benefits and challenges of the approaches explored.

In this chapter, we explore the term 'the curriculum' in its fullest sense, and how the *National curriculum* (Department for Education (DfE), 2013) fits within the broader 'curriculum'. We acknowledge how each school needs to align its curriculum with its aspirations for children's outcomes, not only academically, but also more holistically. We explore how meaningful links can be made across the curriculum to maximise learning, as well as consider how children can be involved in planning the curriculum. The notion of 'porous schools' (Eperjesi and Forster, 2020: 224) is also discussed as a means of enriching children's learning and development.

Defining 'The Curriculum' and 'Rich Learning'

As a student teacher, you are likely to be aware of the *National curriculum* and its role in identifying what should be taught in most primary schools. You may be less aware that the *National curriculum* is part of the wider 'school curriculum', which comprises 'all learning and other experiences each school plans for its pupils' (DfE, 2013: 5). The DfE (2013: 5) states that all state-funded schools must:

offer a curriculum which is balanced and broadly based and which:

- promotes the spiritual, moral, cultural, mental and physical development of pupils at the school and of society, and
- prepares pupils at the school for the opportunities, responsibilities and experiences of later life.

The DfE (2019: 13) also states that 'a school's curriculum enables it to set out its vision for the knowledge, skills and values that its pupils will learn, encompassing the national curriculum within a coherent wider vision for successful learning'. So, while the *National curriculum* focuses on children's academic development and outcomes, the wider curriculum should be much more holistic than that. For example, the Organisation for Economic Co-operation and Development (OECD) (2021: 3) suggests that 'social and emotional skills are the bedrock of students' wellbeing and academic achievement', that these skills 'help us live and work together resiliently and productively' and that 'school is where we can learn and sharpen these skills'. The Education Endowment Foundation's *Teaching and learning toolkit* (2023) indicates that using approaches which develop children's social and emotional learning can have a moderate, positive impact on their academic outcomes. While noting that this is based on limited evidence, they have published a guidance report offering 'practical recommendations' to improve social and emotional learning in primary schools, noting that this is 'especially important for children from disadvantaged backgrounds, and other vulnerable groups' (Education Endowment Foundation (EEF), 2019: 2). While the evidence may be limited, they clearly believe that seeking to develop children's social and emotional learning is worthwhile. The guidance suggests that this goes beyond explicitly teaching social and emotional learning skills through a carefully planned PSHE programme. It indicates that these skills should be modelled and integrated through everyday teaching and reinforced through the whole-school ethos and activities (EEF, 2019).

'How Can I Cover Everything?'

You might now be feeling a little daunted, realising that what you need to teach goes far beyond the *National curriculum* requirements, but it is perfectly possible to address all aspects of the school curriculum. It is often children's development in the less academic aspects which can provide the most satisfaction for you as a teacher and have the most long-lasting and life-enhancing impact on your learners. Academic success, including attaining academic qualifications, is undoubtedly important for later life. Whether going into higher education or straight into employment, there will be expectations about previous qualifications for entry. However, employers are also looking for other qualities and skills, which are considered vital in employment and wider life, such as communication, problem-solving, critical thinking, collaboration, creativity, resilience and social awareness (Baker, 2017). If we can enable children to develop these skills and qualities through our teaching, as well as securing their academic success, then we are preparing them well for 'later life' (DfE, 2013: 5) and having a genuinely life-enhancing impact.

One way to 'cover everything' is to plan carefully, both in considering what you want to teach children and how you might go about it, so that, where possible, you are 'combining' learning opportunities. Think of it like a supermarket 'two for the price of one' offer. For example, in a computing lesson, you might decide to take a collaborative learning approach (see Case Study 9.1), as the EEF's *Teaching and learning toolkit* (2023) identifies this approach as having high impact on academic outcomes. Not only is it likely to increase the likelihood of the children developing the intended computing knowledge, understanding and skills, the collaborative approach has the additional benefit of providing opportunities for children to develop their skills in communication and working well with others. In a science lesson, you might want to consolidate children's understanding of insulation towards the end of a unit of work and you might therefore ask them to produce something of their own choice (e.g., a leaflet, a poster, a podcast) to help home-owners understand how to reduce heat loss. In doing so, you are developing the children's skills in problem-solving and creativity, as well as the intended scientific learning.

Case Study 9.1

Combining Learning Opportunities

Annabeth, an undergraduate student teacher placed in a Year 4 class, has been asked to develop a medium-term plan for geography. The focus for the unit of work is volcanoes.

While developing her own subject knowledge, Annabeth realises that there will not be enough time for the children to learn about all of the volcanoes on earth, even if they just focused on the active ones. She also recognises that, as this is the first time the children will be learning about volcanoes, she needs to spend significant time on the features of volcanoes, how they are formed and what can happen during an eruption. However, she does not want to miss the opportunity for the children to apply and extend their locational knowledge and geographical skills.

Annabeth decides that, towards the end of the unit of work, after the children have developed foundational knowledge and understanding, they will then focus on learning about specific volcanoes. She realises that if different groups focus on different volcanoes, they can share their learning with the rest of the class, adding to the breadth of learning, as well as providing valuable opportunities to work collaboratively and develop spoken language skills.

Annabeth plans carefully, considering how to group the children, which volcano to allocate to each group, which resources each group will be able to access, what information each group will be asked to find out and how they will gather and share their research. She allocates two lessons for this task, so children can work in groups to undertake research on their allocated volcano in the first lesson, plan how to present their findings in the first half of the second lesson and then present their findings in the second half of the second lesson.

Continued

In the first of these lessons, Annabeth uses a whole-class input to revisit the necessary geographical skills, such as using maps, atlases and globes to locate their allocated volcanoes. As a class, they also identify some roles and rules for effective collaborative working. In the second of these lessons, Annabeth and the teaching assistant use the whole-class input to model how to work collaboratively to present their findings to the rest of the class. She works with the children to develop some 'tips for good speaking' and 'tips for good listening'.

After teaching the unit of work, Annabeth is very pleased with the impact on children's geographical learning and on their capacity to work well with others. She notes children referring to the rules for collaborative working during talk partner time and group work in other subjects, and identifies that collaborative working has reduced off-task behaviour. She also notes improvements in their spoken language skills.

Annabeth's approach has a significant impact on the children's learning, both in terms of the depth and breadth of geographical learning, but also in terms of their wider skills. This does not happen by chance and is undoubtedly due to her clear intentions and very thorough planning, as well as her modelling and communication of her expectations.

Rich Learning

Whatever we are aiming for children to learn, the 'richer' the learning experience, the more likely it is that children will make progress and retain their learning. As explored in Chapter 5, learning involves a lasting change and the role of memory in learning is significant (Immordino-Yang and Damasio, 2007). Teachers therefore need to consider how to make learning memorable, and this chapter seeks to support you with that objective through exploring strategies that enrich teaching and learning.

It would be easy to assume that what we mean by rich learning is that pupils are fully engaged. Of course, children do need to be engaged to learn, but it is important to avoid the assumption that engagement automatically equals learning. On its own, engagement is not sufficient and may simply be an indication that children are busy with things they already know or can do (Hendrick and Heal, 2020). What we mean by rich learning is learning which is engaging but also memorable, and which has a genuine and meaningful impact on children's development, ideally in more than one aspect. As we continue through this chapter, we will also consider some of the potential 'tensions' in striving for rich learning across the curriculum.

Making Meaningful Links Across the Curriculum

In this section, we explore the potential benefits and limitations of making meaningful links across the curriculum. This might also be known as 'cross-curricular', 'topic' or 'thematic' planning and teaching.

The Potential Benefits and Limitations of Making Meaningful Links Across the Curriculum

The concept of making links between different subjects across the primary curriculum is not new. Before the *National curriculum* was first introduced in 1989, a 'topic-based' approach, which addressed multiple subjects within one topic, was quite common (Shaw and Shirley, 2018). Since then, many schools and teachers have continued to make links across different curriculum subjects.

One perceived potential benefit of this approach is a very practical one, which is that it may save time. As discussed earlier, there can be concern about how we can fit everything in (EEF, 2019), with so many subjects and the wider school curriculum to consider. With significant emphasis on English and maths, time for science and the foundation subjects can seem to be in short supply, so making links between different foundation subjects (e.g., RE and music), or between a core subject and a foundation subject (e.g., science and geography), may be one way of tackling this.

Another potential benefit of making links across the curriculum relates to contextualising learning for children, so that they are enabled to make connections to real life and to understand *why* they are learning what they are learning. This might increase their engagement and be more memorable, thus increasing the chances of learning being retained. For children who are learning English as an Additional Language (EAL), making links between different subjects can also reduce the new vocabulary that a child needs to learn at any one time.

However, there are also some potential limitations of making meaningful links across the curriculum. Like so many aspects of teaching, in order to harness the potential benefits, it needs to be 'done well', not just 'done'. Some critics of approaches that make links between different curriculum subjects are concerned that the subject-specific knowledge, conceptual understanding and skills of each individual subject can be missed or diluted (Ofsted, 2021). In addition, links can appear forced or contrived at times, and where this is the case, the potential benefits are much less likely to be realised, as it is highly unlikely that there will be meaningful contexts that can relate to children's real lives.

Effective Practice

In order to ensure that an approach which makes links across different subjects is effective, there are some important aspects that need to be considered, at both the planning and teaching stages:

- There should be genuine links between the subjects involved. For example, learning about rivers in geography aligns well with learning about the water cycle in science. Learning about the Great Fire of London in history does not align with learning about Jewish festivals in RE, so these should be taught separately.

- Both/all subjects involved need to be taught well, with a clear development of knowledge, conceptual understanding and skills, so that the benefits relate to both subjects and not just to one subject (Barnes, 2018). Reinforcing learning in science by drawing a diagram does not mean that there is a curriculum link with art, since there is no planned development of art-specific knowledge, conceptual understanding or skills.
- In ensuring that both/all subjects are taught well, it may be that time is not actually saved; you may still need the same number of sessions as you would have done to teach the subjects separately. However, it may be that the learning is richer and that wider aspects, such as working collaboratively or problem-solving, have been developed through a more creative approach.
- Barnes (2018: xv) states that 'cross-curricular learning and separate subject learning are not opposites'. He suggests that developing children's knowledge, conceptual understanding and skills in each subject 'provides the raw materials' that can then be applied in cross-curricular contexts. So, it may be beneficial to make meaningful links across the curriculum later in each unit of work, so that you are able to 'explicitly link new ideas to what has been previously studied and learned' (DfE, 2019: 17).

Case Study 9.2

Making Meaningful Links Across the Curriculum

Ash is the headteacher of a three-form entry urban primary school, which has an average proportion of children with SEND and a slightly higher than average proportion of children with EAL. Below, Ash explains the approach that the school takes to make meaningful links across the curriculum:

> As a team, we believe that making links across the curriculum is important. With so many subjects, it can be a way to fit more in, but, more importantly, we find it helps secure the children's learning more fully as it provides additional opportunities to revisit and apply their learning. It benefits all children, but particularly those with SEND or EAL.
>
> However, our top priority is that our curriculum is coherent and developmental, so we don't make links just for the sake of it: they have to be authentic and valuable. For example, for systematic synthetic phonics, we follow one of the validated schemes and we also teach maths discretely (although our topic might provide a context for problem-solving tasks).
>
> For English, each year group covers the genres set out in our long-term plans; this enables us to ensure that all genres are covered and that they are revisited and extended at appropriate intervals. While there is some flexibility about when each

genre unit is taught, each strand (narrative, non-fiction, poetry) has a recommended order (e.g., non-fiction unit 2 needs to be taught after non-fiction unit 1), so that the knowledge, skills and conceptual understanding are developmental. Year group teams map their genre units across the year, ensuring that they have at least one unit from each strand in each term.

For all other subjects, subject leaders develop long-term plans, identifying which topics and which aspects of the curriculum must be addressed in each year group. For some subjects (e.g., science), the topics are stated in the curriculum, whereas for others (e.g., art and design), the subject leader will suggest topics to address the curriculum requirements. For each topic, they indicate whether it can be taught at any point in the year, or whether it needs to precede or follow other units. Year group teams then work together to map their science and foundation subject topics across the year, seeking to make links between subjects where appropriate, while ensuring the curriculum remains developmental. They consider their English genre units again, making links to other subjects, as appropriate. For example, Year 5 have been learning about particular composers in music this term, and their teachers have positioned an English unit on biographies towards the end of this term, so that they can write biographies about these composers. This enables them to really focus on the features and grammar of biographies in English, as they have already developed the contextual knowledge through the music lessons.

We don't try to fit all subjects under an overarching theme each term as this either leads to some tenuous links or the curriculum requirements not being addressed (or both). We only make links where these are authentic; we teach other subjects separately. Sometimes there are links that could be made, but they won't work developmentally (e.g., between a science unit that the subject leader has identified must be taught near the beginning of a year and a geography unit that the subject leader has identified must be taught near the end of year). Learning development is always our priority.

Year group teams work closely with subject leaders and sometimes it is possible to make changes. For example, Year 4 are focusing on their use of colour in painting in art and design. The subject leader had originally suggested doing this through a topic on clothing design, but the year group team realised that they could address the same curriculum requirements through linking it to their Rainforest topic, which also encompasses some geography and science learning.

The staff in Ash's school have a shared understanding and set of principles which guide their approach to making links across the curriculum. Class teachers, year group teams and subject leaders work together to ensure that their curriculum is coherent and developmental, reaping the benefits of making links across the curriculum and avoiding any of the potential limitations or challenges of doing so.

Involving Children in Planning the Curriculum

Forster and Eperjesi (2020: 5) suggest that most pupils in primary schools will be 'following a curriculum that has been designed by a relatively small group of adults, drawn from a narrow range of fields, focusing on content that they consider to be most important'. In this section, we consider how involving children in planning the curriculum might have a positive impact on their sense of curriculum ownership and engagement.

The Potential Value of Involving Children in Planning the Curriculum

While research on the value of involving learners in planning the curriculum in primary schools is limited, there is plenty of evidence to support the importance of doing so in early years, as well as compelling evidence that co-creation of the curriculum in higher education can have benefits for students and staff (Lubicz-Nawrocka and Bovill, 2021).

Think of a project or task that you were actively involved in setting up recently – perhaps it was your idea or focused on a topic that you feel passionately about. Compare how committed and engaged you felt about working on the project or task with how you felt when forced to work on a project or task that did not interest you or where you could not see any benefit. When we have a sense of ownership, our enthusiasm, motivation, resilience and engagement all tend to be increased. Lubicz-Nawrocka and Bovill (2021) suggest that being involved in planning the curriculum can also help us to become much more aware of ourselves as learners.

Remember also the importance of the 'wider curriculum', such as developing children's social and emotional skills, and some of the skills and qualities that employers are looking for. Involving children in planning the curriculum can certainly support the development of some of these qualities and skills, as children collaborate with each other and with you.

How Children Can Be Involved in Planning the Curriculum

There are several possible approaches that enable children to be more involved in planning the curriculum. Children can be involved in planning the content of the curriculum, within some parameters, such as a particular topic within a particular subject. For example, you can tell your Year 2 class that they will be learning about plants in science (DfE, 2013) and ask them what sorts of things they would like to learn about that topic. How you ask them to share their ideas with you may differ. For example, you can lead a whole-class discussion and create a mind map of the children's ideas, or create a simple survey and ask children to use iPads to complete it individually.

Critical Task 9.1

Responding to Children's Interests

Imagine that you have asked children to share what they would like to learn more about in relation to your history topic for the upcoming half term. Among the ideas shared, one child makes a suggestion which does indeed relate to the topic, but not to the aspects of the curriculum that you were intending to address through the topic. How would you respond in this situation?

Of course, as outlined in Critical Task 9.1, one of the potential challenges of involving children in planning the content of the curriculum is that their ideas may not always match the intended curriculum requirements. You will need to consider how flexible the curriculum requirements are and how much time you have available. For example, is it possible to address the curriculum requirements and have time left over to explore some of the children's other ideas for content? If there is insufficient time within the sequence of lessons, you may consider whether setting an open-ended homework task will provide an opportunity for children to follow their own lines of interest. If they can then be provided with the opportunity to share their independent learning, not only will this be likely to increase their sense of ownership, but it also offers an opportunity to develop their spoken language skills.

Another way of involving children in planning the curriculum is to involve them in planning the mode of learning, rather than the content. For example, they may identify that they would like the opportunity to work in pairs or groups, or they would like to engage in drama, or they may ask if they can make more use of IT.

It may not always be possible to involve children in planning before embarking on a unit of work, but even giving them choices within lessons can be very helpful, both in terms of engagement and considering children's holistic development. The ability to make choices is an important one. As adults, we frequently make choices. Some are less important, such as what to make for dinner, while others hold more importance, such as which higher education course or employment field to apply to. Part of the 'skill' involved in making good choices lies in being able to reflect on the relative pros and cons of the options available. Within lessons, children may be able to make choices about the resources they use, who they work with or the task they complete. As long as all options allow children to meet the intended learning outcomes, offering them some control is likely to have positive impact for many, particularly as the curriculum content is largely imposed upon them.

Porous Schools

In this section, we explore the notion of 'porous schools', defined by Eperjesi and Forster (2020: 224) as meaning 'children get out into the real world as often as possible and ... members of the real world are regularly invited into the school building'. The idea of porous schools may also be thought of as 'visits and visitors', although getting out into the real world may mean staying on the school site on some occasions, rather than visiting another location.

The Opportunities of Learning Outdoors, Visits and Visitors

The use of the outdoor environment as a space for teaching and learning is widely accepted as a fundamental part of effective early years practice. Some schools continue using the outdoor environment in Key Stages 1 and 2, while other schools do not. Anecdotally, it is not unusual for Year 1 children in this latter group to complain that they 'only go outside for play time now'. Why this might be the case will be explored further when we consider the limitations and challenges, but it should be noted that in Waite et al.'s four-year study, commissioned by Natural England, 82% of the 125 schools surveyed suggested that outdoor learning improved their pupils' health and wellbeing, social skills and behaviour (Waite et al., 2016). The study also found that 79% of the teachers surveyed reported positive impacts on their teaching practice when they taught some lessons outdoors, with 72% identifying improvements in their own health and wellbeing (Waite et al., 2016).

Learning outside the classroom seems obvious for some aspects of the *National curriculum*, such as geographical fieldwork and learning about plants, animals and habitats in science. There will also be times when a lesson can be equally effective whether indoors or outdoors, but you choose to undertake it outdoors because of some of the wider benefits mentioned above. With rising numbers of children in primary schools experiencing mental health difficulties, and research demonstrating that spending time in nature can have positive impacts on issues such as anxiety and depression (Pearson and Craig, 2014), the case is even stronger for getting out of the classroom regularly.

Although it may now be seen as somewhat dated, in 2006, the Department for Education and Skills published its *Learning outside the classroom* manifesto, in which claims were made about the positive impact of learning outdoors on children's academic outcomes, as well as aspects such as personal development and social skills. It went on to suggest that learning outdoors could involve the school grounds and the local environment as well as places further afield for visits and residentials. More recently, Behrendt and Franklin's (2014) research supports the notion that visits can have multiple positive impacts, including on academic attainment.

Some aspects of the curriculum can be significantly enhanced by engaging in teaching and learning situations outside the classroom. For example, while it is perfectly possible to explore the work of artists and musicians within the classroom, visiting an art gallery to see the scale of a piece of artwork or listening to a live orchestra will make the experience more meaningful and memorable. Engaging with local businesses and charities can provide a wealth of valuable opportunities to add richness to children's learning, such as providing a context for persuasive writing in English.

There may be other occasions where there is more value in inviting a visitor into the school, rather than undertaking a visit, such as a faith visitor for RE. You may choose a visitor, rather than a visit, due to practicalities such as time or cost, but possibly also because it enables you and the class to have the visitor's undivided attention, which is not always possible if visiting them in their 'local environment'. Inviting visitors into school provides valuable opportunities for children to plan and ask meaningful questions, which in turn gives them more control over their learning, as well as developing their spoken language. When deciding whether to select a visit or a visitor, carefully consider which is most appropriate for your intended learning outcomes.

Critical Task 9.2

Possible Challenges of Using Outdoor Learning, Visits and Visitors

Before reading on, consider the possible limitations and challenges of using outdoor learning, visits and visitors as part of your teaching repertoire.

Now think about how some of those limitations and challenges might be overcome.

The Limitations and Challenges of Outdoor Learning, Visits and Visitors

In Critical Task 9.2, you were asked to consider some of the possible challenges and limitations of using outdoor learning, visits and visitors. It is likely that you identified factors such as cost, safety, time and workload, and we will consider how to overcome these barriers and get the most out of outdoor learning, visits and visitors in the next section.

You may also have identified managing behaviour as a potential challenge. Glackin (2018: 66) suggests that many teachers experience a 'fear of losing control outside'. However, Sjoblom et al. (2021) suggest that, in reality, this is much less of an issue than feared, citing multiple studies in which children's engagement, behaviour and relationship with the teacher were enhanced through learning in alternative environments.

Observation Guide 9.1

Maximising Learning from Visits

The *ITT Core Content Framework* (*CCF*) states that student teachers should 'Learn how to teach and rigorously maintain clear behavioural expectations (in alternative environments)' (DfE, 2019: 10).

Continued

We have already explored how to learn from expert colleagues about managing children's behaviour in Chapter 3, but as concerns about this aspect are often one of the reasons that some teachers are reluctant to engage with learning outdoors and visits, it is worth revisiting it from that perspective. If possible, try to observe a teacher-mentor both before and during an outdoor learning experience or visit:

- Note whether the teacher briefs the children and other adults about the learning experience or visit and what the briefing covers. Does it just focus on organisational aspects, or does it also include intended learning outcomes and/or behavioural expectations?
- If behavioural expectations are included, consider how these align with the usual behavioural expectations in the classroom.
- Observe whether any verbal reminders or non-verbal signals about behavioural expectations are given.
- Observe how the teacher-mentor manages any incidents of more challenging behaviour.
- Consider whether the experience follows a similar structure to lessons in the classroom. Is the teacher explicitly teaching in the same way as they would in the classroom? If not, how would you describe their role?

How to Get the Most Out of Outdoor Learning, Visits and Visitors

In order to overcome the potential challenges or limitations, and harness the potential benefits of outdoor learning, visits and visitors, here are some key considerations:

- Select visits and visitors with care. Given the potential challenges relating to cost, time, workload and so on, choose those visits or visitors that have the most potential to make a positive contribution to children's learning, both academically and more holistically. One or two carefully selected visits are likely to have more impact than multiple, less valuable visits. Learning outdoors in the school grounds is different: try to do this much more regularly.
- Plan and prepare carefully, starting with a pre-visit (or conversation, in the case of a visitor) before making a booking. Ensure that you are considering health and safety as well as learning potential. Plan carefully, just as you would for any other teaching and learning opportunity. You should be very clear about your intended learning outcomes, key teaching points and approaches, organisation and management of the class, what and how you will assess, and so on.
- Seek support from more experienced colleagues at every stage, from identifying possible locations/visitors to completing the risk assessment to briefing additional adults. Like all aspects of teaching, this is a learning process for you, but one that you have perhaps had less experience of.

- Brief and prepare the children. This might mean undertaking pre-lessons, such as composing questions to ask a visitor. At the very least, children should be clear about the intended learning and expectations in relation to behaviour.
- Brief other adults. For visits off-site, there will be adult-to-child ratios to adhere to, so you may need to seek help from parents/carers, who will be less experienced in all aspects. Brief them carefully. If a parent/carer has responsibility for a group of children, pair their group with a group led by a member of staff. Ensure that all adults know how the children have been briefed and share other important information, such as accessing first aid, emergency numbers, timings for the day, and so on.
- Ensure that your planning includes time for following up, so that you and the children are clear about what they have learnt from the experience and how this relates to other learning.

Question Guide 9.1

Curriculum Planning

The *CCF* states that student teachers should:

> Learn how to deliver a carefully sequenced and coherent curriculum by … discussing and analysing with expert colleagues the rationale for curriculum choices, the process for arriving at current curriculum choices and how the school's curriculum materials inform lesson preparation. (DfE, 2019: 13)

To help you understand how schools provide a balanced, broadly based school curriculum with rich learning for pupils, use some of these questions to guide your discussions with an expert colleague:

- Does the school have a mission statement, and how was it developed?
- Is the curriculum based on the *National curriculum*? What else is included in the school's curriculum and why?
- Who decides what is taught and when, particularly in foundation subjects where the *National curriculum* is less prescriptive?
- How do class teachers/year group teams use the curriculum and long-term plans to inform their short-term planning?
- How do class teachers/year group teams plan to develop children's social and emotional skills, and other skills, such as working collaboratively, thinking critically and making decisions?
- Do class teachers/year group teams have the flexibility to make meaningful links across the curriculum and use the outdoors, visits and visitors to extend learning?
- Are children able to take some ownership of the learning, by contributing to the planning of the curriculum or by making choices within lessons?

Chapter Summary

In this chapter, we have considered the importance of understanding that each school's curriculum will be based on its aspirations for its pupils and that it will be wider than the *National curriculum*. We have discussed the notion of 'rich learning' and explored some approaches which might enrich children's learning experiences, noting the potential value of learning outside the classroom, inviting visitors into your classroom and going out on purposeful visits. We have also identified the challenges and limitations of doing so, and considered how to overcome them. Plan carefully, be clear about the rationale for the choices you make and hold on to your own aspirations for the children you are teaching – your impact can be life-changing.

Further Reading

The following texts may be helpful in further developing your knowledge and understanding of approaches that can enrich children's learning experiences.

Barnes, J. (2018) *Applying cross-curricular approaches creatively.* Abingdon, UK: Routledge.

This helpful book can support you in further developing your understanding of how to make meaningful links across the curriculum and enable you to recognise and avoid the potential pitfalls.

Hewitt, D. and Wright, B. (2019) *Engaging, motivating and empowering learners in schools.* London: Sage.

This book, which is aimed at student teachers and early career teachers, helps you to consider both yourself and the children as learners. It is based on the notion that engagement, motivation and empowerment are crucial to successful education.

Waite, S. (ed.) (2017) *Children learning outside the classroom: From birth to eleven* (2nd edn). London: Sage.

This helpful text offers support with all aspects of learning outside the classroom, from identifying the potential benefits, managing the potential challenges and considering possible opportunities across all curriculum subjects.

References

Baker, S. (2017) 'The global university employability ranking 2017', *Times Higher Education,* 16 November. Available at: www.timeshighereducation.com/features/which-countries-and-universities-produce-most-employable-graduates (accessed 1 March 2022).

Barnes, J. (2018) *Applying cross-curricular approaches creatively.* Abingdon, UK: Routledge.

Behrendt, M. and Franklin, T. (2014) 'A review of research on school field trips and their value in education', *International Journal of Environmental and Science Education,* 9, 235–245.

Department for Education (DfE) (2013) *The national curriculum in England: Key stages 1 and 2 framework document.* London: DfE.

Department for Education (DfE) (2019) *ITT core content framework*. London: DfE.

Department for Education and Skills (DfES) (2006) *Learning outside the classroom: Manifesto*. Nottingham: DfES Publications.

Education Endowment Foundation (EEF) (2019) *Improving social and emotional learning in primary schools: Guidance report*. London: EEF.

Education Endowment Foundation (EEF) (2023) *Teaching and learning toolkit*. London: EEF. Available at: https://educationendowmentfoundation.org.uk/education-evidence/teaching-learning-toolkit (accessed 11 April 2023).

Eperjesi, R. and Forster, C. (2020) 'Conclusion', in C. Forster and R. Eperjesi (eds.), *Teaching the primary curriculum*. London: Sage, pp. 221–227.

Forster, C. and Eperjesi, R. (2020) 'Introduction', in C. Forster and R. Eperjesi (eds.), *Teaching the primary curriculum*. London: Sage, pp. 1–9.

Glackin, M. (2018) '"Control must be maintained": exploring teachers' pedagogical practice outside the classroom', *British Journal of Sociology of Education,* 39(1), 61–76.

Hendrick, C. and Heal, J. (2020) 'Just because they're engaged, it doesn't mean they're learning', *Impact,* 10, Autumn.

Immordino-Yang, M.H. and Damasio, A. (2007) 'We feel, therefore we learn: the relevance of affective and social neuroscience to education', *Mind, Brain and Education,* 1(1), 3–10.

Lubicz-Nawrocka, T. and Bovill, C. (2021) 'Do students experience transformation through co-creating curriculum in higher education?', *Teaching in Higher Education,* 17 May. DOI: 10.1080/13562517.2021.1928060.

Ofsted (2021) *Research review series: Geography*. London: Ofsted. Available at: www.gov.uk/government/publications/research-review-series-geography (accessed 11 April 2022).

Organisation for Economic Co-operation and Development (OECD) (2021) *Beyond academic learning: First results from the survey of social and emotional skills*. Paris: OECD Publishing.

Pearson, D.G. and Craig, T. (2014) 'The great outdoors? Exploring the mental health benefits of natural environments', *Frontiers in Psychology,* 5, Article 1178, 1–4.

Shaw, S. and Shirley, I. (2018) 'History of education', in H. Cooper and S. Elton-Chalcraft (eds.), *Professional studies in primary education* (3rd edn). London: Sage, pp. 17–43.

Sjoblom, P., Eklund, G. and Fagerlund, P. (2021) 'Student teachers' views on outdoor education as a teaching method: two cases from Finland and Norway', *Journal of Adventure Education and Outdoor Learning,* 23(3), 286–300. DOI: 10.1080/14729679.2021.2011338.

Waite, S., Passy, R., Gilchrist, M., Hunt, A. and Blackwell, I. (2016) *Natural connections demonstration project, 2012–2016: Final report and analysis of the key evaluation questions*. Natural England Commissioned Reports, Number 215. York: Natural England.

10
THE POTENTIAL OF HOMEWORK TO ENRICH THE CURRICULUM

Colin Forster

Chapter Objectives

- To explore the varied nature of homework.
- To reflect on some of the potential benefits and limitations of homework.
- To consider ways in which to maximise the impact of homework as part of a planned curriculum.

In this chapter, we explore the endlessly fraught issue of homework. Roberts (2009: 14) notes that 'homework is usually seen as an intrinsically good thing, particularly by those who don't have to do it or set it', but for those who do have to do it (children) or set it (teachers) there is a wide range of views about it, many of which are very strongly held. In this chapter, we explore some of the issues that underpin this variety of opinions, by identifying both the benefits and limitations associated with homework, before discussing ways in which to utilise homework effectively as part of a planned curriculum.

The Nature of Homework

Homework has been a feature of secondary education for many years and, over recent decades, has become more prevalent in primary schools. While there are no mandatory requirements related to homework, it is clear that the Department for Education (DfE) sees it as an important element of children's education, while recognising that not all kinds of homework are equally useful:

> Homework can improve pupil outcomes, particularly for older pupils, but it is likely that the quality of homework and its relevance to main class teaching is more important than the amount set. (DfE, 2019: 18)

What is Homework?

This is a difficult question to answer, as 'homework' looks very different in different schools and in different classrooms. Some homework is in the form of worksheets that need to be completed and returned to school. Some homework might be project-based, and involve preparing presentations, making models or baking cakes. Some might involve a large degree of choice, while others might give the children no choice at all. Some schools might choose to describe their homework as 'home learning', to help shift the emphasis from task completion to learning-oriented activity. So, when discussing 'homework' in this chapter, we have to keep in mind that schools take a very wide range of approaches to planning and transacting this element of their curriculum, and this aspect of 'out-of-school learning' can mean many different things.

Critical Task 10.1

Potential Benefits and Downsides of Homework

Reflect on your own experiences of homework when you were in school (either primary or secondary). From your personal perspective, and using Table 10.1, what do you see as some of the potential benefits and downsides of homework?

Table 10.1 Potential benefits and downsides of homework

Potential benefits	Potential downsides

Potential Benefits of Homework

Homework is so much a part of everyday life in many primary schools that we rarely stop to ask ourselves what we hope the benefits might be, as noted by Kohn (2006: 3):

> After spending most of the day in school, children are typically given additional assignments to be completed at home. This is a rather curious fact when you stop to think about it, but not as curious as the fact that few people ever stop to think about it.

In this section, we critically explore some of the research evidence about the potential benefits associated with homework in the primary years.

Impact on Learning

Research into the impact of homework on pupil learning is difficult to undertake for a number of reasons: as we have already established, the term 'homework' means different things in different contexts; the same piece of homework will be completed in many different ways, with varying levels of support (or even completion) by parents; there are many factors that impact on pupil progress (quality of teaching, socio-economic conditions, opportunities outside school) so trying to isolate the impact of homework is tricky. The complexities and challenges inherent in researching the impact of homework on pupil progress might account for the range of findings from research in this area, and so it is important to read any such research with a good degree of criticality.

The Education Endowment Foundation (EEF) (2023) suggests that homework can support the educational progress of children and young people. In their headline figure, based on a meta-analysis of several research reports, and presented as part of their *Teaching and learning toolkit*, they suggest that homework can add up to five months of additional progress in an academic year. This is an impressive claim. However, this headline figure needs to be read with caution, and the underlining research explored with criticality. First, it should be noted that the EEF identifies that the research evidence to support this claim is not very robust, as there has not yet been enough rigorous research undertaken in this area to make confident assertions. Second, of the 44 research studies reviewed, only 11 were focused on primary education and, of these, none was undertaken in the United Kingdom (almost all were undertaken in the United States of America). Third, the EEF meta-analysis draws a distinction between primary and secondary homework: in line with research findings over many years (e.g., Cooper, 1989), it identifies a greater impact for homework in the secondary years (+ five months) than the primary years (+ three months). Finally, an examination of the research reports selected for analysis by EEF that relate specifically to homework in the primary years reveals that these focused on just two areas: mathematics and reading. Taking all this into account, the headline figures presented by EEF should be treated with caution and compared with other research.

According to Farrow et al. (1999: 323), research:

> did not lend support to the 'more is better' view of homework. Our contention is that assumptions about the value of homework (largely derived from secondary school practice and experience) should not be automatically 'grafted on' to primary practice.

Jerrim et al. (2020) undertook an international study, in which they compared the reported amount of time spent on homework with outcomes of assessments conducted by the International Association for the Evaluation of Educational Achievement. From their analysis of data from 24 countries, they conclude:

> We found almost no association between the amount of homework set by teachers and children's achievement in any of our 24 countries. This is consistent across various sub-groups and survives a series of robustness tests. We thus conclude that the homework teachers assign in primary school does not produce a meaningful positive influence on achievement. Homework needs to be improved if this time-consuming activity is to become a worthwhile investment. (Jerrim et al., 2020: 250)

Reading and Early Maths

Although there appears to be evidence of only a limited impact of homework on children's learning, there are some elements of home learning that are more broadly accepted as having some recognised benefits. In my own research, there was broad agreement among teachers that regular home-reading and simple early maths homework can be useful to help lay the foundations for children's learning.

Reading is recognised as being fundamental to children's long-term success, both in education and in life. In this context, Reilly (2017) reports that some schools have decided to reduce or abandon all other forms of homework, so that they can focus purely on reading at home.

The EEF (2020) identify the benefits of involving parents in supporting their children's understanding of early mathematics, and this can be done through a variety of informal approaches, such as playing board games, counting in real-life contexts and talking about other mathematical concepts, such as capacity or time.

Other Potential Benefits of Homework

Cooper (2015) suggests that homework has other perceived benefits, beyond any immediate impact on learning or progress, including the development of study habits and skills and an improvement in personal organisation and independence.

In the UK, a common argument for setting children homework in primary schools is that it helps to prepare children for the homework that they might receive in secondary schools. In Medwell and Wray's (2019) research, 82% of the primary teachers who responded to their survey agreed that homework in primary school prepares children for the demands that secondary schools will make on them. This is an interesting argument and there may be an alternative view: giving children lots of homework in primary schools might mean that they are thoroughly bored of it by the time they finish Year 6 and perhaps 'saving' it as something new to be experienced at secondary school might increase its impact at that stage.

Question Guide 10.1

Understanding the Detail of Effective Use of Homework

The *ITT Core Content Framework* (*CCF*) states that 'it is likely that the quality of homework and its relevance to main class teaching is more important than the amount set' (DfE, 2019: 18).

When reflecting on effective practice when on placement, here are some questions to ask your teacher-mentor or another member of the teaching team about how they ensure the high quality of homework and its relevance to the planned curriculum. Remember to frame your questions professionally and positively, to avoid any suggestion of implied criticism.

- Do you agree that the quality of homework is more important than the amount set?
- When considering setting a piece of homework, what kinds of issues do you think through?
- How do the children generally respond to the homework?
- How do you use homework as part of your planned curriculum?
- How do you provide feedback on completed homework?

Potential Limitations of Homework

Homework is a regular feature in many primary schools and yet, as we have seen, the evidence suggests it may have a limited impact on pupil progress, which should probably be enough of a reason for us to ask ourselves whether it is worthwhile. In this section, we will consider some other issues that make some kinds of homework problematic for many children. As Kohn (2006: 11) notes, 'no discussion about homework should be taken seriously if it fails to address the impact on real children'.

Stress and Arguments

Many researchers have identified that homework is a 'site of tension' (Solomon et al., 2002: 603) between parents and their children, with Lacina-Gifford and Gifford (2004: 279) suggesting that 'almost half of parents reported having a serious argument with their children over homework'.

This was confirmed in my own research (Forster, 2011), with many parents and children admitting to having arguments related to homework. In one particularly vivid example given by a child in Year 6:

> Mum says 'you're doing it and that's final' and I say 'But what if I don't want to do it right now?' and then Dad will get involved and he'll start shouting and stuff. You'll have Mum out in the garden doing something she wants to do, and Dad will be sat watching the rugby in a sulk, and I'll be in my room playing on the Playstation. (Forster, 2011: 87)

The interesting thing about this example is that the homework has caused a row and every member of the family is feeling disgruntled and they have all gone off in different directions, yet the homework still has not been done!

Diminished Enthusiasm for Learning

It is easy with teaching to get absorbed in the 'here and now', to focus on the short-term impact of our actions on children's learning. It is important to remind ourselves, now and again, that our job as teachers is not just to support children with their learning in the short term, but to help them learn the skills and engender the enthusiasm for learning over the longer term.

In this context, homework can, for some children, be problematic. While, in the short term, it might help children to reinforce their knowledge of number bonds or spellings, it can often have a longer-term negative impact on their enthusiasm for learning. This was a key finding in my own research, in which it was clear that, for some children, homework is a painful activity that does not enhance their excitement about learning. Take this example, in which a parent is talking about their child's response and approach to homework:

> It does become a real drag, I have to say, to do it, and actually we do find that we get into that 'Let's just get it done.' And he doesn't want to talk about it, you know, so it is just a 'Let's get it done, and over and done with'. (Forster, 2011: 82)

— Observation Guide 10.1 —

Impact of Homework on Emotions and Relationships

When observing how homework 'works' in a school, there are routine and practical things to note, as we will explore in Observation Guide 10.2, but there are some more important (and more subtle) things to notice, related to children's emotional responses to homework and any potential impacts on relationships within the classroom:

- How do the children respond when the teacher is giving homework? Watch closely and try to interpret their reactions: are they excited, downbeat, happy, frustrated, engaged or apathetic?
- When homework is due to be handed in or is being handed in, how do the children respond? Watch closely and try to interpret their reactions: are they excited, nervous, confident, worried or indifferent?
- If a child has not handed in homework on the expected day, how does this affect them during the day? Watch closely and try to interpret their actions: are they more or less engaged than usual? Does there seem to be any impact on their relationship with the teacher?

Corrosive Impact on Relationships

One area that is often overlooked when considering the potential drawbacks of homework is the impact it has on the relationships between teachers and parents and, more importantly, between teachers and their pupils. This mostly relates to the rather fraught question of what a teacher should do when a child has not handed in their homework. If they do nothing, they risk giving the message that they believe the homework is not all that important, but if they berate the child for non-submission, they run the risk of damaging their relationship with both that child and their parent. In my own research study, one teacher confessed:

> I always feel I'm nagging about it, the handing in of it, especially Year 6 ... it's always the same culprits every week forgetting it, so I do feel I'm nagging. One child I'm thinking of never does it, is always pulled up on it by us. We then moan to the parents about it at parents' evening, and she gets a hard time for it. (Forster, 2011: 63)

Of course, as professionals, teachers will aim to ensure that any 'nagging' of a child about non-submission of homework will be quickly forgotten and that all children will be treated equally and supported equally throughout the rest of the school day. However, the same research study (Forster, 2011: 93) reveals that this is not always how children perceive it, as shown by this insight given by a child in Year 6:

> There's one boy and he always does his homework and everything, but when he doesn't bring his homework in the teachers are a bit off with him. So sometimes you think 'I have to do it because if I'm stuck with something they're not going to be as helpful'. They will be helpful but they won't be as much because they're a bit annoyed with you because you haven't done your homework or brought it in.

Assessment of Homework

One of the challenges that teachers face when integrating homework as part of their planned curriculum is considering how they will provide meaningful feedback on the work or engage the children in a formative assessment process. In my research, I found that much assessment of homework tends to be 'binary': it is either handed in or it isn't! Beyond that, many teachers struggle to find time to provide meaningful feedback on homework tasks and, even if they do, it is hard to know how independently the work was completed and whether they are providing feedback for the children or their parents.

Exacerbation of Inequalities

International research by the Office for Economic Co-operation and Development (OECD) (2014) found that, in many countries, homework can have the unintended impact of widening the gap in educational outcomes between children in families from different socio-economic backgrounds. Some of the reasons for this are explained by the EEF (2023) in their *Teaching and learning toolkit*:

> Surveys in England suggest that pupils from disadvantaged backgrounds are less likely to have a quiet working space, are less likely to have access to a device suitable for learning or a stable internet connection and may receive less parental support to complete homework and develop effective learning habits. These difficulties may increase the gap in attainment for disadvantaged pupils.

It suggests that teachers need to think carefully about the kind of homework that they set and the ways in which they support children who might struggle to complete the tasks at home. One approach is to establish a 'homework club', to which all children are welcome but which some children in particular are encouraged to join.

─── **Observation Guide 10.2** ───

Management of Homework

When observing practice related to homework, there is a range of elements to notice about the management of the homework process:

- How does the teacher decide on the most appropriate homework task?
- How does the teacher introduce and explain homework tasks to the children?
- How does the teacher manage the process of collecting in homework?

- What happens if a child has not handed in their homework?
- How does the teacher provide feedback on the homework?
- How does the teacher use the homework tasks to inform or enhance the in-class learning?

Homework That Minimises the Limitations and Maximises Potential

When considering how to make the best use of homework, it is important to reflect on ways in which to limit any of the potentially negative impacts that we have discussed in this chapter, and identify ways to maximise impact, not just on learning but on enthusiasm for learning. The aim is to reduce the potential for stress, arguments and corrosive impacts on relationships, and maximise the potential for effective, creative, purposeful and joyful learning.

Pencil-free Homework

One potential approach to reducing some of the downsides associated with homework is an approach known as 'pencil-free homework' (Forster et al., 2010). The distinctive features of this kind of homework are that it focuses on doing and talking activities and there are no spaces on the homework sheet for children to fill in the blanks or provide answers: the homework is 'pencil-free' as there is no requirement to write anything down.

The pencil-free approach is based on what we know about effective learning: talking about ideas in a safe, social context enables children to learn from adults. It also allows them to demonstrate their own knowledge and understanding, which reinforces their learning and clarifies their thinking. It also provides good opportunities for them to express their own questions, which is an important and often overlooked element of effective learning.

The approach also addresses several of the known limitations of homework: children are less stressed about the homework, as there is nothing to hand in and nothing to 'get wrong'. Since the homework itself is less stress-laden, there are fewer arguments in the home about it and, importantly, the relationships between teachers and children cannot be eroded by nagging about handing in homework, as there is nothing to hand in. Instead, the teacher can organise group and class discussions in order to formatively assess and acknowledge the children's learning, which has the added benefit for children who, for whatever reason, had been unable to give the homework task a go at home, because they are able to learn from others and contribute their ideas at this stage.

Homework to Enhance Social Capital

Another approach to homework is to consider children's 'social capital' and identify ways in which this might be encouraged and recognised by the school. It is worth considering the kinds of activities that are likely to enrich children's lives, develop a range of skills and enhance their future prospects. For example, learning to play a musical instrument as a member of a community group is rich with life-enhancing benefits, such as developing listening skills, contributing to a group, learning about teamwork and experiencing the benefits of working hard on a new skill.

Other activities might include talking to your grandparents about their childhoods, walking with a member of your family to a local park, reading the names on a local war memorial or learning a new skill of your choice. This approach will require some thought to make it worthwhile, relevant to the children and manageable in the local area; there is no point asking children to visit a museum if the nearest one is ten miles away. The school may create links with local community groups and organisations to create valuable experiences for the children. Such activities may take a little effort but, once you start to see it as a choice between asking children to spend two hours a week filling in worksheets or engaging in life-enriching activities, the answer is obvious.

Case Study 10.1

School Leaders' Examples of Effective Practice

We asked a couple of school leaders to tell us about some of the best homework they set in their school, and they suggested two similar tasks that they have found valuable over the years:

1 Learn a poem by heart. This leads into a class recital of the poem, with rich learning in relation to reading skills, vocabulary development, understanding of intonation and performance skills.
2 Learn the lines for the Year 6 end-of-year play. This is an enriching task, in terms of both language and memory, that the children are keen to engage in because it has a real purpose related to an event to which they feel committed and emotionally invested.

The benefit of both tasks is that they avoid the trap of being 'homework for homework's sake' (i.e., homework that lacks purpose and is probably set just because it's the day homework needs to be set).

Homework as Part of a Planned Curriculum

One of the challenges with homework is making it both manageable and to some extent predictable for parents, so that they know what to expect and how best to support their children. The reason this is a challenge is that, if you always give maths homework on a Thursday, it can be tricky to ensure that the homework is always directly relevant to the current learning.

It is important to avoid this 'bolt-on' approach to homework, or as Martin Hughes describes it, in an interview with Roberts (2009), 'homework for homework's sake'. As identified by the EEF (2023):

> In the most effective examples, homework was an integral part of learning, rather than an add-on. To maximise impact, it also appears to be important that students are provided with high-quality feedback on their work.

Integrating Homework in Planning

Broadly, you might think about planning for homework in two ways: activities that can be done after classroom-based learning to consolidate key ideas, or activities that can be done in advance of a specific teaching episode, to prepare the children for the content or to help them understand the context or the significance of the learning.

Critical Task 10.2

Benefits of Planning Homework Tasks to be Done *Before* Teaching

Most homework follows on from lessons taught in school, with the aim of consolidating learning. In this task, we would like you to consider the benefits of planning creative, interesting and/or collaborative homework activities that can be given *before* the relevant lessons are taught in school. Complete Table 10.2.

Table 10.2   Potential benefits of homework tasks before teaching

Potential benefits of giving a homework task before relevant teaching	Can you give an example of the kind of task that might be effective?

The important thing is that your planning for homework should be done as an embedded element of your planning for the sequence of learning, rather than as a last-minute bolt-on.

Response to Critical Task 10.1

Potential Benefits and Downsides of Homework

In this task, we asked you to reflect on your own experiences of homework when you were in school, to identify what you see as some of the potential benefits and downsides of homework. In Table 10.3, we present an overview of some of the issues explored in the chapter to give a research-informed summary of the pros and cons of homework.

Table 10.3 Suggested benefits and downsides of homework

Potential benefits of homework	Potential downsides of homework
Potential preparation for secondary school	Arguments at home
Parents are given insights into their children's learning	Inequality can be exacerbated
Parents learn about 'current' approaches to teaching and learning	Children's stress and anxiety increased
Reinforcement of fundamental skills: reading and basic number work	Negative impact on children's enthusiasm for learning
	Corrosive impacts on teacher/pupil relationships
	Assessment can be challenging

Response to Critical Task 10.2

Benefits of Planning Homework Tasks to be Done *Before* Teaching

In this task, we asked you to consider the benefits of planning creative, interesting and/or collaborative homework activities that can be given *before* the relevant lessons are taught in school. Table 10.4 offers some examples of the kinds of task that might be effective.

Table 10.4 Suggested benefits of giving homework before teaching

Potential benefits of giving a homework task before relevant teaching	An example of the kind of task that might be effective
Opportunity to elicit the children's initial ideas about a topic, and to understand how others in their home influence their thinking	Give a key question for discussion at home, such as: • Does the Earth travel around the Sun or does the Sun travel around the Earth?
Initiate interest in a new topic	Give the children something to observe or notice, such as: • Look for the moon every evening this week. On Monday next week, we'll discuss what you notice.
Identify the relevance of a new topic to real-life contexts	Ask the children to bring in an object that might relate to the new topic, such as: • In science, we're going to start learning about sound, so please could you ask at home if you have any musical instruments that you could bring in on Tuesday.

Chapter Summary

In this chapter, we have considered some of the potential benefits of homework and some of the potential limitations. While the case for giving homework is relatively strong in secondary schools, the potential impact on learning for children of primary age appears to be limited, although there are some benefits associated with parents developing an understanding of what their children are learning at school. Meanwhile, there are several limitations to homework, including its impact on stress levels in children and parents, its contribution to arguments within the home, its potentially negative impact on children's enthusiasm for learning and its likely corrosive impact on the relationship between teachers and children. For homework to be most effective, approaches should be considered that reduce these negative impacts and promote authentic learning, with rich, life-enhancing approaches that are embedded as part of a well-planned curriculum.

Further Reading

Kohn, A. (2006) *The homework myth*. Philadelphia, PA: Da Capo Press.
This insightful book provides a great summary of published research on the limitations of homework. Kohn brings his usual rigour to examining the issues, based on the available evidence, and helps the reader to consider the impact of homework on the 'lived experience' of the child.
Education Endowment Foundation (EEF) (2020) *Supporting the learning of mathematics at home*. Available at: https://educationendowmentfoundation.org.uk/news/blog-supporting-the-learning-of-mathematics-at-home
This blog is an accessible guide that summarises some of the key findings of EEF's research on supporting young children's learning in maths at home.

References

Cooper, H. (1989) 'Synthesis of research on homework', *Educational Leadership*, 47(3), 85–91.
Cooper, H. (2015) *The battle over homework: Common ground for administrators, teachers, and parents* (3rd edn). New York: Carrel Books.
Department for Education (DfE) (2019) *ITT core content framework*. London: DfE.
Education Endowment Foundation (EEF) (2020) *Supporting the learning of mathematics at home*. Available at: https://educationendowmentfoundation.org.uk/news/blog-supporting-the-learning-of-mathematics-at-home (accessed 16 February 2023).
Education Endowment Foundation (EEF) (2023) *Teaching and learning toolkit*. Available at: https://educationendowmentfoundation.org.uk/education-evidence/teaching-learning-toolkit (accessed 16 February 2023).

Farrow, S., Tymms, P. and Henderson, B. (1999) 'Homework and attainment in primary schools', *British Educational Research Journal*, 25(3), 323–341.

Forster, C. (2011) *The application of constructivist learning theory to homework practice: A case study of a trial of pencil-free approaches to home-learning in Key Stage Two Science.* Unpublished EdD thesis, University of Gloucestershire. Available at: https://eprints.glos.ac.uk/3524/ (accessed 11 April 2023).

Forster, C., Parfitt, V., McGowan, A. and Brookes, D. (2010) *Science homework for key stage 2: Activity based learning.* London: David Fulton.

Jerrim, J., Lopez-Agudo, L.A. and Marcenaro-Gutierrez, O.D. (2020) 'The association between homework and primary school children's academic achievement: international evidence from PIRLS and TIMSS', *European Journal of Education*, 55(2), 248–260.

Kohn, A. (2006) *The homework myth.* Philadelphia, PA: Da Capo Press.

Lacina-Gifford, L.J. and Gifford, R.B. (2004) 'Putting an end to the battle over homework', *Education*, 125(2), 279–281.

Medwell, J. and Wray, D. (2019) 'Primary homework in England: the beliefs and practices of teachers in primary schools', *Education 3–13*, 47(2), 191–204.

Office for Economic Co-operation and Development (OECD) (2014) 'Does homework perpetuate inequities in education?', *PISA in Focus*, No. 46. Paris: OECD Publishing.

Reilly, K. (2017) 'A Florida School District is eliminating homework in favor of reading', *Time.com*, 19 July.

Roberts, C. (2009) 'A benefit – or a burden?', *Professional Teacher*, Autumn, 14–15.

Solomon, Y., Warin, J. and Lewis, C. (2002) 'Helping with homework? Homework as a site of tension for parents and teenagers', *British Educational Research Journal*, 28(4), 603–622.

SECTION 4
ASSESSMENT

11
DECIDING WHAT TO ASSESS

Ruth Hollier

Chapter Objectives

- To consider why assessment is critical to effective teaching and learning.
- To explore what to assess and when, and how to undertake and use assessment to maximise children's learning.
- To reflect on assessment as an integral part of the teaching and learning process, and how it should be deliberately connected to planning, evaluation and adaptive teaching.

In this chapter, we explore what assessment means and consider how teachers decide what to assess and when, why and how that happens. It may seem straightforward if we take assessment as simply the act of setting and marking tests in particular subjects, but, in fact, assessment is a much more complex activity than that. It is a crucial part of every moment of teaching, and is vital to effective learning. We explore different types of assessment and how these are enacted within the classroom, and consider why it is important to plan deliberately for high-quality assessment.

What is Assessment?

'Assessment', in its broadest meaning, refers to the ways in which teachers find out and make judgements about what children know, can do and understand. As you might imagine, this is a complex process and, to be effective, it relies on teachers being 'assessment literate' (DeLuca and Johnson, 2017: 121). This means that teachers need to understand the aims of assessment and know a range of useful approaches before they can enact it well in their classrooms.

Towards a Definition or Shared Understanding of Assessment

While it is accepted as a part of everyday practice, it is important to recognise that there is a range of ways in which the word 'assessment' can be used and understood. Often, assessment is linked to ideas about pencil and paper testing and exams, especially at secondary school. In primary schools, assessment approaches are often more practical in nature and based on the teacher's knowledge of the pupils as well as what children can commit to the page. Nevertheless, there is a tendency to think of assessment in general terms as something concrete and tangible which is 'done to' children as part of their experience of school.

It can be said that this is a rather simplistic view which loses the true meaning and intention of assessment as a central part of teaching and learning. The word 'assessment' originates from the Latin word 'assideo', meaning 'to sit beside'. If we think of our assessment of a child's learning as being the act of 'sitting beside' them, it carries some added meaning. In this interpretation, the teacher must not only make a judgement on a child's level of knowledge, but also see learning from the child's point of view and understand their thinking, attitude and motivation. Understanding 'assessment' in this way brings value to the act beyond merely judging a child's attainment and progress in a certain subject.

In addition, assessment is a 'value-laden' activity (Earle, 2019: 5), a driver for what is taught and when and how. As such, it shapes children's experience of education (Earle, 2019) because if children are expected to meet certain criteria set by statutory guidance, it is likely that teaching will focus on those things. Assessments also influence children's emotional engagement with learning. Although research evidence remains inconclusive, some forms of assessment (such as the end of Key Stage 2 SATs tests) are commonly thought to be associated with stress (Bradbury, 2019). Regular use of tests, such as spellings and times tables tests, can provide useful retrieval practice and help to embed knowledge through the 'testing effect' (Wiliam and Christodoulou, 2017: 34). However, they arguably offer little of value in assessing children's learning, as, for example, they offer no insight into how children use spellings in context.

According to Black and Wiliam (1998: 140), 'assessment' should be a general term which we use 'to refer to all those activities undertaken by teachers – and by their students in assessing themselves – that provide information to be used as feedback to modify teaching and learning activities'. Thus, assessment can take many forms but should always make a difference to the teaching, and therefore the learning, that follows. It should not happen accidentally or incidentally: it is an integral part of teaching and should be considered deliberately. This puts assessment at the heart of effective teaching.

Types of Assessment: Statutory, Summative, Formative, Informal, Formal

Most education systems have some form of statutory assessment structure. These are usually a set of national, legally required assessments, used as benchmarks for expected attainment and to show progress across time. They are 'summative' assessments, providing a snapshot of children's attainment and capabilities at a point in time. Assessments like these tend to be narrow, focusing on what is easy to assess in a standardised way, rather than revealing the depth and detail of a child's understanding. Although critics propose many limitations to statutory assessments (Hall and Sheehy, 2018), the results are often used to hold schools, and teachers, accountable for children's outcomes.

Accountability measures, such as published league tables, which are drawn from these statutory assessments, mean they are high profile, so some might assume assessment in school is almost entirely 'summative'. This would be to overlook those assessment approaches which are continuous and provide feedback to teachers (and to pupils) that directly inform teaching and learning strategies. These are 'formative' assessment approaches with the specific purpose of supporting learning, as set out by Black and Wiliam (1998). The formative Assessment *for* Learning (AfL) should be considered separately from summative assessments used for the purposes of grading, reporting and comparison, which can be termed Assessment *of* Learning (AoL) (Assessment Reform Group (ARG), 1999).

Formative assessment can have a significant impact on learning when used effectively, as Wiliam explains in discussion with Christodoulou:

> The biggest improvements in student learning happen when teachers use assessment minute-by-minute and day-by-day as part of regular teaching, not as part of process monitoring. (Wiliam and Christodoulou, 2017: 34)

However, it is worth noting that it is not the *mode* of assessment which dictates whether it is summative or formative, but how the information is used. Assessment becomes formative 'when the evidence is actually used to adapt teaching to meet pupil needs' (Black and Wiliam, 1998: 140). So intertwined is assessment with teaching that Wiliam more recently regretted that he had used the term 'formative assessment' to describe the process at all, saying that the term 'responsive teaching' would be more appropriate (Wiliam and Christodoulou, 2017: 23).

You may also hear assessment described as formal or informal. The naming really depends on the way in which the mode of assessment is carried out. A formal approach would be planned for, set and applied to many children at one time; an informal approach might be *ad hoc*, individual or involve dialogue between child and teacher or completion of an individual task.

We will explore the different types of assessment activity undertaken by teachers in this chapter. Ways in which feedback can impact on learning will be discussed in Chapter 12 and how pupils can become engaged in their own assessment is addressed further in Chapter 13.

What Should We Assess?

For assessment to be purposeful it must be precisely targeted. Most importantly, we should assess children's learning and skills development, with a targeted and precise focus matched very closely to learning intentions. This will enable us to 'avoid being over-influenced by potentially misleading factors, such as how busy pupils appear' (Department for Education (DfE), 2019: 23).

However, we must also go beyond the usual perception of teaching and learning activities. Valuable assessment links not only to subject-related learning objectives specifically, but also to other things we value but do not necessarily assess formally. Within any lesson we may also assess children's speaking and listening, collaboration, emotional response or resilience. These are not often planned for as assessment within a lesson, but gauging these aspects of children's learning and development is useful to you as a teacher to judge how to support their progress in a broader sense. In fact, as Black and Wiliam acknowledge (1998: 140), teachers must manage the 'personal, emotional and social pressures of a group of 30 or more youngsters in order to help them learn immediately and become better learners in the future', so these assessments may be vital. Teachers need to know their pupils holistically, not just academically. Without assessing these personal aspects of development, it would be difficult to facilitate children's learning effectively or comment on character, perseverance or collaborative skills at parents' evening, for example.

When Should We Assess?

Simply, all the time. As we will explore through the rest of this chapter, assessment should be considered at each stage of teaching: before, during and after. Assessment in readiness for teaching ensures that lessons are 'pitched' appropriately and build effectively on the children's prior knowledge. Assessment 'on the go' during teaching is required in order to ensure effective, responsive teaching, adapted to children's needs. Assessment after teaching is essential to determine next steps for both pupils and teachers.

This does not mean that we should only focus on assessment, though, as the rest of this book makes clear. Teaching is a complex activity. To create and deliver worthwhile learning experiences for the children, we need to consider how we focus the use of our time as teachers. We should not spend more time on assessing and gathering data than on planning how we can teach in an engaging, adaptive and focused way, meeting the academic and wider needs of the children we work with.

Assessment in Readiness for Teaching

In the plan–teach–assess–review cycle, we often think of assessment as the 'after' part of the teaching process. However, assessing *before* planning and teaching is very important, so much so that the *Special educational needs and disability code of practice* (DfE, 2015: 86) refers to a graduated approach which prioritises assessment as the first of 'four stages of action: assess, plan, do and review'.

The Importance of 'Pitching Your Teaching'

In order to move children forwards on the next step of their learning journey, you need to know where they are to begin with and teach them the next step that they need to take, as explored in Chapter 5. You should also consider how to match your approach to children's interests, or to create a 'hook' for learning which aims to engage the children with your teaching. This is why 'pitching your teaching' to match children's prior knowledge and interests is vital. Assessing prior learning allows teachers to ascertain what children already know and what skills they have that they can apply. Building a relationship with children in your class can help you determine what contexts might interest them in learning new knowledge. Knowing this, teachers can plan for a precise next step, define a clear learning intention and understand the scaffolding children may need to access new learning. They can design learning opportunities that appeal to children, 'start their expositions at the point of current pupil understanding' (DfE, 2019: 17) and plan for meaningful review of previous learning at the start of lessons, which, as explored in Chapter 5, Rosenshine (2012) suggests can have a significant effect on learning.

Critical Task 11.1

Pitch Perfect: Why is it Important to Get Assessment Right before Teaching?

Reflect on what might happen if teachers' assessments of children's knowledge and understanding before teaching are inaccurate or flawed. What might be the impact on learning if:

- A teacher overestimates what children know and can do within a subject they are planning to teach?
- A teacher underestimates what children know and can do within a subject they are planning to teach?
- A child has a gap in their foundational knowledge that teachers have not identified? For example, in mathematics if they have not secured understanding of place value before tackling two-digit column addition?
- A child holds a pre-existing misconception? For example, in science, if children hold the belief that plants get their food from the soil? Or that light travels from their eyes to an object so they can see it? Or in history that all shiny things must be 'new'?

Consider how a teacher might address such knowledge gaps and/or pre-existing misconceptions in their teaching.

Uncovering Pre-Existing Misconceptions

If we accept that 'pupils learn new ideas by linking those ideas to existing knowledge, organising this knowledge into increasingly complex mental models (or "schemata")' (DfE, 2019: 14), then we must also recognise that children having the *correct* concept as existing knowledge is essential. A misconception, which might be based on faulty or immature thinking or understanding, will only provide flawed and unreliable foundations on which children build their mental models or new understanding. This is especially complex because, while there are common misconceptions which teachers can become aware of through their own study and subject knowledge development, children can also form individual and unpredictable misconceptions based on the way in which they understand or make sense of their own experiences. So, assessments and elicitation tasks must be carefully designed to ensure that all misconceptions are revealed.

Finding Out About Prior Knowledge and Attainment: Strategies for Elicitation

As a teacher, you will know what you expect children in your class to know and understand based on information from previous assessments, but it is always wise to check for yourself to make sure knowledge gaps have not appeared. There are many techniques which can be used to elicit children's understanding. Salter and Earle (2019: 22) suggest that these can be divided into 'open' and 'closed' strategies, depending on whether you want to know what children know more generally, for example at the start of a topic, or whether you intend to check on whether they know something specific.

While there are often subject-specific approaches to eliciting children's prior knowledge, some general open elicitation strategies include:

- open dialogue with children
- observing pupils
- mind mapping with children
- pupil drawings or model making
- pupil question-raising
- open investigations.

Strategies to check on specific aspects of knowledge include:

- question and answer activities
- quizzes
- matching and grouping activities
- diagrams and labelling
- challenge tasks
- tasks with one expected outcome.

Observation Guide 11.1

Assessing Prior Knowledge

The *ITT Core Content Framework (CCF)* states that student teachers should 'learn how to check prior knowledge and understanding … by … using assessments to check for prior knowledge and pre-existing misconceptions' (DfE, 2019: 23).

While observing in school, pay particular attention to how the teacher frames their expectations at the beginning of a sequence of teaching and learning:

- How does the teacher use evidence from previous assessments before teaching?
- How does the teacher structure tasks and questions early in the teaching to enable them to identify other knowledge gaps and misconceptions about new material?
- How do these tasks and questions vary in different subjects in the primary curriculum?

Assessment 'On The Go': During Teaching

As discussed earlier, assessment is indivisible from teaching within a lesson. Assessment 'on the go' allows us to track children's learning throughout the lesson and make adaptations to teaching in real time, to address difficulties and misconceptions as they arise, in a responsive approach to adaptive teaching. We should make sure that we assess the important elements of learning, such as whether children have gained deep and secure understanding of the knowledge or skill intended within a lesson. We should be wary that we do not simply assess the 'easy to assess' elements, such as task completion. In order to achieve accurate assessment, teachers use a wide range of visible and covert assessment strategies. We will explore a range of these in this section.

Visible Assessment Strategies

Visible assessment strategies are assessment strategies that are explicitly part of each lesson and are readily observable in practice. For the most part, they can be planned for in an overt way in advance of the lesson, offering opportunities for assessment through the use of structured tasks and questions and by planning for moments within the lesson where you can take stock of the situation and gauge children's progress. They will all be easily noticed when observing practice in the classroom, which is why we have termed them as 'visible' here.

Clarity of learning intentions: As Wiliam (2018: 80) says: 'It seems obvious that to get anywhere, it helps to be clear about where you are going.' So, in your mind, there should be absolute clarity, based on your assessment of prior learning and on knowledge of the necessary next steps in the subject in hand, about what the key point of the learning intention in any lesson should be.

You should also be very clear about how children are intended to achieve the learning intention, whether or not you write and share these matching success criteria with the children in an explicit way. Clarity enables you to 'plan formative assessment tasks linked to lesson objectives and think ahead about what would indicate understanding' (DfE, 2019: 23). Thus, your aim for pupils' learning, and ways for them to demonstrate that learning, become visible to all within the lesson.

Design assessment tasks for insight: For the purpose of assessment, if the intention is to inform teaching, it is important to ensure that tasks include elements that provide insights into the pupils' thinking and understanding. As Wiliam says, 'if all you discover in giving students a mathematics exercise is that they couldn't do it, … [it] is because you didn't design the task in a way that illuminated aspects of that student's thinking' (Wiliam and Christodoulou, 2017: 33).

So, structuring assessment tasks within a lesson deserves careful thought and deliberation, to ensure that what you are asking them to do at any given point will allow you to gain the information you need to move forward. It may be as simple as presenting a small, closed task to assess recall of a particular fact, or it may be a longer and more involved task, such as writing a paragraph or building a model to explain a process. A common way to ensure that your assessment tasks allow you to identify knowledge gaps and misconceptions is to make use of them within the task itself, such as by including 'common misconceptions within multiple-choice questions' (DfE, 2019: 23).

Mark as you go: Whether you have designed open or closed assessment tasks for the lesson, it is important to check children's understanding as you go along, so you can respond in a timely way if difficulties arise. One way to do this is to undertake 'live' marking; that is, to mark children's work while they are still working on it. This is especially useful in subjects like mathematics where it allows misconceptions to be quickly identified and tackled. Other ideas for opportunities and strategies for giving effective feedback are explored further in Chapter 12.

Ask the right question at the right time: One key tool in the teacher's repertoire is to use questioning to enable assessment. Much has been written on how to ask effective questions (e.g., see Salter and Earle, 2019: 23–25), which, like assessment task design, need to be constructed carefully to elicit the desired (and therefore useful) responses.

For effective assessment, questions need to be targeted to match specific learning points at the right moment in the lesson. Wiliam (2015: 41) refers to the right moment as the 'hinge' of the lesson, where teachers should 'get on-the-spot evidence about what students do and don't understand before moving forward'. Black et al. (2004) say that you need to have detailed subject knowledge in order to choose a good question. You will also need to plan your hinge questions carefully, based on the intended learning outcomes, and practise gauging when the right moment to ask them arrives. Based on the responses to your question, Wiliam (2015: 42) suggests you can then 'decide whether to go forward or back' in your teaching.

It is also worth remembering that in whole-class situations, question answering can be dominated by confident pupils. Assessment value is limited when your questions only attract answers from confident children, so you also need to make use of effective strategies to ensure everyone has a voice. Chapter 13 provides more information to support you in developing this aspect of your practice.

Question Guide 11.1

Assessment in Action

The *CCF* states that student teachers should 'learn how to avoid common assessment pitfalls and how to check ... knowledge and understanding during lessons' (DfE, 2019: 23).

For many expert teachers, decisions about what and how to assess during a lesson will have become intuitive, based on their prior experience of teaching. As a result, a focused discussion with an experienced teacher may be very helpful in revealing their thought processes, which may not be evident in their own planning or practice. The best way to approach such a focused discussion may be to follow up a specific lesson that you have observed with questions such as:

- What was your focus for assessment during the lesson?
- How did you decide what you needed to assess?
- What assessment strategies were you using during the lesson?
- How did you decide which assessment strategies would be most useful?
- How effective do you think your assessment was in giving you the information you needed?

After this discussion it is useful to follow up with a focused observation of the next lesson in the sequence, to see some of these strategies in action.

Covert Assessment Strategies

Not all assessment strategies are easily visible to the observer. Just as valuable as structured assessment tasks are the 'soft' skills of assessment (observation, listening, reading body language), which serve to 'round out' the teacher's assessment of a child's learning beyond knowing about their academic attainment. When we do this kind of covert assessment of children, they are often unaware that they are being assessed, which can offer an unguarded view of their learning. So, it is not only overt responses, recorded or written outcomes that we are interested in detecting here, but also more covert signs which reveal attitudes, confidence and engagement.

During the lesson, we need to consider where we position ourselves in the classroom. While observing and listening in on children while they work, we might ask ourselves:

- Are children really showing interest and engaging with the learning or are they simply looking busy?
- Are they completing the task entirely independently or are they surreptitiously copying from children around them or relying heavily on support materials?
- Are they fully engaged and comfortable with the task, feeling confident in their learning, or are they fidgeting and avoiding concentration?

We can also eavesdrop on the dialogue between children as they focus on a task to help us pick up on misconceptions or difficulties which the child may not reveal to an adult.

These are things which can be observed using a covert approach but would not necessarily be visible in the outcomes from assessment tasks alone. Using covert assessment strategies alongside assessing the more visible outcomes from the tasks and responses to direct questions can help you to build a convincing and rounded picture of the children's learning. It is important that your assessment is holistic, that it ensures that children have secured the intended knowledge and understanding, and that they feel confident and engaged in their learning.

Observation Guide 11.2

Seeing Assessment in Action: Noticing Covert Strategies

Following on from the previous discussion, observe closely how the teacher assesses children within a lesson.

- Make a note of any structured (visible) assessment strategies which are obvious as planned tasks or questions within the lesson. Consider what you think the teacher intends to assess through a particular task or question.
- Try to notice when the teacher uses covert assessment strategies, which may be hidden within their interactions with children during the lesson or in their general movement around the classroom. Consider which children the teacher targets and why. Think about what the teacher might be observing or listening to. How does the teacher adapt their approach as a result of this covert assessment?

Assessment After Teaching: What Next?

Whether assessment information has been gathered during the course of a lesson or from one-off summative assessment, the key thing that teachers should focus on is making sure that it makes a difference to the teaching and learning experience for children.

Question Guide 11.2

Using Assessment *for* Learning

The *CCF* states that 'effective assessment is critical to teaching because it provides teachers with information about pupils' understanding and needs' (DfE, 2019: 23).

So, what do teachers *do* with that information?

When reflecting on a lesson you have observed while on placement, here are some questions you can ask your teacher-mentor or another member of the teaching team about how they ensure assessment information is used effectively to make an impact on children's learning. Remember to frame your questions professionally, to avoid any implied criticism.

- What does your assessment from today's lesson tell you about children's understanding and their needs?
- Did the children respond in the way you expected?
- What notes or records will you keep of your assessments from today, if any?
- For the children who did not meet the learning intention or had specific needs today, how will you follow up in the next lesson?
- What impact do you expect that to have on the learning for those children? How will you manage that, practically, in the classroom?
- Will there be anything which needs a more long-term follow-up or intervention? How will you address it?

Uses of Assessment Information

There are different uses of assessment information at individual, class and whole-school level.

As we have discussed, experienced teachers gather vast amounts of assessment information, related to both academic attainment and personal development, as an intrinsic part of their teaching. Much of this information is acted on immediately within the lesson to influence individual children's learning. Beyond that, unless there is a reason for gathering or recording additional assessment information, you should not do it. As Wiliam says, 'Students don't get any extra benefit from testing when a teacher records a score in a mark book' (Wiliam and Christodoulou, 2017: 35). Generally, teachers should use summative assessment information gathered about their own class at the end of a sequence of teaching to inform their near-future class teaching and interventions for children.

However, recording assessment information often forms part of school policy for wider reasons. Teachers must assess and track pupils' attainment and progress against expected standards over time and need records to support this process, as well as to report to parents, governors and higher authorities. Schools use a range of ways to record and process such data, including software packages that are specifically designed for the purpose.

Data collection at the school level is not synonymous with assessment of individual children but is linked to whole-school planning and accountability measures, which, at first thought, may not seem to make much difference to children, day to day, in your classroom. In fact, summative assessments are not necessarily designed to be diagnostic or to support responsive teaching, but to inform future planning in the long term. This is assessment *of* learning, and is used to influence the way schools operate: 'the purpose for the [data] analysis is to confirm what teachers and children do well so they can continue doing it, what they need to stop doing because it does not work, and what they could do instead' (McKay, 2019: 76).

Case Study 11.1

Using Assessment *of* Learning

The *CCF* states that, 'before using any assessment, teachers should be clear about the decision it will be used to support and be able to justify its use' (DfE, 2019: 23).

One experienced teacher describes below how their school uses assessment information to support decisions about future teaching, target setting and interventions.

> Our school's maths scheme provides assessment tasks for every unit taught, which offer a useful 'snapshot' of children's understanding. When I analyse the outcomes of these assessments, it highlights specific strengths and weaknesses of children, which means I can make judgements about their next steps at the end of the teaching. Where there are misconceptions or a lack of understanding of a key learning point, I make a note to re-cap in the following week or next term, to ensure the children know and remember more about the topic over time. In English, there are reading tests to see whether children can move to the next level of reading book, and in writing, we set individual targets for children to work on based on termly assessments of pieces of writing they have completed. I use these assessments to inform the content of interventions too. Where I can see there's a particular weakness, I can ask my TA to target that with a small group.
>
> All classes use these assessments and then they are looked at by the relevant subject leader, who carries out analysis to look for consistent strengths and weaknesses across the whole school. Class teachers are then advised on what to address, for example in maths daily fluency sessions, helping the children to know more and remember more in their weaker areas. This also enables us to have targeted professional development to support our teaching where we need it.

While schools have different assessment policies and work in different ways, the use of assessment as described here is a typical picture of effective approaches. It is used by teachers to inform their planning in the medium and long term, to link to target-setting and planning for interventions, and to inform whole-school improvement and development.

Assessing Deliberately

Having explored some ideas about when and how to assess, and given its importance in effective teaching and learning, it should now be quite clear that the main thing about assessment is that it should be something done both deliberately and with discernment. It should not be an afterthought, and the quality rather than the quantity of assessment is key. You may find it useful to reflect on your own approach and on how deliberate and discerning you are in your planning for and use of assessment.

Critical Task 11.2

How Deliberately Do You Plan for Assessment?

While it is vital to plan structured tasks and questioning as part of your lessons to enable you to gather useful assessment information, many of the most impactful strategies that teachers employ are covert and seem to happen intuitively. It is often these strategies which enable teachers to interact responsively with children during the lesson.

Until this practice becomes intuitive for you, you will need to plan when and how to use these covert strategies in your lessons. This means planning opportunities to listen to and observe children while they are learning. So, next time you plan a lesson or sequence of learning, consider the following things:

- Have you planned any structured tasks to gather assessment information? What do you intend to find out from these tasks?
- Have you planned any questions you can use to gather assessment information?
- What opportunities are there for you to stand back and observe the class while they are engaged in learning activities?
- Where will you position yourself?
- Are there any children you will target individually to assess?
- What will you look or listen for at various points in the lesson?
- What will you expect to see or hear?
- How will you respond if a misconception or misunderstanding is evident?

Response to Critical Task 11.1

Pitch Perfect: Why is it Important to Get Assessment Right before Teaching?

In this task, we asked you to reflect on what might happen in the lesson if teachers' assessments of children's knowledge and understanding before teaching were inaccurate or flawed, and what the impact on children's learning might be.

Continued

By now, you have probably realised that assessment is the foundation on which effective teaching and learning is built. It is not only vital to get it right before you start teaching a new lesson or sequence of learning, it is also important to plan deliberately for effective assessment throughout the teaching cycle. Effective assessment will be crucial both during and beyond the lesson you are teaching to ensure that you are able to respond and adapt your teaching to the needs of your pupils in the moment, and over time.

Chapter Summary

In this chapter, we have considered assessment in its broadest sense, which means assessing and understanding children's academic, personal and skills development. We have explored how teachers decide what to assess and when, why and how that happens, and the importance of matching deliberate, structured assessment tasks with the 'soft', covert skills of assessment. In doing so, we can see that assessment can be complex to master, but essential to good teaching and learning. The next chapters will explore further how teachers provide effective feedback and how they usefully involve pupils with assessment processes in order to maximise learning.

Further Reading

Earle, S. (ed.) (2019) *Assessment in the primary classroom: Principles and practice*. London: Learning Matters/Sage.
This helpful book is useful for a more in-depth look at all aspects of assessment. In Salter and Earle's chapter, the summaries of formative assessment questioning strategies on pp. 23–25 are particularly useful.
Hendrick, C. and McPherson, R. (eds.) *What does this look like in the classroom? Bridging the gap between research and practice*. Woodbridge, UK: John Catt Educational Ltd.
Chapter 1 of this book contains a very interesting discussion between Dylan Wiliam and Daisy Christodoulou relating to assessment, marking and feedback.

References

Assessment Reform Group (ARG) (1999) *Assessment for learning: Beyond the Black Box*. Cambridge: University of Cambridge School of Education.
Black, P., Harrison, C., Lee, C., Marshall, B. and Wiliam, D. (2004) 'Working inside the Black Box: assessment for learning in the classroom', *Phi Delta Kappan*, 86(1), 9–21.

Black, P. and Wiliam, D. (1998) 'Inside the Black Box: raising standards through classroom assessment', *Phi Delta Kappan*, 80(2), 139–148.

Bradbury, A. (2019) *Pressure, anxiety and collateral damage: The headteachers' verdict on SATS.* More than a Score [website]. Available at: www.morethanascore.org.uk/wp-content/uploads/2019/09/SATs-research.pdf (accessed 9 November 2022).

DeLuca, C. and Johnson, S. (2017) 'Developing assessment capable teachers in this age of accountability', *Assessment in Education: Principles, Policy and Practice*, 24(2), 121–126.

Department for Education (DfE) (2015) *Special educational needs and disability code of practice: 0 to 25 years.* London: DfE. Available at: www.gov.uk/government/publications/send-code-of-practice-0-to-25 (accessed 9 November 2022).

Department for Education (DfE) (2019) *ITT core content framework.* London: DfE.

Earle, S. (ed.) (2019) *Assessment in the primary classroom: Principles and practice.* London: Learning Matters/Sage.

Hall, K. and Sheehy, K. (2018) 'Assessment and learning: summative approaches', in T. Cremin and C. Burnett (eds.), *Learning to teach in the primary school* (4th edn). Abingdon, UK: Routledge, pp. 288–303.

McKay, D. (2019) 'Using data to support school improvement', in S. Earle (ed.), *Assessment in the primary classroom: Principles and practice.* London: Learning Matters/Sage, pp. 73–85.

Rosenshine, B. (2012) 'Principles of instruction: research-based strategies that all teachers should know', *American Educator*, 36(1), 12–19.

Salter, L. and Earle, S. (2019) 'Formative use of assessment by teachers', in S. Earle (ed.), *Assessment in the primary classroom: Principles and practice.* London: Learning Matters/Sage, pp. 19–32.

Wiliam, D. (2015) 'Designing great hinge questions', *Educational Leadership,* 73(1), 40–44.

Wiliam, D. (2018) *Embedded formative assessment* (2nd edn). Bloomington, IN: Solution Tree Press.

Wiliam, D. and Christodoulou, D. (2017) 'Assessment, marking and feedback', in C. Hendrick and R. McPherson (eds.), *What does this look like in the classroom? Bridging the gap between research and practice.* Woodbridge, UK: John Catt Educational Ltd, pp. 22–44.

12
FEEDBACK AND FEEDFORWARD

Michelle Walton

Chapter Objectives

- To consider the potential significance of feedback.
- To explore how to plan for and provide effective feedback.
- To reflect on the importance of timing, both in providing feedback and for pupils to respond to feedback.

In this chapter, we explore the potential impact that feedback can have, both positive and negative. We consider how to plan for providing meaningful feedback as well as exploring the features of effective feedback, whether written or verbal. We identify the importance and challenges of identifying when to provide 'appropriately timed feedback' (Education Endowment Foundation (EEF), 2021: 19). We reflect on the learner's central role in this process by identifying factors that influence the ways in which pupils receive and use feedback to further their own learning.

The Power of Feedback

Feedback has the potential to have significant impact on children's learning. The EEF's *Teaching and learning toolkit* (2023), based on meta-analysis of available research, identifies that effective feedback can have very high impact for very low cost. Based on extensive evidence, the EEF suggests that this can be an average impact of six additional months of progress in one academic year.

However, that is not to say that all feedback will have that effect. The EEF (2021: 4) states that 'done badly, feedback can even harm progress'. The EEF (2021) also notes that providing feedback can be time-consuming, so it is important for you to learn how to give effective feedback, while ensuring that providing feedback does not 'become onerous and have a disproportionate impact on workload' (Department for Education (DfE), 2019: 24).

Feedback or Feedforward: Is There a Difference?

Technically, feedback means providing learners with information about where they are in their learning and how well they have done in relation to a specific learning goal. Feedforward, as the name suggests, is forward-looking and provides learners with information about how to make further progress in the future. It is said that both are needed to 'ensure that assessment has a developmental impact on learning' (JISC, 2016: 20).

In primary education, we tend to use the term 'feedback' to mean both traditional feedback *and* feedforward. Indeed, the DfE (2019: 23) argues that 'high-quality feedback ... is likely to be accurate and clear, encourage further effort, and provide specific guidance on how to improve', demonstrating that both are incorporated in the same term. The EEF (2021: 5) takes this further, stating that the 'main role of feedback, at least in schools, is to improve the learner, not the work', with the intention that it will enable them to be more successful when undertaking new tasks in the future.

In Chapter 11, we explored the importance of formative assessment and its role in furthering learning. The same is true of formative feedback, and this is highlighted by Wiliam (2017: 140), who notes: 'If educators intend the information fed back to the learner to be helpful but the learner cannot use it to improve his or her performance, it is not formative'. He goes on to identify that 'feedback must provide a recipe for future action' (Wiliam, 2017: 141). This feedforward is not only important for learning, but also for children's motivation and self-esteem, so that they know that their teacher believes they can make further progress.

— Critical Task 12.1 —

Different Forms of Feedback

Reflect on your own experiences of receiving feedback.

- Can you think of an occasion when you received positive feedback? How did it make you feel? Did it improve the way in which you continued/completed a task?
- Can you think of an occasion when you were given constructive feedback that encouraged you to develop or change something? How did it make you feel? How was

this response different from how you responded to receiving only positive feedback? Did it encourage you to develop/change the task you were engaged in?

- Have you experienced an occasion when you were given only negative feedback? What was your response? How did it differ from receiving positive and/or constructive feedback?

Now relate your own experiences to the context of the primary classroom. How might these personal experiences shape your own professional practice and the teacher you would like to become?

Planning for High-quality Feedback

To provide pupils with effective feedback that can move learning forwards, it is useful to consider carefully, at the planning stage, when you might build in opportunities to give feedback throughout the lesson and throughout the day. For example, when planning your lessons, consider:

- How will the children know what you and they are looking for?
- When in the lesson might you pause to refer back to learning objective(s) or success criteria?
- How will you enable children to become active participants in the feedback process?

Laying the Foundations

Hattie and Timperley (2007: 82) state that 'feedback has no effect in a vacuum', so before you can plan for or provide high-quality feedback, there are some foundations that need to be laid. First, you need to plan, and then deliver, some effective teaching: 'Feedback can only build on something; it is of little use when there is no initial learning or surface information. Feedback happens second' (Hattie and Timperley, 2007: 82).

However, the EEF (2021) suggests that feedback does not happen second, but third. They argue that before feedback can be given, teachers need to plan for, and then undertake, 'clarifying, sharing and understanding learning intentions and success criteria' and 'eliciting evidence of learning' (EEF, 2021: 14). In relation to eliciting evidence of learning, they also suggest that 'the quality of feedback that a teacher can provide depends crucially on the quality of the evidence about learners' achievement' (EEF, 2021: 5). We cannot provide effective feedback, if we do not know how children are getting on in their learning and our feedback won't be effective if it is not sharply focused on the intended learning and success criteria (Kluger and DeNisi, 1996). So, feedback comes after teaching, and it comes after other aspects of formative assessment.

Planning to Use Errors and Misconceptions as a Form of Whole-class Feedback

Your assessment from a previous lesson may have identified some common errors and misconceptions shared by many of the pupils in your class. Ideally, you will have noticed this during that lesson and engaged in individual or small group responsive teaching to address it (we will consider the importance of timing of feedback later in this chapter), but the reality is that it won't always be possible to undertake responsive teaching in the moment. In such a scenario, providing individual feedback that is similar for many children is not an effective use of your time. The DfE (2019) states that whole-class feedback can be an efficient alternative.

However, simply telling children that lots of them made the same mistake is unlikely to be effective. If they knew *how* to avoid that mistake, it is likely that they would have done so in the first place. Again, the importance of feedforward is highlighted, so that you move 'from a statement to a specific action' (Christodoulou, 2019: no page). For example, you might have noticed that many children were forgetting to carry across the tens when adding two two-digit numbers. Telling them that lots of them forgot to do that is much less helpful than telling them that and then showing them *how* to do it with some worked examples, some 'spot the error' type activities and some further independent practice at the start of the next lesson.

Remember that 'whole class' does not have to be taken literally; it can be 'most' of the class. Those to whom it does not apply can instead have individual or group feedback with a well-primed teaching assistant (TA). Whole-class feedback can be very valuable, in its potential impact on learning and in time saved for you. However, Riches (2021: no page) cautions that it is just 'one piece of the puzzle' and should be used 'in conjunction with other feedback methods' that allow for personalised feedback for individuals.

Case Study 12.1

Whole-class Feedback Using Errors and Misconceptions

John, an experienced teacher-mentor, explains to the student teacher working with him how he uses children's errors and misconceptions to plan for and provide whole-class feedback for his Year 2 class:

> When marking children's written work, I get an overview of the high frequency words that children can and cannot spell independently. I plan to focus on some of these words in subsequent lessons, exploring some common errors (e.g., whith, rather than with). I work with the children to unpick why some of them might be finding it difficult to spell and to develop strategies for remembering the correct spelling. I find this is much more effective than just correcting spellings in individual children's books or just telling the

whole class the correct spelling. Sometimes, I will include common errors in my own spelling, but this has to be carefully timed to ensure children are already secure enough to spot the error; otherwise, I just run the risk of reinforcing the incorrect spelling.

John is making efficient use of his time by identifying the knowledge gaps within the class and responding to these in his daily planning and teaching. He is encouraging children to feel confident in identifying and talking about errors in a positive manner.

Verbal and Written Feedback

The DfE (2019: 23) note that 'high quality feedback can be written or verbal'. In this section, we focus on 'the principles of good feedback' (EEF, 2021: 4), whether written or verbal, and explore some of the potential challenges or limitations of each form.

Critical Task 12.2

Verbal Feedback or Written Feedback?

Before reading on, pause and think about the impact of using written or verbal feedback. Draw on your experiences to consider the strengths and challenges of using each of these approaches and complete Table 12.1.

Table 12.1 Verbal and written feedback

Verbal Feedback		Written Feedback	
Pros	Cons	Pros	Cons

When completing Critical Task 12.2, one of the potential challenges you may have considered for written feedback is that it can be time-consuming, something that the Education Endowment Foundation (2021) suggests can apply to both forms of feedback, but particularly written feedback, describing it as an 'opportunity cost' (EEF, 2021: 8). What the EEF means by this is that it can have an impact on workload (and potentially on wellbeing) and that spending significant time on feedback can reduce time spent on other important aspects of teaching. Feedback therefore needs to be as effective and as efficient as possible.

It is also possible that one of the potential limitations that you considered for verbal feedback is that pupils can forget it quickly. Technology, such as dictaphones and 'talking tins', can provide support by allowing you to record your feedback and enabling children to listen to it again. It is unlikely that all children will need such supports and you will quickly learn which children benefit from being able to replay your verbal feedback.

You may also have noted that younger children may struggle to read written feedback. You may therefore prioritise giving verbal feedback until their reading skills are sufficiently developed. The important thing is to consider and identify the potential challenges so that you can plan how to overcome them and harness all of the potential benefits of providing feedback.

Principles of Good Feedback, Whether Written or Verbal

Hattie and Clarke (2019: 4) identify that feedback should provide information 'that "closes the gap" between where a student is and where the student needs to be', reinforcing the earlier point that effective feedback is actually a combination of both feedback (where they are) and feedforward (how they might get to where they need to be).

The EEF (2021: 21) suggests that feedforward should focus on task, subject or self-regulation strategies, noting that 'feedback that focuses on a pupil's personal characteristics is less likely to be effective'. For example, comments such as 'You're so clever.' or 'You are fantastic at art.' are unlikely to move learning forward in any way. Skipper and Douglas (2012) agree. They state that personal feedback, even when positive, can have a negative impact when children experience challenging situations in the future, as they may then doubt their 'cleverness', lose confidence and even refuse to engage with tasks for fear of failure. It goes without saying that negative personal feedback (e.g., 'Goodness, you aren't very good at PE, are you?') is to be avoided at all costs.

Task feedback focuses on 'improving a specific piece of work or specific type of task' (EEF, 2021: 22). For example, you may give feedback in maths relating to the need to carefully check whether they have added on any numbers carried over when solving addition calculations with two-digit and three-digit numbers. Not only does this feedback allow pupils to revisit any errors in the current piece of work, but it will also assist them next time they encounter adding numbers comprising multiple digits.

Subject feedback will focus on 'the underlying processes in a task, which are used across a subject' (EEF, 2021: 22). Subject feedback differs from task feedback because it is likely to be applicable in far more situations. For example, feedback relating to the accurate use of punctuation in English is likely to apply to all writing undertaken in English and across the curriculum.

Self-regulation strategy feedback will focus on aiming 'to improve the learner's own ability to plan, monitor, and evaluate their learning' and will often be provided 'as prompts and cues' (EEF, 2021: 22). For example, a child who is frustrated about their inaccurate catching in PE can be asked to consider what had helped them to improve their throwing skills in previous PE lessons. The intended impact is not only to help the child improve their catching, but also to develop their self-regulation skills, which can then be applied in multiple learning situations across the curriculum and beyond.

Praise, Effort and Structuring Feedback

Hattie and Clarke (2019: 43) suggest that 'we all like to be praised', but that 'praise can also interfere with learning' as we can be 'inclined to remember the praise more than the feedback about the learning'. If we are going to let children know how well they have done in relation to a specific learning goal, then it may well involve some praise. The EEF (2021) states that praise is more likely to have a positive impact on learning if it is clear and specific, rather than generic. 'Well done for using such a range of adjectives today' is likely to be much more effective than 'Great writing', as the pupil knows exactly what they did well and is therefore more likely to do it again in the future.

Nevertheless, Hattie and Clarke (2019: 43–44) caution against the overuse of praise, suggesting that pupils can become 'praise junkies', focusing far more on the pursuit of praise than on the learning itself. They distinguish between 'positive reinforcement', where the focus is clearly on what has been done well, and praising the individual.

Commenting on effort can be similarly complex. The DfE (2019: 23) propose that high-quality feedback should 'encourage further effort', but explicitly commenting on a child's effort can be challenging, as effort can be hard to assess. Some pupils can perceive positive feedback about their effort as an unspoken negative comment about their achievement, almost like a 'consolation prize' (Dweck, 2016, quoted in Hattie and Clarke, 2019: 44). The EEF (2021: 24) advocates that, if teachers do comment on effort, the comment should provide possible actions for the pupil to take 'to improve at the task, the subject, or their self-regulation rather than a comment on a pupil's general effort'. For example, you might say 'I think that a little more time spent checking your measurements carefully might have helped you to construct your vehicle more easily', rather than 'You needed to work harder in this DT lesson'.

The need for effective feedback statements (whether written or verbal) to include both feedback and feedforward has led to the development of a number of ways to structure feedback. Two examples are 'the feedback sandwich', where the feedforward is sandwiched between two positive feedback comments, or 'two stars and a wish', where the feedback starts with two positive comments and finishes with an 'even better if...' feedforward statement. Some have argued that 'the feedback sandwich' is better, as it finishes on a positive and is therefore better for self-esteem. However, others have suggested that the feedforward comment can get lost in this method. The important thing to remember is that there is no research evidence that either approach (or indeed any other similar approach) is best. Indeed, there is no research which concludes that feedback needs to have a ratio of 2:1 for positive feedback:feedforward comments. As the feedforward is likely to have the most impact on future learning, some argue that it should outweigh feedback.

Clarke (2014) advises that feedforward comments can be scaffolded, according to individual needs. She suggests that some children will be able to locate for themselves where they may act on a feedforward comment (e.g., identifying where they may have provided more description in a piece of writing), whereas other children may need a pointer, perhaps in the form of an arrow indicating the location. Other children may need even more scaffolding, in the form of a 'specific improvement suggestion' (Hattie and Clarke, 2019: 103), such as: 'You could use one of these two describing words to add more detail about the building: dusty, spooky. Or you could choose one of your own'.

You will learn to use your own judgement about what is most appropriate in each particular context for each particular pupil, and then monitor the impact of your feedback. Throughout your placements, you should take the opportunity to discuss with expert colleagues 'how pupils' responses to feedback can vary depending on a range of social factors (e.g. the message the feedback contains or the age of the child)' (DfE, 2019: 24) to help you to develop your skills in making these decisions.

Reducing the Opportunity Cost

In 2017, Christodoulou argued that 'we've got into a bit of a situation where we think that feedback and marking are the same thing and actually they're not' (2017: 33). As we have already established, the content of the feedback is much more important than the method, so it is perfectly possible to give feedback without undertaking marking. Elliott et al.'s research (2020) into feedback practices in primary and secondary schools in England found that there has been a gradual shift in schools from having a marking policy to having a feedback policy, noting also that there has been a decrease in providing lengthy written feedback and an increase in giving verbal feedback.

Providing verbal, rather than written, feedback can certainly be one way of reducing the workload involved in providing effective feedback. There are also ways of reducing the time needed to provide written feedback. 'Live marking' is undertaken during the lesson, rather than afterwards. If you are working with a target group, you may mark their work during the lesson and your TA may mark the work of another group. You may also choose to use a visualiser to mark an anonymous piece of work with the whole class, so that pupils can consider how the feedback relates to their own work. Live marking can be combined with verbal feedback. For example, you may mark the maths calculations that are correct and those that are incorrect, and then give verbal feedforward to support the pupil in revisiting the incorrect ones. Live marking can also allow you 'to assess misconceptions and identify the trends across the class' (Riches, 2021: no page), meaning that you can then be responsive, perhaps stopping for a mini-plenary and addressing misconceptions and errors immediately, rather than waiting until the end of the lesson or the start of the next one.

Another approach to save time on written feedback is to use coded marking, where the teacher uses codes, such as letters or numbers, to represent whole comments. The important thing is that children need the key so that they know what the letters and numbers refer to. For example, the letter D on a piece of English writing might mean that the pupil could have included more dialogue between the characters in that section. The EEF (2021) suggests that the children might even be involved in designing the code with the teacher, using the success criteria as a starting point. Elliott et al.'s (2020) research found that the use of coded marking is growing in popularity in primary schools, with some school's feedback policies actively encouraging this method as a way of reducing teacher workload.

There will be times, though, when it will be perfectly appropriate to provide pupils with feedback in the form of individual written comments. You will need to be selective about when to do this. If you are going to put the time into providing individual written comments, then the anticipated impact should be worth the time you are investing, so ensure that you consider how to make these comments as effective as possible, following the advice given earlier. You also need to give pupils time to respond to the feedback, which we will explore later in the chapter.

There are two very important things for you to remember in terms of verbal and written feedback. The first is that, whatever approach you take, it should be in line with the school's policy. The second is that, whether feedback is written or verbal, quality is more important than quantity.

Timing Matters

As we have explored in the previous sections, the content of our feedback is highly significant. Timing is equally important, although there is no consensus in the research about the perfect timing for feedback to be provided. The EEF (2021: 10) concludes from its meta-analysis that 'there is not one clear answer for when feedback should be provided'.

Immediate or Delayed

Many sources, including Hattie and Clarke (2019: 82), state that immediate feedback can have most impact, arguing that this is 'the golden moment, when the context is alive, the student is "in flow" and the learning is gaining momentum'. The EEF (2021: 19) notes that immediate feedback 'could prevent misconceptions from forming early on'. However, they also note that rather than providing an answer too quickly, delayed feedback may be more effective in encouraging pupils to persevere and be resilient, suggesting that holding back may help them recall the learning more fully (EEF, 2021). Wiliam (2017: 127) supports this view, stating that 'if it is given too early, before students have had a chance to work on a problem, then they will learn less'.

Elliott et al.'s research (2020: 96) revealed that there has been a shift away from delayed feedback to more immediate feedback. They note that many teachers believe that feedback 'should be given in the moment as close as possible to the point of the student doing the work'. Clarke (2014: 139) agrees, describing this as 'within-lesson feedback'. She suggests the use of visualisers to:

- look at good examples during the lesson and not just at the end
- assess a piece of work against the success criteria partway through the lesson, identifying which have been met and how well, and which still need to be considered
- edit a piece of work in order to make improvements based on feedback.

As noted above, there can also be benefits to delaying feedback, in terms of developing children's resilience and problem-solving skills. Hattie and Clarke (2019) suggest that higher attainers may benefit more from delayed feedback than lower attainers, who might need more immediate feedback to avoid extended struggles which damage self-esteem, but perhaps it is not as clear-cut as this, as we consider below.

Developing Your Teacher Judgement

Hattie and Timperley (2007: 100) state that to 'make the feedback effective, teachers need to make appropriate judgements about when, how, and at what level to provide appropriate feedback'. This is a skill to develop and you can learn a great deal from expert colleagues during your placements about how to do it. You also need to really get to know the children in your class and assess effectively to inform the decisions you make about the timing and content of feedback. As established in Chapter 7, children will learn at different rates and find different things easier or more challenging. Some children will be more willing to persevere than others. As Hattie (2012: 122) asserts, 'the aim is to provide feedback that is "just in time", "just for me", "just for where I am in my learning process" and "just what I need to help me move forward"'. It suggests that the most effective timing and content of feedback is likely to be highly individual to each child and learning situation.

Of course, we have to be realistic and accept that giving timely, personalised, individual feedback won't always be possible. We can apply the principles explored earlier in this chapter about good feedback, doing our best to ensure that it has as much positive impact as possible, without having a 'disproportionate impact on workload' (DfE, 2019: 24). We should also bear in mind the purpose of providing feedback (to move learning forward), who it is for and what the school's feedback policy requires. We should also remember that other adults working in our classrooms can give feedback to children and that children can also engage in self- and peer-assessment (which we explore in Chapter 13) to identify how they are doing and what they may do next.

Reacting and Responding to Feedback

The DfE (2019: 23) suggest that 'to be of value ... pupils must be able to act on feedback for it to have an effect'. It is therefore important that we think about how and when pupils will be able to respond to the feedback given, but, before we can do that, we also need to consider how they may react to it. Think back to your own reflections in Critical Task 12.1 and how different types of feedback made you feel. Ultimately, you want your feedback to support pupils in moving forward with their learning, rather than evoking a negative emotional reaction, and that depends on your classroom culture.

Observation Guide 12.1

Pupils' Response to Feedback

The *ITT Core Content Framework (CCF)* states that student teachers should 'learn how to ... provide high-quality feedback by ... [understanding] how pupils' responses to feedback can vary depending on a range of social factors (e.g., the message the feedback contains or the age of the child)' (DfE, 2019: 23).

On your next placement, choose four pupils to observe and use Table 12.2 to make a note of their reactions to the feedback they receive. If possible, discuss your observations with your teacher-mentor.

Table 12.2 Pupil response to feedback

Pupil	Type of feedback	Pupil reaction
A	Written Verbal Assessment/test score	
B	Written Verbal Assessment/test score	
C	Written Verbal Assessment/test score	
D	Written Verbal Assessment/test score	

Classroom Culture

To maximise the impact of our feedback, we need to develop a classroom culture where pupils are open and receptive to feedback, valuing it and understanding its potential for furthering their learning and themselves as reflective, life-long learners.

The EEF (2021: 27) proposes that there are four factors which influence how receptive learners are to feedback: 'motivation', 'self-confidence and self-concept', 'trust in the teacher' and 'working memory'. They suggest that strategies such as 'discussing the purpose of feedback', keeping the feedback 'clear, concise and focused' and checking that pupils understand the feedback can help to enhance these factors and increase children's receptiveness to feedback (EEF, 2021: 27).

Put simply, children need to understand that you are on their side, that you believe in their capacity for learning and that the feedback you give is to help them to make progress. Giving feedback that relates explicitly to the stated learning intentions and success criteria helps children to trust you; telling them that you are looking for one thing but then comment on something different does not. Developing children's metacognitive and self-regulation skills (discussed further in Chapter 13), as well as involving them in the assessment process directly, will also make them more receptive to feedback.

Devote time to engage in open dialogue, talk to and listen to individuals, groups, classes about what they know, what they understand and what they don't. By involving your pupils in the process, it is *done with* the children you work with, rather than *done to* them. The value you place on the process will be apparent to your pupils and enable you to cultivate a learning environment where feedback is received positively and proactively.

Hattie (2012: 124) suggests that feedback 'thrives when there is error or incomplete knowing or understanding' and that 'errors invite opportunities'. We therefore need to establish a classroom environment where 'marvellous mistakes' and incorrect answers are welcomed, explored and celebrated. It enables children to learn from these errors and thus move forward in their learning. The power of the word 'yet' can also be harnessed, as we seek to reframe 'I can't do this' into 'I can't do this yet', recognising that the children can now do lots of things that they couldn't do before and focusing their attention on the strategies that have helped them to learn in the past. This shift of emphasis can transform pupils' attitudes to learning in the long term and develop that intrinsic love of learning, which can be regarded as the Holy Grail of teaching.

Time to Respond

The shift towards more immediate, within-lesson feedback makes identifying time for children to respond to it more straightforward, as there is still time in the lesson for the children to act on the feedback they have been given, whether that is individual feedback through live marking or verbal feedback, whole-class feedback based on a common misconception, or whole-class feedback on a sample of work. Similarly, we can plan for children to engage in peer assessment partway through a lesson or sequence of connected lessons, rather than at the end, so that they can act on their partner's feedback.

When feedback is not given until after the lesson (e.g., written feedback in the form of marking), it will need more careful consideration. Indeed, the DfE (2019: 24) suggests that you will need to 'practise, receive feedback and improve at … providing time for pupils to respond to feedback' during your placements. You will need to think carefully about when would be the best time for children to engage with and act upon their feedback and this is likely to depend on the context. If your marking has identified some careless slips in maths calculations, it may be perfectly appropriate for children to read that feedback quietly during registration and correct their errors. If your marking has identified some more fundamental errors or misconceptions, which are shared by lots of children in the class, it may be more appropriate to engage in whole-class feedback, as discussed earlier, at the start of the next lesson. If your marking has identified a wide range of areas of improvement, children may need time at the start of the next lesson to read their feedback and act on it, while you (and your TA) work with targeted individuals and groups. You may even find it helpful to ask children with similar feedback to work together.

Remember: if you are not going to give children the opportunity to respond to the feedback given, there is little point in providing it. We established at the start of this chapter that, when done well, feedback has the potential to have a significant impact on learning. So don't just focus on improving your provision of feedback; improve how you engage pupils meaningfully with your feedback.

Question Guide 12.1

Effective Feedback

The *CCF* states that student teachers should:

> Learn how to … make marking manageable and effective, by … discussing and analysing with expert colleagues how to identify efficient approaches to marking and alternative approaches to providing feedback (e.g. using whole class feedback …) and deconstructing this approach. (DfE, 2019: 24–25)

To help you understand how schools provide feedback effectively, use some of these questions to guide your discussions with an expert colleague:

- Can you tell me about the different forms of feedback a child may receive when they are engaged in learning?

Continued

- How do you know what type of feedback to give?
- Do all children in your class receive the same type of feedback?
- When do the pupils receive feedback?
- Is this always the same or can this change from day to day?
- Do you expect children to respond to your feedback? How and when?
- Do you have a feedback policy?

Chapter Summary

In this chapter, we considered the potentially empowering and transformative value of effective feedback, recognising that its value is dependent on its quality. We explored the principles of providing good feedback, whether written or verbal, alongside the need to ensure that it does not negatively impact on workload or other aspects of practice. We considered the importance of timing, in terms of when feedback is given and when pupils are given the opportunity to respond to it. We also reflected on how to create a classroom culture in which pupils are positive about receiving and acting on feedback.

Further Reading

Earle, S. (ed.) (2019) *Assessment in the primary classroom: Principles and practice.* London: Learning Matters/Sage.
This book is helpful as a starting point for understanding assessment in the primary school and the underpinning principles of assessment and common practices used, including where feedback fits into assessment.
Hattie, J. and Timperley, H. (2007) 'The power of feedback', *Review of Educational Research,* 77(1), 81–112.
This influential article explains the potential impact that feedback can have on learning as well as exploring the significance of the purpose and type of feedback.

References

Christodoulou, D. (2017) *Making good progress? The future of assessment for learning.* Oxford: Oxford University Press.
Christodoulou, D. (2019) 'Whole-class feedback: a recipe, not a statement', *No More Marking* [Blog]. Available at: https://blog.nomoremarking.com/whole-class-feedback-a-recipe-not-a-statement-e2a6704ea434 (accessed 14 March 2023).

Clarke, S. (2014) *Outstanding formative assessment: Culture and practice*. London: Hodder Education.

Department for Education (DfE) (2019) *ITT core content framework*. London: DfE.

Education Endowment Foundation (EEF) (2021) *Guidance report: Teacher feedback to improve pupil learning*. London: EEF.

Education Endowment Foundation (EEF) (2023) *Teaching and learning toolkit*. Available at: https://educationendowmentfoundation.org.uk/education-evidence/teaching-learning-toolkit (accessed 11 April 2023).

Elliott, V., Randhawa, A., Ingram, J., Nelson-Addy, L., Griffin, C. and Baird, J. (2020) *Feedback in action: A review of practice in English schools*. London: Education Endowment Foundation.

Hattie, J. (2012) *Visible learning for teachers: Maximising impact on learning*. Abingdon, UK: Routledge.

Hattie, J. and Clarke, S. (2019) *Visible learning: Feedback*. Abingdon, UK: Routledge.

Hattie, J. and Timperley, H. (2007) 'The power of feedback', *Review of Educational Research*, 77(1), 81–112.

JISC (Joint Information Systems Committee) (2016) *Transforming assessment and feedback with technology*. Available at: www.jisc.ac.uk/guides/transforming-assessment-and-feedback (accessed 14 March 2023).

Kluger, A.N. and DeNisi, A. (1996) 'The effects of feedback interventions on performance: a historical review, a meta-analysis, and a preliminary feedback intervention theory', *Psychological Bulletin*, 119(2), 254–284.

Riches, A. (2021) '*Whole-class feedback: practical tips and ideas', SecEd: The Voice for Secondary Education*. Available at: www.sec-ed.co.uk/best-practice/whole-class-feedback-practical-tips-and-ideas-assessment-pedagogy-teaching-marking/ (accessed 14 March 2023).

Skipper, Y. and Douglas, K. (2012) 'Is no praise good praise? Effects of positive feedback on children's and university students' responses to subsequent failures', *British Journal of Educational Psychology*, 82, 327–339.

Wiliam, D. (2017) *Embedded formative assessment* (2nd edn). Bloomington, IN: Solution Tree Press.

13
ENGAGING LEARNERS IN ASSESSMENT

Jude Penny

Chapter Objectives

- To reflect on why it is important to engage pupils in the assessment process.
- To consider the nature and value of metacognition and self-regulation.
- To explore how teachers can engage learners in the assessment process.

In this chapter, we consider who 'owns' pupil assessment, who it is useful for and how pupils can be encouraged to engage with the process of assessment, with the aim of extending their learning.

The Importance of Involving Learners in the Assessment Process

You would be forgiven for thinking that involving learners in the assessment process is a 'modern' or contemporary idea. However, as far back as 1916, American philosopher, psychologist and educational reformer John Dewey (1916: 6) maintained that children must actively participate in their education because, 'if the pupil has no initiative of his own in this direction, the result is a random groping after what is wanted, and the formation of habits of dependence upon the cues furnished by others'. What Dewey seems to be warning against is the development of passive learners who are reliant on the instruction of an authority source (in this case, a teacher), and who have little opportunity for active involvement in the choices and processes of the learning environment.

Furthermore, it has been suggested that an education system that overemphasises the value of testing pupils' knowledge can result in a 'training' of children's minds at the expense of developing holistic and transferable thinking skills and dispositions that the children of today will require in an unpredictable tomorrow (Claxton, 2008). Wiliam and Leahy (2015: 16) believe that 'as automation and offshoring change the world of work and as society becomes more complex, what students learn at school will never be enough'. In order to navigate an uncertain future, learners will be required to have agency, be self-directed and responsible for their own actions, all of which can be nurtured through involving learners in the experience of education, including the assessment process.

Who Owns Learning and Assessment?

William and Leahy (2015: 169) suggest that 'the curious task of teachers is to work towards their own redundancy'. Obviously, they do not mean this in a literal sense, but that teachers should aim to support their pupils to need them less and less through developing 'ownership' of their learning. Ownership of learning (and, it can be argued, assessment) has been referred to as 'the development of a sense of connectedness, active involvement and personal investment in the learning process' (Voltz and Damiano-Lantz, 1993: 18) and research suggests that, when students are involved in the assessment process specifically, they become more engaged in their learning.

Traditionally, teachers have been regarded as being responsible for establishing where learners are in their learning, where they are going and what needs to be done to get them there (pretty daunting, especially for novice teachers!). However, Black and Wiliam (1998) emphasise the necessity of taking into account the role that the learners and their peers play in these processes, and that a shared responsibility should be established. According to Chan et al. (2014: 106), student engagement becomes more meaningful 'when teachers go beyond assessment *of* learning and use assessment *for* learning'. It is worth pausing here to consider the impact of changing just one small word. Clarke (2012: 9) defines assessment *of* learning as 'any summative test or assessment, whether class-based, school-based or national'. Assessment *for* learning is thought to be 'part of everyday practice by students, teachers and peers that seeks, reflects upon and responds to information from dialogue, demonstration and observation in ways that enhance ongoing learning' (Klenowski, 2009: 264). This latter approach is also referred to as 'formative assessment' and, according to Chan et al. (2014: 106), 'student ownership is key to a formative system of teaching and learning in classrooms' and there should be 'a shared and clear understanding of where pupils are, where they are going and how to "close the gaps" in order to accomplish the intended learning outcomes'.

Assessment for learning is central to this process and, according to Jagals (2021), assessment can serve as a tool that facilitates metacognition, alongside promoting self-directed learning.

The Nature and Value of Metacognition and Self-regulation

According to the Educational Endowment Foundation (EEF) (2021: 8), 'there is a strong body of evidence from psychology and education demonstrating the importance of metacognition and self-regulation to effective pupil learning'.

Metacognition

Metacognition has been referred to as 'an elusive topic' (EEF, 2021: 4), mainly due to the fact that it can be difficult to describe what it means in the classroom. Perhaps a good starting point is its etymology (the origin of the word and the historical development of its meaning): *meta* refers to 'transcending' or 'beyond', and *cognition* to the process of knowing. So, metacognition is more than simply 'thinking' or 'knowing' and can be described as the ability to be aware of (think about) and to control (regulate) one's thinking for learning. Branigan and Donaldson (2019) suggest two main components:

- metacognitive knowledge (e.g., knowledge of persons, strategies and tasks that support thinking)
- metacognitive regulation (e.g., controlling thinking through planning, monitoring and evaluating one's thinking).

Self-regulation

According to Boyle and Charles (2014: 175): 'For the child to become an autonomous learner, s/he should be involved in and sharing in the construction of their own learning. This philosophy is known as self-regulated learning'.

In Chapter 4, we explored the notion of self-regulation in relation to emotions and behaviour. In this chapter, we explore self-regulation it relation to learning. The EEF (2021: 8) suggests that self-regulation relates to the ways in which learners 'are aware of their strengths and weaknesses and the strategies they use to learn'. If learners are aware of their strengths and limitations, are guided by self-defined personal goals and employ task-related strategies, they will be proactive in their efforts to learn. Such learners monitor their behaviour in terms of their goals and self-reflect on their increasing effectiveness. This enhances their self-satisfaction and motivation to continue to improve their methods of learning.

Metacognition and self-regulation are inherently learner-centred concepts, and so they are inextricably linked to the idea of self-assessment. In fact, Siegesmund (2017) suggests that self-assessment not only increases metacognition, but learners also become more proficient at evaluating their progress towards completing a task, a key facet of self-regulated learning.

It is worth considering the classroom culture that you hope to establish and the relationships that you hope to form with learners: how would you like it to *feel* to be a learner in the classroom that you teach? As explored in Chapter 3, positive relationships underpin great teaching and the culture you create in your classroom will impact greatly on children's abilities to regulate their own approach to learning, to reflect on their own progress and engage in meaningful self-assessment.

Strategies for Engaging Learners in the Assessment Process

In this section, we will consider some practical approaches that teachers can utilise to promote children's metacognition and to engage them in meaningful formative assessment.

Facilitating Metacognition in the Classroom

Mulholland (2021a) proposes three simple classroom strategies that can encourage metacognition or 'thinking about thinking'. The first is to 'talk more about less'. In a nutshell, teachers should plan fewer questions, but discuss them in greater depth. This method helps thinking to become more visible and possible misconceptions can be revealed (to both teacher and learner), which aids the ongoing assessment process.

'Thinking out loud' while modelling a writing task or reflecting on a piece of text is another strategy that will help broaden learners' understanding of the types of thinking they can draw on and the strategies that teachers or more knowledgeable others use in their own work. The EEF (2021: 6) also recommends that 'teachers should verbalise their own metacognitive thinking (e.g., "What do I know about problems like this? What ways of solving them have I used before?") as they approach and work through a task'.

The third strategy is to 'make questions key', particularly those that shift the emphasis from the answer or learning outcome towards the process used to achieve it. Mulholland (2021a) suggests that teachers encourage learners to explain their reasoning through using questions such as: 'How do you know?', 'What could you do to improve?', 'What went well, and why?' and 'What helped you to be successful?'. We shall return to the important issue of teachers' questioning later in the chapter.

Formative Assessment: Some Key Strategies

According to Wiliam and Thompson (2007: 76), 'the "big idea" is that evidence about student learning is used to adjust instruction to better meet student need – in other words, that teaching is adaptive to the student's learning needs'. One of the key messages about implementing formative assessment successfully is that strategies and techniques have very little impact if the culture of the classroom does not support the key principles.

The following framework draws on the work of Harrison and Howard (2009), Wiliam and Thompson (2007) and Clarke (2012) to consider strategies for formative assessment that can support such a culture:

- Create a learning culture in which all involved see ability as incremental rather than fixed.
- Clarify learning objectives and establish pupil-generated and pupil-owned success criteria (this will be addressed later in this chapter).
- Encourage learners to analyse what quality consists of: the meeting of the success criteria and *how to best meet them*.
- Plan and facilitate effective classroom discussions, dialogue and worthwhile questioning (we will explore classroom talk in the next section).
- Provide feedback that moves learners on and, importantly, provide time to act on that feedback (as discussed in Chapter 12).
- Enable pupils to engage in effective self- and peer-evaluation (also to be explored later in this chapter).

Critical Task 13.1

A Framework of Strategies for Formative Assessment

Reflect on a lesson that you have taught where the formative assessment was not as effective as you would have liked it to be. Using Table 13.1, see if you can identify some tweaks and adaptations that may have led to more effective formative assessment, and therefore a more positive impact on the children's learning.

Table 13.1 Strategies for formative assessment

Aspect of framework	What might you have done to support effective formative assessment?
Creating a classroom culture in which all involved see ability as incremental rather than fixed.	
Clarifying learning objectives and establishing pupil-generated/pupil-owned success criteria.	
Involving pupils in analysis and discussion about what excellence in their work 'looks like' and how best to meet success criteria.	
Enabling and planning effective classroom dialogic talk and worthwhile questioning.	
Establishing continual opportunities for timely review and feedback from teachers and pupils, focusing on recognition of success and improvement needs, and provision of time to act on that feedback.	
Enabling pupils to be effective self- and peer-evaluators.	

'Let's Talk': The Potential Benefits of Dialogue and Dialogic Teaching

'If you have to talk, you have to think. I get to learn things from other people I didn't know.' (Five-year-old child, quoted in Clarke, 2012: 35)

According to Mulholland (2021b: 83), 'there is substantial evidence that increasing opportunities for pupil talk can lead to increased engagement in learning, as well as strengthening progress and attainment'.

Is There a Difference Between 'Talk' and 'Dialogue'?

Watkins (2005: 35) believes that 'the human capacity for language and meaning is at its highest in dialogue'. According to Clarke (2012), pupil talk is central to active learning. However, before we consider the role of pupil talk in engaging learners in assessment, it is worth taking time to establish what we consider to be 'productive talk' and how, as teachers, we might facilitate it (note the term 'facilitate' as opposed to 'teach').

Another important consideration is the meaning of the word 'dialogue', so perhaps it is time for some more etymology. Notice the roots of the word dialogue: *dia* meaning 'through' and *logos* meaning 'speech', 'word' or 'reason'. This last word, 'reason', alludes to exploratory talk rather than mere communication. Alexander (2008: 104) highlights a distinction between 'conversation' and 'dialogue'. The sequence of exchanges that take place in a conversation may be unchained and the participants perhaps not fully engaged with each other. In a dialogue, he sees attention and engagement as 'mandatory', where exchanges are 'chained together' into a 'meaningful sequence'.

So, dialogue can be thought of as *constructive talk* and, according to Clarke (2012), constructive 'dialogic' pupil talk is a key identifier of a formative assessment approach.

What is Dialogic Teaching?

Alexander (2008) describes dialogic teaching as powerful discourse to stimulate and extend learners' thinking and advance their acquisition of knowledge and understanding. He describes dialogic teaching in a classroom context as an activity which is:

- **Collective**: teachers and children address tasks together.
- **Reciprocal**: teachers and children listen to each other, share ideas and consider alternative viewpoints.
- **Supportive**: children articulate their ideas freely without fear of embarrassment over 'wrong answers' and they help each other to reach a common understanding.

- **Cumulative**: teachers and children build on their own and others' ideas and chain them into coherent lines of thinking and enquiry.
- **Purposeful**: teachers plan and steer classroom talk with educational goals in view. (Alexander, 2008: 187)

We have already considered the importance of a positive classroom culture to support formative assessment practices and, when considering the characteristics of dialogic teaching, Alexander (2008) contributes to this idea, believing that, by making a classroom ethos more collective, reciprocal and supportive, the dynamics of classroom talk can change. To be effective, teachers need to be able to elicit *authentic* responses from learners, possibly via questioning strategies, and then facilitate dialogue to incorporate their students' ideas and experiences into the lesson. On the topic of teachers' questioning, Forster et al. (2019: 176) identify that 'many teachers over-rely on the use of closed questions (those with just one "correct" answer), that tend to promote little intelligent response'. Open questions that allow divergent responses, and promote and value dialogue, can support meaning-making and the application of concepts to new situations, which seems to make sense if our ultimate aim is for assessment to be transformative and to have a positive impact, not just on learning, but on children's perceptions of themselves as learners.

In the following section, we will consider the sorts of questions that might support dialogue between pupils in the context of peer- and self-assessment, but, before that, it may be beneficial for you to reflect on your own teaching and the extent to which *you* are a dialogic teacher.

— Critical Task 13.2 —

Becoming a Dialogic Teacher

If possible, video- or audio-record one of your lessons. Ensure that you seek advice and take into consideration ethical issues such as informed consent, anonymity and deletion of the recording once you have analysed it. Create a typed transcript from the audio-recording and analyse the talk in terms of the number of interactions of the following types (Mortimer and Scott, 2003: 34):

- **Interactive (I)**: allows for verbal participation of both teacher and learner.
- **Non-interactive (N-I)**: involves the teacher only.
- **Dialogic (D)**: the teacher asks the learner for their point of view and takes account of their response.
- **Authoritative (A)**: ideas which do not contribute to the 'learning goals' are reshaped or ignored.

The ultimate aim is to create an interactive style that is also dialogic (and it is worth noting that it is quite possible to have an interactive style that is not dialogic). You may be able to review your interactions and categorise them using the Caroll diagram in Table 13.2 with reference to the definitions below (adapted from Lehesvuori et al., 2011).

Continued

Table 13.2 Analysing interactions

	Interactive	Non-Interactive
Dialogic	A	B
Authoritative	C	D

A **Interactive Dialogic (I/D)**: Children's ideas are intentionally explored and exploited with no evaluation. The teacher does not seek a specific point of view; rather, the teacher purposefully elicits student perspectives and works with these contrasting views.

B **Non-Interactive Dialogic (NI/D)**: The teacher works with contrasting views, perhaps previously expressed pupil perspectives, and intentionally moves away from the authoritative view. While the teacher may lecture, diverging ideas are still present and the way in which the teacher-talk manages both the everyday and expert understandings means that the teacher talk is dialogic in nature.

C **Interactive Authoritative (I/A)**: Question–answer routines often feature, with pupil responses often being evaluated in line with the authoritative view, leaving little space for the consideration of alternative or diverging ideas.

D **Non-Interactive Authoritative (NI/A)**: The teacher explicitly presents the authoritative view, often by lecturing, without addressing contrasting views.

Post-analysis, consider some of the more authoritative interactions (C and D): could you have been more dialogic at this point? What tweaks and adaptations would enable a more dialogic interaction? Is it possible to plan for dialogic episodes in your lesson planning? Try to identify the best opportunities for engaging children meaningfully in assessment, such as clarifying learning objectives, negotiating success criteria, eliciting prior knowledge, checking understanding or discussing next steps.

The Role of Talk in Assessment

We have established that 'pupil talk is central to active learning' (Clarke, 2012: 35). Through dialogue, individual learners' perspectives can be shared and compared in an open and supportive environment, and collaborative decisions can be made about next steps. Ideas can be explored through 'peer review', enabling the selection of productive ideas and new ways of thinking about a topic or skill (Harrison and Howard, 2009).

Earlier in this chapter, we considered Mullholland's (2021a) suggested questions that teachers can use to encourage learners to explain their reasoning, such as: 'How do you know?', 'What could you do to improve?', 'What went well, and why?' and 'What helped you to be successful?'. These seem to be useful prompts to encourage learners to reflect on their experiences and to begin to articulate their learning. Questions that enable children to communicate, reason and justify their responses are key. For example, consider the difference between 'Which metals are magnetic? Which metals are not magnetic?' and 'All metals are magnetic. Do you agree or disagree, and why?'. The former are limited, recall questions and the latter question is reframed into a statement for children to agree or disagree with and, most importantly, give their reasons.

— Observation Guide 13.1 —

The Role of Talk in Assessment

The *CCF* states that student teachers should 'learn how to … consider the factors that will support effective collaborative or paired work … [and] provide scaffolds for pupil talk to increase the focus and rigour of dialogue' (DfE, 2019: 18).

Clarke (2012: 35) suggests that: 'Establishing talk partners is often the first step teachers take in experimenting with formative assessment, as it is relatively straightforward to embark on and the impact can be seen immediately'.

When observing how pupil talk can contribute to formative assessment in school:

- Note the characteristics of the classroom culture that support pupil talk.
- Take note of how the talk partners/triplets are arranged or decided on.
- Notice how learning objectives/success criteria are established/reviewed.
- Notice how the teacher uses questions or prompts to instigate peer talk.
- Notice the nature of pupil–teacher feedback.

Facilitating Effective Peer-assessment and Self-assessment

Peer-assessment and self-assessment are much more than children just marking each other's work or completing a checklist. Peer-assessment involves learners giving feedback to each other to grade their work or performance using relevant criteria. According to Chin (2016), numerous studies have shown that peer-assessment offers real educational benefits for learners. Self assessment enables children to reflect on their own learning and progress in relation to certain criteria. Chin (2016) warns that some students are prone to overestimate or underestimate their own achievements, relative to their assessment of others, and we will consider this issue later in the chapter.

— Question Guide 13.1 —

Self-assessment and Peer-assessment

The *ITT Core Content Framework* (CCF) states that student teachers should 'learn how to … scaffold self-assessment by sharing model work with pupils, highlighting key details … [and] ensure feedback is specific and helpful when using peer or self-assessment' (DfE, 2019: 24).

Continued

To support reflection on effective practice when on placement, here are some questions to ask your teacher-mentor or another member of the teaching team about how they support children to engage with peer- or self-assessment. As always, remember to frame your questions professionally and positively.

- Do you think self-assessment and peer-assessment are important or impactful?
- What do you think are the key factors that support successful self-assessment and peer-assessment?
- How do you encourage children to understand the learning intentions and success criteria?
- How do you use the information gained from pupil self-assessment and peer-assessment?

A simple strategy that is often used to get children started on reflecting on their own learning is to ask them to indicate their confidence or success with a particular task or concept, usually with a thumbs up/down, a smiley face or a traffic light colour. This functional 'checklist' approach may be fine as an initial strategy to encourage children to consider their performance, but it is important to consider the potential limitations associated with this approach, as the following case study reveals.

— Case Study 13.1 —

Beyond the Traffic Lights: Meaningful Engagement with Self-assessment and Peer-assessment Strategies

Khadeeja, an undergraduate student teacher in her second year of training, is keen to implement some self-assessment strategies that she had been reading about. During her placement in a Year 4 class, she implements a 'traffic light system', whereby, at the end of a lesson, the learners were asked to circle a traffic light based on their confidence and success with the learning. A green light indicates 'I understand this very well', an amber light indicates 'I need a bit of help but I understand a bit' and a red light indicates 'help, I don't understand'. Khadeeja had read that it is important to share the success criteria with the learners, so these have been stuck into children's books alongside the traffic lights.

Upon collecting the children's books, Khadeeja is a little disappointed to find that, often, the work that was produced did not match the learners' traffic light assessment. For example, there are clear misconceptions shown in an individual's completed work, even though they have circled green. This makes her lose confidence in the method and during her weekly professional discussion, she shares her experience with her mentor.

It is not surprising that the children's responses are not authentic. There are a range of possible reasons why individuals may choose certain traffic light colours. For example, a learner may choose green because they feel unsure about something, but don't want to look 'stupid' in front of their peers. Amber or red may be chosen because the learner feels confident but doesn't want to be placed in the 'spotlight' – last time they were asked to explain something to the whole class, which was embarrassing. Or perhaps a learner might choose *any* colour because they are keen to go out to play! Even though the success criteria are shared in the books, Khadeeja has not provided the opportunity for the learners to discuss and 'internalise' them. Khadeeja selected a strategy which is fine as a starting point in engaging learners in thinking about their learning, but unless the system is developed, it will continue to provide a potentially superficial picture. In order to be fully engaged, the learners need to be able to express *why* they think they have succeeded or *why* they found the task challenging or *what* it is they don't understand. This will support them to engage more fully in making decisions about their next steps and, importantly, how to get there.

Khadeeja might consider modelling authentic engagement with the assessment process, perhaps by using anonymous examples of work and supporting children to identify misconceptions. She could plan in time to allow children to reflect, clarify, then talk about their responses before making their traffic light judgements, and emphasise the importance of expressing opinions, agreeing, disagreeing and giving reasons.

Learning Objectives and Success Criteria

It seems such an obvious point but, for a learner to assess how well they have done and why, they need to know (and, importantly, understand) what the intended learning is. You will no doubt be familiar with the terms 'learning objective' (LO), 'learning intention' or 'learning outcome'. These guide a lesson and are often written on the board for children to copy or stick into their books. It is worth considering whether children simply copying the learning objective into their books at the start of each lesson has a positive or negative impact on their engagement with the lesson content. If we expect children to make authentic judgements about their learning, we should aim to facilitate this through supporting them to know and understand what they are supposed to be learning. The LO must be presented to them in a way that they can understand.

Success criteria are a series of statements that guide the learner to understand the extent to which they have met the learning objectives. Once children have access to success criteria, they have a framework for a formative dialogue, which Clarke (2011) suggests enables them to:

- ensure appropriate focus
- clarify understanding
- identify success
- determine difficulties
- discuss strategies for improvement
- reflect on overall progress.

The danger with any set of success criteria is that they can be seen by the children as a kind of 'tick list' of things they need to do or include in their work. If peer-assessment is going to be effective, it must be done in a way that helps children to engage with and reflect on each other's work and consider how the work can be improved in a focused and meaningful way. It is thought that peer-assessment helps learners to develop and hone their self-assessment skills

(Harrison and Howard, 2009) because it is a reciprocal process in that the learner who provides feedback also benefits from having to critique and review someone else's work, and thereby reflect on their own understanding or performance. So, for learners who have little experience, or as stated earlier, tend to overestimate or underestimate their achievements, perhaps peer-assessment is a good place to start in order to gain experience, confidence and accuracy with the process.

Chapter Summary

In this chapter, we have considered the importance of engaging pupils in the assessment process, the value of metacognition and self-regulation, and the potential benefits of dialogic teaching. We have also considered the strengths and limitations of some established strategies and tools to support learners to reflect on, clarify, articulate and improve their learning through engaging them in the assessment process. Empowering learners by giving them ownership enables them to engage authentically in the assessment process, establishing learning and personal skills that will have a significant impact beyond the year that they spend in your classroom.

Further Reading

Black, P. and Wiliam, D. (1998) *Inside the Black Box: Raising standards through classroom assessment*. London: King's College School of Education.
The pioneers of assessment for learning discuss the self-esteem of pupils, self-assessment by pupils and the evolution of effective teaching. This is a 'must read' for all teachers.
Education Endowment Foundation (EEF) (2021) *Guidance report: Metacognition and self-regulated learning*. London: EEF.
This guidance report is relevant to the teaching of all learners, within any subject area.
It introduces a simplified framework for self-regulated learning and metacognition.

References

Alexander, R. (2008) *Essays on pedagogy*. London: Routledge.
Black, P. and Wiliam, D. (1998) 'Inside the Black Box: raising standards through classroom assessment', *Phi Delta Kappan*, 80(2), 139–148.
Boyle, B. and Charles, M. (2014) *Formative assessment for teaching and learning*. London: Sage.
Branigan, H.E. and Donaldson, D.I. (2019) 'Learning from learning logs: a case study of metacognition in the primary school classroom', *British Educational Research Journal*, 45(4), 791–820.
Chan, P., Graham-Day, K., Ressa, V., Peters, M. and Konrad, M. (2014) 'Beyond involvement: promoting student ownership of learning in classrooms', *Intervention in School and Clinic*, 50(2), 105–113.

Chin, P. (2016) 'Peer assessment', *New Directions in the Teaching of Physical Sciences,* 3(1), 13–18.

Clarke, S. (2011) *Formative assessment in action.* London: Hodder Education.

Clarke, S. (2012) *Active learning through formative assessment.* London: Hodder Education.

Claxton, G. (2008) *What's the point of school? Rediscovering the heart of education.* Oxford: Oneworld Publications.

Department for Education (DfE) (2019) *ITT core content framework.* London: DfE.

Dewey, J. (1916) *Democracy and education: An introduction to the philosophy of education.* New York: The Macmillan Company.

Education Endowment Foundation (EEF) (2021) *Guidance report: Metacognition and self-regulated learning.* London: EEF.

Forster, C., Penny, J. and Shalofsky, R. (2019) 'Questioning the role of questions: new primary teachers' realisations of over-reliance on questions in scientific dialogue', *PRACTICE: Contemporary Issues in Practitioner Education*, 1(2), 173–185.

Harrison, C. and Howard, S. (2009) *Inside the primary Black Box: Assessment for learning in primary and early years classrooms.* London: King's College School of Education.

Jagals, D. (2021) 'Assessment as an epistemological tool to facilitate metacognitive awareness and promote self-directed learning', in E. Mentz and A. Lubbe (eds.), *Learning through assessment: An approach towards self-directed learning (NWU Self-Directed Learning Series Volume 7)*, Cape Town: AOSIS Publishing, pp. 123–142.

Klenowski, V. (2009) 'Assessment for learning revisited: an Asia-Pacific perspective', *Assessment in Education: Principles, Policy and Practice*, 16(3), 263–268.

Lehesvuori, S., Viiri, J. and Rasku-Puttonen, H. (2011) 'Introducing dialogic teaching to science student teachers', *Journal of Science Teacher Education*, 22(8), 705–727.

Mortimer, E.F. and Scott, P.H. (2003) *Meaning making in secondary science classrooms.* Maidenhead: Open University Press.

Mulholland, K. (2021a) 'Three simple ways to bring metacognition to your class', *TES Magazine*. Available at: www.tes.com/magazine/archived/3-simple-ways-bring-metacognition-your-class (accessed 30 March 2023).

Mulholland, K. (2021b) 'Improving the quality of children's discussions about learning', in A. Gillespie (ed.), *Early careers in education: Perspectives for students and NQTs.* Bingley, UK: Emerald, pp. 77–84.

Siegesmund, A. (2017) 'Using self-assessment to develop metacognition and self-regulated learners', *FEMS Microbiology Letters*, 364(11).

Voltz, D.L. and Damiano-Lantz, M. (1993) 'Developing ownership in learning', *Teaching Exceptional Children*, 25(4), 18–22.

Watkins, C. (2005) 'Classrooms as learning communities: a review of research', *London Review of Education*, 3(1), 47–64.

Wiliam, D. and Leahy, S. (2015) *Embedding formative assessment: Practical techniques for K-12 classrooms.* West Palm Beach, FL: Learning Sciences International.

Wiliam, D. and Thompson, M. (2007) 'Integrating assessment with learning: what will it take to make it work?', in C.A. Dwyer (ed.), *The future of assessment.* New York: Routledge, pp. 53–82.

SECTION 5
PROFESSIONAL BEHAVIOURS

14
PROFESSIONAL LEARNING

Graham Parton

Chapter Objectives

- To reflect on the importance of professional learning for teachers.
- To consider the strengths and limitations of some of the key models of professional learning in schools.
- To explore the key factors involved in effective professional learning.

In this chapter, we discuss the vital role of professional learning in a teacher's career and how to take control of your own professional learning. We evaluate some models of professional learning, explore what effective professional development looks like and discuss the importance of critical, research-informed practice. Reading this chapter should help you to plan and implement your own professional learning to thrive in the classroom and make the most of your career as a teacher.

What is Professional Learning and Why Is It Important?

As a student teacher, it is important that you explore your own professional learning journey and professional identity as a teacher. Taking control of your professional learning provides you with a solid platform for becoming a critical and adaptable teacher. You will be constantly learning about yourself as a teacher and yourself as a learner.

Teaching is a demanding career, and it is important that you have a long and rewarding career, not just for yourself, but also for the children you teach. Professional learning is an important aspect of ensuring that teachers are teaching to the best of their capabilities.

Wiliam (2016: 182) states that, 'the quality of teachers in our classrooms is one of the most important determinants of how much children learn in those classrooms, with the very best teachers generating four times as much progress for their students as the least effective'.

Professional learning is defined by Lloyd and Davis (2018) as a practical model of teacher development that isn't just concerned with the performance of a teacher regarding the management of the classroom, but also looks at practical and research-informed ways to increase the attainment of children and to unlock their learning potential. Professional learning and professional development are linked but do have explicit differences. Professional learning is personal to each teacher and provides a space for each teacher to reflect on their own development. Professional development is the vehicle for professional learning to happen and, with an understanding of their own learning, each teacher will be able to develop their own personalised learning journey.

Teacher professional development is defined by Fletcher-Wood and Zuccollo (2020) as the learning of teachers to improve their own practice and support the learning of pupils. They go further by stating that the quality of professional development in schools has a direct correlation to the effectiveness of teaching and learning in the classroom. Obviously, this has significance for all children's progress, but as the Department for Education (2019: 9) note, 'high-quality teaching has a long-term positive effect on pupils' life chances, particularly for children from disadvantaged backgrounds'. The Education Endowment Foundation (EEF) carried out research on the support given to children who are classed as disadvantaged and how teachers can maximise their educational outcomes. One major finding from this research was that professional development had a large role to play in improving educational outcomes for children who were in receipt of pupil premium. Good teaching was found to be the most important factor in improving the educational outcomes of disadvantaged children. The study goes on to highlight that schools should use some of the pupil premium funding to provide impactful professional development for teachers to improve their teaching quality (Sims et al., 2021).

In a survey conducted by Teacher Tapp, a daily survey app for teachers, only 34% of classroom teachers agreed that their school's professional development provision was helping them to become better teachers. It is also interesting to note that 67% of headteachers believed that they were providing effective professional development. The discrepancy highlights a significant gap between the perceptions of headteachers, who design professional development within their schools, and teachers' sense of the effectiveness of this provision. It is therefore important for teachers to understand their own professional learning needs and work with senior leadership teams to improve opportunities for effective professional development in their schools.

Professional Autonomy

Worth and Van den Brande (2020) suggest that teachers' feelings of being in charge of their own professional learning can make a huge difference to their morale and resilience to stay in teaching. Providing a collaborative environment for professional learning to happen is seen to be vital. Research by the Organisation for Economic Cooperation and Development (OECD) indicated that a collaborative environment, where staff can learn from one another and explore areas of practice together, is just as important as what they learn from their professional development sessions (OECD, 2017).

It is important, therefore, for student teachers looking for their first teaching position to choose a school where they will feel supported in their professional learning. It is always a good question to ask at interview about the provision for professional development and how the school supports new teachers in their early career development. As a student teacher, you should seek to take control of your own professional learning from early in your training and as an early career teacher.

What are the Dominant Models of Professional Development Seen in Schools?

There are four main models of professional development:

- standards-based training model
- deficit model
- coaching/mentoring model
- action research model.

Each has advantages and disadvantages for high-quality professional learning. It is important to understand these models so that, as a student teacher, you can identify which modes of learning best support your own learning preferences, and are therefore likely to have more impact on your own professional development.

The Standards-based Training Model

The standards-based training model has traditionally been the dominant model for teachers' professional development in the UK (Kennedy, 2005). The model infers a standards-based, skills-led view of teaching. Professional development in this model provides teachers with the opportunity to develop their skills and therefore demonstrate competence in teaching. The model usually takes place outside the classroom and seeks to transmit knowledge to a group of teachers in an efficient way. It is argued that there is a lack of connection to the classroom context, to pupils' learning and to teachers' professional learning. Day (1999) states that this lack of connection results in failure to connect with the essential moral purposes that are at the centre of teachers' views of professionalism.

Hoban (2002) suggests that the standards-based training model is popular with the government because of the high degree of central control of standards-based education from the government. However, it is argued that the standardisation of professional development over-shadows the need for teachers to be proactive in identifying and meeting their own develop-ment needs. The standards-based training model of professional development supports the notion that from this training, improvements in teaching, learning and pupil attainment will be seen. This is criticised by Kennedy (2005: 5), who states: 'the training model provides an effective way for dominant stakeholders to control and limit the agenda and places teachers in a passive role as recipients of specific knowledge'.

The standards-based training model can be seen to favour the idea of teaching as based on a practical 'craft knowledge' rather than a model which has research-informed practice at its centre. Solomon and Tresman (1999) argue that this model focuses too heavily on classroom practice, rather than looking at issues that are personal to the teachers, such as the values and beliefs of the teacher when designing learning experiences with children, and the style of teaching employed by the teacher.

The Deficit Model

The deficit model uses professional development as a way to remedy perceived weaknesses in teacher performance. It attributes blame for underperformance and does not include any col-lective responsibility. This model underpins the way that the performance of a teacher is man-aged in some schools: a senior leader or mentor will be responsible for observing a teacher's lesson and identifying a 'deficit' in their performance. The teacher will then be required to attend a course or programme to respond to that deficit. The deficit model is critiqued by Rho-des and Beneicke (2003), who argue that the root causes of poor teacher performance should be related not only to individual teachers, but also to organisational and management practices. The model also assumes the need for a baseline competence measure which is not owned by the teacher, but by senior leaders within the school.

The Coaching/Mentoring Model

The coaching/mentoring model is characterised by the importance of a one-to-one relation-ship, generally between two teachers. The distinction between coaching and mentoring is subtle but, generally, mentoring involves an element of counselling and critical friendship, whereas coaching involves one teacher helping another to find their own solutions to prob-lems or challenges they face. Mentoring can assume a relationship where one partner is a novice and the other a more experienced member of staff. Coaching can be carried out by a more experienced teacher, but this is not vital. Coaching between two student teachers or early career teachers can be a very effective model of professional learning, as the coach does not need to have all the answers and can provide an environment in which solutions to problems can be thought through and researched by the teacher and coach.

Key to the coaching/mentoring model is that, unlike other models, professional learning can take place within the school context rather than outside the classroom. It enables a shared and developmental dialogue between teachers. The model is very similar to the mentoring experience you will be experiencing as part of your placements, where a more experienced teacher supports you through the experience, providing feedback on your performance and helping you identify targets for personal development.

The Action Research Model

The action research model 'provides a framework within which professionals can identify problems or challenges in their work, ask themselves questions about "how they are doing", and seek solutions or improvements through reviewing appropriate evidence' (Forster and Eperjesi, 2021: 2). It is a research-informed, enquiry-based approach to professional learning that can be very powerful if approached in the right way, but can be more complicated to carry out than the models outlined above. Teachers need time to be educated in action research and to practise using research tools and methods. It is argued that a model of action research, which is a collaborative venture between a community of teachers and academic researchers, provides the most effective impact on children's progress and the professional learning of teachers (Noffke and Somekh, 2011).

Case Study 14.1

Action Research As a Student Teacher

Artie, a postgraduate student teacher, is reflecting on an action research enquiry that he undertook during one of his placements, as one of the academic requirements of his PGCE course:

> To begin with, I viewed the need to undertake an action research enquiry and to write it up for submission for one of my modules as a hurdle to overcome. With help from my tutor, I identified a focus on questioning, as this was something that I really needed to work on after previous placements, and I developed an enquiry plan.
>
> As I began to read more about effective questioning before undertaking my enquiry, I began to feel more enthusiastic about the project, as I had found some great research about what had worked in practice for others and was excited to try to apply this in my own practice. As I reflected on the evidence after each cycle, I could see that I really was using questioning more effectively and that it was having a positive impact on children's learning. This made me excited to plan and implement the subsequent cycles.
>
> At the end of the enquiry, I was so pleased with the progress I had made in my questioning skills and it was identified as one of my strengths in the end-of-placement

Continued

report. It didn't end there, though. When I wrote up the enquiry as an assignment, I continued to reflect, as I could see the big picture of the enquiry as a whole, and I learnt even more to apply to my future practice. The impact has been huge and I know I can use action research to improve other aspects of my practice.

From a somewhat reluctant start, Artie has engaged well with the process of action research, from planning and reading, to undertaking the enquiry and reflecting on the evidence gathered in a cyclical manner. It has enabled him to see the transformational potential of the action research approach to professional learning.

Having discussed the dominant models of professional learning, it is important not to try to evaluate which is the best as, with everything in education, there will be advantages and disadvantages to each of the models. It is more fruitful to investigate which models most effectively align with the purpose of the professional development required and its capacity to increase your own professional autonomy. Table 14.1 illustrates this.

Table 14.1 Comparison of models of professional development

Model of professional development	Purpose of model	Capacity for professional autonomy
Standards-based training model	Transmission	Limited
The deficit model	Transmission	Limited
The coaching/mentoring model	Transitional	Good
The action research model	Transformation	Good

Observation Guide 14.1

Professional Development

The *ITT Core Content Framework* (*CCF*) states that student teachers should 'learn how to develop as a professional by … [understanding] how to engage in professional development with clear intentions for impact on pupil outcomes, sustained over time with built-in opportunities for practice' (DfE, 2019: 29).

Observe the professional development opportunities available to staff during your placements, through staff meetings, inset and other continuous professional development (CPD). In particular, note the following:

- Which model(s) of professional development are used?
- Is it just for teachers or do support staff engage as well? Does this depend on the focus?
- Who decides what the professional development should focus on and who leads it?

- Are teachers expected to (a) apply what has been covered in their practice and (b) reflect and report back on it?
- Are teachers encouraged to work collaboratively, or to work individually, to implement what has been covered?

Research by Bergmark (2020) strongly suggests that successful professional development is dependent on teachers taking ownership of their own development, based on their own authentic questions, rather than expecting schools and training establishments to take control for them. As a student teacher, it is likely that your teacher training provider is already encouraging you to take some control. For example, you may be setting targets in relation to subject knowledge development and practice development while on placements.

What Makes Effective Professional Learning?

Another important aspect of engaging with your own professional development is understanding your own emerging professional identity as a teacher. Understanding and becoming aware of your own professional identity is an important milestone in becoming the best teacher you can become.

Understanding Your Own Professional Identity

Professional identity is an important concept to understand as a teacher and is all about how teachers consider or 'see' themselves as educators (Tao and Gao, 2017). Your professional identity impacts on everything you do and think about when you are teaching. Your values, ideas and decisions are all informed by and impact on your professional identity. Once you are aware of your professional identity, it will give you the agency and autonomy to be able to make important decisions about your professional learning.

Critical Task 14.1

The Rollercoaster Ride

You will need a large piece of paper and some coloured pens for this task. Think about your journey to becoming a teacher as a rollercoaster ride which has ups, downs and critical moments. Consider your education so far – a good starting point is primary school, say Year 4. Think about the critical incidents in your education and consider the following themes:

Continued

- specific challenges that you faced in your education or life
- key moments of success (e.g., SATs, GCSEs, A levels)
- teachers who either positively or negatively impacted your education
- when you decided you wanted to be a teacher, and what motivated you.

Once you have thought about these themes and noted them down, start to map your rollercoaster journey from left to right on your paper, including these critical incidents. It may look something like the example in Figure 14.1.

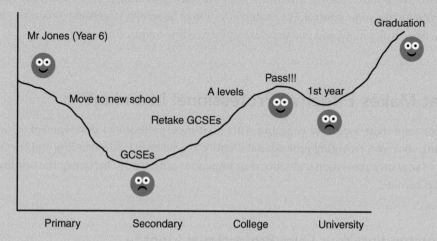

Figure 14.1   The rollercoaster of personal development

Once you have completed Critical Task 14.1, consider how the positive incidents impacted your confidence and resilience to achieve more. Also reflect on the negative incidents in your education, which, for me, would include when I failed my GCSEs. This really impacted my identity, as I felt like a failure. It was only when I attended college that I believed that I could achieve and succeed in my education, due to the excellent teachers and friends I made. Negative incidents can be positive for your identity as they can provide a reality check and drive you to success.

Critical incidents are an important part of your professional identity formation. A good example of this is a story I hear a lot from trainee teachers. Many student teachers recall a learning barrier, such as dyslexia or dyspraxia, and how it had a negative impact on their education. They feel that the strategies they used to overcome these barriers made them want to become a teacher to help and support other children with specific learning needs. This is a part of their professional identity and influences the decisions they make as teachers. As Slay and Smith (2011) state, professional identity is an image of yourself and the ideas, values, reasons and experiences employed to describe your professional learning. It is important for teachers to understand and reflect on their professional identity in order to maximise their professional learning and to choose opportunities that align with their professional identity.

Working in a School that Prioritises Professional Learning

When you are looking for your first teaching post, it is important to look for a school that fits your professional identity and will allow you to grow as a teacher. So you will want to find out as much as you can about each school that you apply to. You may want to work in a large Multi-Academy Trust (MAT) or in a school supported by the local authority. In either case, the school's website will tell you about their vision and ethos. Visiting the school or MAT before applying can be helpful, as it will give you a 'feel' for the school. Ask questions about induction and professional development opportunities as an early career teacher. Once you have found a school that you feel will allow you to grow, you can then put all your efforts into securing a position in the school.

Research by Stoll and Kools (2017) introduced the concept of the 'school as a learning organisation', not just for pupils, but for all members of the school community, including staff, leaders, parents and the wider community. They identified some key elements of collective endeavour that are central to a school's ambition to become a learning organisation:

- creating and supporting continuous learning opportunities for all staff
- promoting team learning and collaboration among staff
- establishing a culture of enquiry, innovation and exploration
- embedding systems for collecting and exchanging knowledge and learning
- learning with and from the external environment
- modelling and growing learning leadership.

Collaborating Effectively

Professional learning is more than knowledge and skill acquisition. For learning to be optimal, the process of learning should be active rather than passive. Effective professional development is also about creating a learning community where people can interact with one another and share experiences. Wenger (1998) argues that teachers are social beings and learning takes place in social contexts. Our professional identity is developed and moulded in the process of learning, which involves a process of self-awareness that promotes meaning-making.

In a report by the Department for Education (2022) regarding teachers' views on professional development, collaboration was highlighted as being especially important. Teachers felt that sharing good practice and sharing resources were hugely beneficial. Perry et al. (2022) found that having key staff who act as 'Challenge Champions' had a significant impact through organising professional development with the support of senior leaders in the school. Furthermore, the headteacher's role in nurturing effective professional development was seen as critical to the success and ongoing improvement of a school. A positive school culture with a good atmosphere and understanding of teachers' learning, in addition to teachers working together collaboratively, was identified as positively impacting professional development (Postholm, 2012).

Evidently, a positive aspect of engaging with your own professional learning is having a group of fellow student teachers or early career teachers with whom to discuss important educational issues and being active in creating an environment where you can discuss your own emerging ideas. Your fellow student teachers are such an amazing resource for your own professional learning so equipping yourself with the skills needed to interact effectively with your peers is crucial. Having access to this community of learning is seen as a very important part of professional learning (Farnsworth et al., 2016).

Working collaboratively is not always a natural or easy process and requires specific skills, attitudes and behaviours to be truly effective in progressing learning as a teacher. Some of the skills, attitudes and behaviours necessary for effective collaboration with your peers are:

- demonstrating patience, trust, empathy and mutual respect
- promoting active participation and open communication
- developing shared decision-making and shared values
- being a critical friend and research-informed.

Becoming a Critical, Reflective Student Teacher

Becoming a confident critical thinker can be a daunting skill to acquire. However, it is crucial to learning and developing as a student teacher and early career teacher. Criticality is defined as the ability to analyse an issue or idea and to be able to evaluate its usefulness. The key critical thinking skills are analysis, interpretation, inference, explanation, self-regulation, open-mindedness and problem-solving. There are so many learning myths in teaching, and therefore it is crucial to evaluate their effectiveness before you implement the findings into your teaching. A good example is the Visual, Auditory and Kinaesthetic (VAK) theory, which is based on the idea that everyone has a specific learning style. As discussed in Chapter 5, the evidence for this theory is minimal and it has failed to live up to the hype around it, despite still being used in some schools (Willingham et al., 2015). It is therefore important to be able to critically evaluate research so that you can feel confident in implementing teaching and learning approaches that are research-informed and stand up to scrutiny. Another important part of thinking critically is having the confidence to communicate your ideas to your peers without feeling like you will be criticised.

--- **Case Study 14.2** ---

Voicing Opinions

Amelie is an undergraduate student teacher participating in a seminar on the inclusion of children for whom English is an Additional Language (EAL).

The tutor has asked the students to work in groups to discuss the practical ways in which teachers can include children with EAL. One of Amelie's peers in the group, Finn, begins the discussion by stating that he doesn't see why we should be talking about this as he has only worked in schools where the main home language is English and there is only a small minority who cannot speak English. Finn goes on to say that these children should be taken out of the classroom with a teaching assistant and have specific provision and interventions to improve their English. Amelie completely disagrees with this statement and believes that all children's needs should be included in the classroom, as far as is possible, and it is the responsibility of the classroom teacher to provide practical support for these children. Amelie has read widely on the subject and the research supports her views. However, she is nervous about sharing her views with the whole group and risking being the only person with this view.

I am sure you have been in this situation before, where you would really like to voice your opinion, and can support your views with research findings, but find it difficult because you fear how your opinion may be perceived by others. Not all student teachers or early career teachers will have the confidence in themselves to voice their opinions or trust in their peers to be empathetic to others' views and opinions.

As you can see from Case Study 14.2, it is not easy to become a confident critical friend to others, but it is so important for your professional learning as a student teacher. Here are a few ways that will set you on the path to becoming a confident critical friend:

- Try not to take criticism personally. Any criticism coming from other school members should not be seen as a personal attack on you.
- It is not your role to force opinions on other people. Critical discussions are not a contest. Everybody wins in good, open critical conversations.
- Try to be as open as you can to other people's opinions. Try to see these opinions from multiple angles. Why do you think they hold these opinions?
- Reflect on why you hold your own opinions and where they have come from. Try to articulate the opposite view, to help you to reflect on it.
- Try to base your views on research that you have read which supports your view. In that way, you can de-personalise the feeling of criticism, as it is about the research, not about you.

Adopting a Research-informed Teaching Mindset

It is argued that developing a research-informed mindset is a crucial element to professional learning and effective teaching (Menter and Flores, 2021). As a busy teacher, it is important to be able to evaluate teaching strategies that will have the most impact on children's learning. A research-informed mindset can help you to reflect critically on any current 'fads' in education. Research carried out by Joseph-Richard and Jessop (2020) identified the key characteristics for developing a research-informed teaching mindset:

- An understanding that there is a difference between the content of a lesson and the teaching approach(es) used to teach it.

- An understanding that *how* content is taught makes a big difference in developing children's understanding and learning outcomes.
- A willingness for teachers to position themselves as a lifelong learner and not as experts.
- A commitment to recognise that all knowledge is open to challenge, and to explore and reflect on why teaching ideas work or do not work.
- A willingness to co-produce knowledge with colleagues in a collaborative manner.

The Education Endowment Foundation's (EEF) *Teaching and learning toolkit* (2023) is a good starting point to help you become research-informed as a student teacher. The EEF website provides a clear, research-informed summary of evidence of various approaches that schools can choose to use and provides an indication of their potential impact on children's progress. For each approach covered in the toolkit, there is an indication of average impact on attainment, cost and the strength of the evidence underpinning it. You can 'dig deeper' into the research base for each approach and consider:

- How many studies are there and in how many schools have they taken place?
- How recent is the evidence?
- How similar are the studies to regular classroom practice?
- How much variation is there in the outcome data collected in the research?
- Were the studies conducted independently and with a rigorous methodology?

It is important to stress that becoming research-informed is a developmental process and requires perseverance. As a busy teacher, it is easy to pick a teaching approach 'off the shelf' and implement it. However, understanding the limitations and the evidence underpinning an approach will provide you with a much richer teaching experience and learning experience for the children.

Question Guide 14.1

How Teachers Maintain Their Development

The *CCF* states that student teachers should 'learn how to develop as a professional by ... strengthening pedagogical and subject knowledge by participating in wider networks ... [and] engaging critically with research and using evidence to critique practice' (DfE, 2019: 29).

To help you understand how teachers make use of professional networks and research to develop their practice, use these questions to guide your discussions with an expert colleague:

- Are you involved in any networks for teachers outside the school, such as subject leader networks? How do these help you to develop your own practice?
- Are you or any of the other teachers in this school undertaking any of the National College qualifications? What benefit does this have for their own practice and is there any benefit for the school more widely?
- How is research and evidence used to inform practice in this school? Please can you give me a specific example?

Chapter Summary

In this chapter, we have considered the importance of professional learning to maximise your successful career as a teacher. We have considered what professional learning is and why it is important to your career. We have considered the dominant models of professional development seen in schools and reflected on their capacity for professional learning and autonomy. We have also explored some of the important factors that maximise effective professional learning, such as professional identify, working in a school that prioritises professional development, working collaboratively and becoming critically reflective, adopting a research-informed teaching mindset. These factors will provide you with a toolkit for effective professional learning and open up a career in teaching that allows you to constantly learn new and different ways to help children learn more effectively. Effective professional learning not only impacts on children, but also allows you to steer yourself through the winding paths of a career in teaching.

Further Reading

Forster, C. and Eperjesi, R. (2021) *Action research for student teachers* (2nd edn). London: Sage. This excellent text provides a step-by-step guide for student teachers to plan, undertake and write up an action research enquiry and will be equally useful for other teachers engaging in action research.

Sherrington, T. and Caviglioli, O. (2020) *Teaching walkthrus: Five-step guide to instructional coaching*. Woodbridge, UK: John Catt Educational Ltd.

This book makes a compelling case for considering how to implement evidence-based pedagogy clearly and concisely. It provides a clear and concise explanation on current theories of learning and how to implement these in your planning.

References

Bergmark, U. (2020) 'Teachers' professional learning when building a research-based education: context-specific, collaborative and teacher-driven professional development', *Professional Development in Education*, 49(2), 1–15.

Day, C. (1999) 'Professional development and reflective practice: purposes, processes and partnerships', *Pedagogy, Culture & Society*, 7(2), 221–233.

Department for Education (DfE) (2019) *ITT core content framework*. London: DfE.

Department for Education (DfE) (2022) *Delivering world-class teacher development*. London: DfE.

Education Endowment Foundation (EEF) (2023) *Teaching and learning toolkit*. Available at: https://educationendowmentfoundation.org.uk/education-evidence/teaching-learning-toolkit (accessed 11 April 2023).

Farnsworth, V., Kleanthous, I. and Wenger-Trayner, E. (2016) 'Communities of practice as a social theory of learning: a conversation with Etienne Wenger', *British Journal of Educational Studies*, 64(2), 139–160.

Fletcher-Wood, H. and Zuccollo, J. (2020) *The effects of high-quality professional development on teachers and students: A rapid review and meta-analysis*. London: Education Policy Institute/ Wellcome. Available at: https://epi.org.uk/publications-and-research/effects-high-quality-professional-development/ (accessed 20 December 2022).

Forster, C. and Eperjesi, R. (2021) *Action research for student teachers* (2nd edn). London: Sage.

Hoban, G.F. (2002) *Teacher learning for educational change*. Buckingham: Open University Press.

Joseph-Richard, P. and Jessop, T. (2020) 'A phenomenographic study of research informed teaching through the eyes of Masters' students', *Studies in Higher Education*, 45(4), 847–861.

Kennedy, A. (2005) 'Models of continuing professional development: a framework for analysis', *Journal of In-Service Education*, 31(2), 235–250.

Lloyd, M. and Davis, J.P. (2018) 'Beyond performativity: a pragmatic model of teacher professional learning', *Professional Development in Education*, 44(1), 92–106.

Menter, I. and Flores, M.A. (2021) 'Connecting research and professionalism in teacher education', *European Journal of Teacher Education*, 44(1), 115–127.

Noffke, S. and Somekh, B. (2011) 'Action research', in B. Somekh and C. Lewin (eds.), *Theory and methods in social research* (2nd edn). Los Angeles, CA: Sage, pp. 94–101.

Organisation for Economic Co-operation and Development (OECD) (2017) *The OECD handbook for innovative learning environments*. Paris: OECD Publishing.

Perry, E., Halliday, J., Higginson, J. and Patel, S. (2022) *Meeting the challenge of providing high-quality continuing professional development for teachers: The Wellcome CPD challenge pilot delivery report February 2022*. London: Wellcome Trust. Available at: https://cms.wellcome. org/sites/default/files/2022-02/wellcome-cpd-challenge-pilot-delivery-report.pdf (accessed 11 May 2023).

Postholm, M.B. (2012) 'Teachers' professional development: a theoretical review', *Educational Research*, 54(4), 405–429.

Rhodes, C. and Beneicke, S. (2003) 'Professional development support for poorly performing teachers: challenges and opportunities for school managers in addressing teacher learning needs', *Journal of In-service Education*, 29(1), 123–140.

Sims, S., Fletcher-Wood, H., O'Mara-Eves, A., Cottingham, S., Stansfield, C., Van Herwegen, J. and Anders, J. (2021) *What are the characteristics of teacher professional development that increase pupil achievement? A systematic review and meta-analysis*. London: Education Endowment Foundation.

Slay, H.S. and Smith, D.A. (2011) 'Professional identity construction: using narrative to understand the negotiation of professional and stigmatized cultural identities', *Human Relations*, 64(1), 85–107.

Solomon, J. and Tresman, S. (1999) 'A model for continued professional development: knowledge, belief and action', *Journal of In-service Education*, 25(2), 307–319.

Stoll, L. and Kools, M. (2017) 'The school as a learning organisation: a review revisiting and extending a timely concept', *Journal of professional capital and community*, 2(1), 2–17.

Tao, J. and Gao, X. (2017) 'Teacher agency and identity commitment in curricular reform', *Teaching and Teacher Education*, 63, 346–355.

Wenger, E. (1998) *Communities of practice: Learning, meaning and identity*. Cambridge: Cambridge University Press.

Wiliam, D. (2016) 'The secret of effective feedback', *Educational Leadership*, 73(7), 10–15.

Willingham, D.T., Hughes, E.M. and Dobolyi, D.G. (2015) 'The scientific status of learning styles theories', *Teaching of Psychology*, 42(3), 266–271.

Worth, J. and Van den Brande, J. (2020) *Teacher autonomy: How does it relate to job satisfaction and retention?* Slough: National Foundation for Educational Research (NFER).

15
WORKING COLLABORATIVELY

Simon Hyde-White

Chapter Objectives

- To explore the importance of effective collaboration with others.
- To reflect on some of the potential benefits, challenges and principles of working with teaching assistants and other adults.
- To consider how to work well with parents to maximise pupils' learning.

In this chapter, we explore the important issue of working collaboratively with others in the classroom and beyond. Brown (2018) highlights the need for all effective practitioners to view vulnerability as a strength and to recognise that you should not expect to have all the answers. This key principle is at the heart of this chapter. However, working collaboratively with others requires sensitive and strategic planning. We explore some of the benefits and challenges of working well with teaching assistants (TAs) as well as exploring good practice. We also consider how to maximise the potential and expertise of parents and other adults in and beyond the classroom.

The Importance of Effective Collaboration

A culture of teamwork should exist in all primary schools. Class teachers do not work in secret isolation behind an impenetrable classroom door. In any one classroom, you may well find a teacher or two and a host of TAs, parents/guardians, other volunteers, student teachers and work experience pupils. Class teachers will also work collaboratively with a range of other colleagues within the school, such as the SENCo, the lead for children with English as an Additional Language (EAL), the pastoral team, and subject leaders. As a student teacher, you will also work closely with your teacher-mentor, as outlined in Chapter 1; as an early career teacher (ECT), you will continue to receive support, monitoring and training from a mentor and/or induction tutor. There may also be times when you will need to work collaboratively with people from outside the school, such as advisory teachers, speech and language therapists or staff from a feeder setting. Working with such a diverse range of other people will require you to develop your skills in working collaboratively. In this chapter, we focus particularly on working effectively with TAs and parents, but the principles explored can be applied to your work with all colleagues.

Interestingly, while the number of teachers in mainstream schools in England has remained relatively steady since 2000, the number of full-time equivalent TAs has more than trebled over the same period, from 79,000 to 243,700 (Department for Education (DfE), 2018; Education Endowment Foundation (EEF), 2018). This figure now outnumbers the nursery and primary teachers employed in state-funded English nursery and primary schools. The increase was designed to support teachers in delivering the curriculum, ease teacher work-load, improve teacher wellbeing and provide support in challenging circumstances. Blatch-ford et al. (2012) suggest that it is not uncommon for headteachers to make claims about schools 'falling apart' without their TAs. However, despite research suggesting that effective deployment of TAs can improve pupils' attitudes and have a positive impact on their attain-ment (Blatchford et al., 2009), there is also research that indicates that the effective deploy-ment of TAs is not necessarily straightforward, and that ineffective deployment can actually have a negative impact. It is therefore vital that new teachers learn to be effective leaders of this expanded 'workforce'.

Embracing the Contribution of Teaching Assistants

A ship cannot sail alone. When considering the complexities of promoting young learners' progress and welfare, it makes sense that effective leadership of this vessel should utilise the strengths of a diverse crew. How effectively you deploy teaching assistants will depend largely on your attitude towards them. Valuing the contribution of TAs, and regarding them as piv-otal facilitators of pupils' learning, should prompt you to adopt participative and delegative styles of classroom leadership in creative and powerful ways. Indeed, beyond the contribution they can make in releasing teachers from routine practical and clerical tasks to focus on core teaching tasks, TAs are increasingly expected to contribute more directly to pupils' academic achievement, prompting many schools to regard them as 'teaching partners' rather than teach-ing assistants.

Critical Task 15.1

Utilising TAs

Reflecting on your school placement experiences, use Table 15.1 to consider up to 10 helpful ways you can employ TAs to impact positively on children's learning. You may find it helpful to think about how TAs can work collaboratively with you, as well as directly with the pupils.

Table 15.1   Utilising TAs

Partnering the teacher	Supporting pupils directly

Welcoming Your Vulnerability

To view TAs as pivotal partners in raising standards, and to work effectively with all stakeholders, you must embrace the humility required to recognise your own limitations and the potential attributes and contributions of others. Having this mindset will give you the confidence to ask others for help and advice without any feelings of inadequacy or threat. Brown (2018: 24) argues that 'our daily lives are defined by experiences of uncertainty, risk and emotional exposure', and that 'to grow up is to accept vulnerability'. We should not derive our strength from our rugged determination to 'go it alone', but rather from our ability to plan, communicate and work together. For example, gaining trust from teaching assistants is earned in the small moments of listening to their contributions, remaining curious, being honest, and valuing their suggestions and feedback. In a complex, problem-solving profession such as teaching, cultivating reciprocal relationships involves viewing 'mistakes' not as failures but as gateways to more effective ways to meet the needs of pupils. As Myatt (2016) points out, believing one must always 'be right' stifles innovative thinking. Similarly, when a TA might be struggling with a professional issue, asking them a question such as 'What does support from me look like?' can lead to a culture of generosity and creativity, not judgementalism. In short, when adults resist having to 'be right' in the short term in favour of 'doing the right thing' in the long term, teachers, TAs and pupils all benefit.

Some student teachers (and indeed, some qualified teachers) can find receiving feedback about their practice challenging, but the DfE (2019a: 29) states that 'seeking challenge, feedback and critique from mentors and other colleagues in an open and trusting working environment' will help you to 'develop as a professional'. It is an integral part of training to teach and of continuing to develop your practice throughout your teaching career. Again, embrace your humility. Remember that feedback is not a personal criticism, but a tool to support you in reflecting on and developing your own practice. The person providing the feedback wants to help you become a more effective teacher, which is also your aim, I'm sure. Warwick and Wolpert (2018: 41) advise that you should be 'receptive, open-minded and active' when receiving feedback and that you should be aware of your own 'body language, tone of voice and level of engagement'. Asking questions and engaging in dialogue, rather than sitting passively and listening, will enable you to get the most of these feedback opportunities.

Potential Limitations of TA Deployment

One reason for the growth in the numbers of TAs has been to support the inclusion of a greater number of pupils who have special educational needs and disabilities (SEND) in mainstream schools. TAs often provide the key means by which inclusion is facilitated. However, despite the anticipated benefits of utilising this enlarged workforce, research into the effective deployment of TAs reveals that effects vary (EEF, 2018). Extensive studies found that deploying TAs on a regular basis to provide general classroom support to groups of lower-achieving pupils or those with identified learning difficulties most often leads to no additional impact on pupils' learning outcomes. This is despite many class teachers believing TAs possess 'more experience helping children who have difficulties with learning' and so are better placed to meet their needs (Blatchford et al., 2012: 2). Undoubtedly, TAs may develop a great deal of experience of working with such children, but this does not mean they are all well qualified or well trained.

   Indeed, Webster et al. (2015) stated that their findings from a large and detailed six-year study showed that support from TAs often had a negative impact on the academic progress of pupils. Alarmingly, the more support pupils with a statement of special educational needs (SEN) received from a TA, the less academic progress they made, relative to similar pupils receiving minimal TA support. Furthermore, despite some headteachers and teachers in the above report maintaining that TAs working with lower-attaining children have a positive impact on the pupils' behaviour, confidence, motivation and independent working, these claims are unsubstantiated and conflict with the report's other findings. Importantly, TAs themselves were not deemed culpable for these findings, but rather the decision to deploy them as an informal teaching resource for low-attaining pupils.

   Other research suggests that TAs can have a positive impact on the attainment outcomes of lower-attaining pupils and those eligible for free school meals when following a specified intervention approach that they have been trained to deliver. Sibieta (2016) claims that brief, regular intervention sessions with clear objectives and expectations that last for a finite period can add up to four months of additional progress, and this aligns with the findings in the EEF's *Teaching and learning toolkit* (EEF, 2023). However, such research evidence must be closely interrogated. First, the impact on pupils seems to be maximised only when working with a TA alone or in small groups, and for no less than three sessions per week over a minimum of 20 weeks. This level of intervention is costly to sustain when only impacting a limited number of pupils. Second, there is a lack of evidence for the holistic benefits of such intervention programmes since most only target improvement in reading, spoken language and mathematics. One might reasonably question what other curriculum areas and social learning were negatively impacted by implementing such intensive catch-up programmes.

Critical Task 15.2

Potential Reasons for Negative Impact

Using Table 15.2, consider the reasons why TAs, through no fault of their own, are not being as effective as we might hope in raising standards, and how these issues can be addressed.

Table 15.2 Potential reasons for negative impact of TAs

Unhelpful practice	How this might be addressed

Limitations in Pupil–TA Discourse

Since TAs have the capacity to provide considerable individual attention to the pupils allocated to them, you may have found completing Critical Task 15.2 rather challenging. However, the key lies in the quality and nature of the TA–pupil interactions, rather than the quantity. Research suggests that TAs often feel under pressure to 'drill' lower-achieving pupils in the right answers required to be successful in external tests, irrespective of whether the pupils truly understand the concepts involved (Webster et al., 2015). This practice reflects the current advocacy for 'direct instruction' pedagogy (Kirschner et al., 2006) to underpin a knowledge-rich curriculum. Yet learning involves pupils acquiring strategies 'to increase comprehension, competence, control and character', not just being kept 'on task' (Claxton, 2021: 120). Merely helping pupils to 'get the right answer' prevents them from thinking for themselves and constructing their own knowledge through cognitive, dialogic approaches to learning (Bryan et al., 2010). Webster et al. (2015) suggest that while class teachers tend to facilitate communities of enquiry, where pupils justify their reasoning and explain their strategies, TAs tend to reduce their discourse with pupils. They commonly ask closed questions, and often end up answering these questions themselves to prioritise task completion over learning.

There is an old joke about two people chatting in a bar. The first announces, 'I've taught my dog to speak French'. 'Let's hear her then', the other person replies. 'I said I taught her; I didn't say she can speak it!'. It is the same when teaching children. They are unlikely to have properly learnt something when they are cut adrift from frequent, high-quality peer interaction and when the requirement to produce a worthwhile outcome using the knowledge they are exploring is removed. The practice of working exclusively with the same targeted children and providing sparse explanations of misunderstood concepts merely induces feelings of 'learned helplessness' and failure in those who become overly reliant on adult support.

Effective Principles and Practice for Working with TAs

Despite the limitations explored in the previous section, all is not lost. There are plenty of schools demonstrating the highly effective deployment of TAs, despite the practical constraints imposed by the busy realities of a typical school day. In such schools, leaders focus on using TAs to add value to what teachers do, not to replace them. This section will therefore explore how you can best deploy TAs more fluidly to facilitate high-quality teaching and learning across the attainment range. This in turn will enable you to spend at least as much of your time working skilfully with the pupils who are most in need of support as you spend with the other children.

Partnering Throughout a Lesson

At the beginning and end of lessons, it might be tempting to engage TAs in administrative tasks while you interact with the class, but this is a wasted opportunity. Consider the ways listed in Table 15.3 to more purposefully utilise your assistant.

Clearly, this is not an exhaustive list. You will discover many other ways during school placements in which TAs can partner you more visibly during whole-class input.

Interacting with Pupils

You should emphasise to TAs that their primary role during group and independent work is to help pupils develop independent learning skills and to manage their own learning, rather than focusing on completing tasks with significant support. To improve the nature and quality of TAs' talk and interactions, they should adopt a hierarchical approach to scaffolding by waiting to see whether pupils can respond to the question or task independently before providing

Table 15.3 Purposefully utilising your TA

Role during whole-class interaction	Impact on learning
Support you in providing feedback to individuals or small groups on the previous day's learning.	Facilitates personalised feedback through showcasing examples of good understanding and common errors.
Engage in role-play, e.g., to model asking or responding to questions 'in character' during English, history or RE hot seating.	Encourages pupils to lead in asking and reflecting on fruitful questions for the 'Gruffalo', 'Mary Seacole' or 'Moses' that delve into relevant themes.
Represent a maths concept using manipulatives as you verbalise and record the procedure.	Seeing visual representations alongside the written recording supports long-term understanding and mastery.
Record key points from your modelling on a flow diagram.	Deconstructs a class teacher's input to avoid cognitive overload and support children in recalling information, developing their thoughts and rehearsing their answers.
Practically model a PE technique or collaborative/ competitive task with you or a pupil.	Explicitly seeing a skill helps pupils more readily disregard strategies that are less effective and spend more time purposefully exploring and refining effective strategies.
Scribe responses during whole-class questioning, discussion and brainstorms, and record key words.	Children can use this as a scaffold when working independently.
Observe and note individual pupils' learning difficulties and achievements.	Identifies required support and challenge for the main part of the lesson or next session.

any prompts (EEF, 2018). When interacting with a group of 'self-scaffolding' pupils displaying high levels of independence, a TA's primary role should be to observe and listen to how they use appropriate knowledge and resources to problem solve and plan their approach to a task. Useful questions to cement understanding and prompt further thinking are:

- What did you notice when…?
- Can you explain what you have done and why?
- Could there be an alternative method/suggestion/example…?
- What do the rest of you think?

When individuals are unable to self-scaffold, prime TAs with question prompts or clues, such as:

- Can you remind us of the learning objective and success criteria?
- Have you got all the information and resources you need?
- What previous knowledge or task can you draw on that might help you?
- Can you talk me through what you need to do first or have done so far?
- What did you do last time? What is different this time?

Both sets of questions can be utilised in any subject.

Providing More Direct Support

There will, however, be occasions when pupils are unable to proceed independently, even with skilful prompting. This is most likely to occur when they encounter a task that requires a new skill, strategy or body of knowledge. It may be when studying a picture source in an unfamiliar period of history or employing attacking strategies for the first time in a small-sided invasion game in PE. In such contexts, encourage your TA to drip-feed key vocabulary or information, break the task down into smaller steps, or deconstruct a modelled example. However, this form of adult-led scaffolding should be reduced as soon as the pupils' competency increases. Alternatively, TAs can act as a 'teacher triage' (EEF, 2018: 14), circulating the classroom to identify those pupils who are having difficulty with a particular task or process, while you are perhaps working with a target group.

Observation Guide 15.1

The Role of TAs

The *ITT Core Content Framework (CCF)* states that student teachers should 'learn how to build effective working relationships by … [learning] how to ensure that support provided by teaching assistants in lessons is additional to, rather than a replacement for, support from the teacher' (DfE, 2019a: 29–30).

As we have established, there are several ways in which TAs can be asked to partner teachers in the classroom. During your placements, particularly note:

- The many ways in which TAs support teachers to facilitate learning during the entirety of a lesson.
- How they support pupils to respond to feedback.
- Whether TAs provide opportunities for pupils to think and work independently.
- The prompting and probing questions TAs ask, and how they wait for, and facilitate, cumulative responses.
- Which groups of learners TAs are supporting.
- How they adapt input and tasks for the pupils they are supporting.
- Whether they demonstrate high expectations of their learners.

Effective Teacher–TA Communication

It goes without saying that to be effective partners in curriculum delivery, TAs must be fully prepared for this role (DfE, 2019b). Good teachers make the role they want TAs to adopt in lessons explicit; TAs should not be left to mindread. However, finding sufficient teacher–TA liaison time can be a challenge. Unfortunately, TAs often go into classes without knowing what will be taught or what the teacher expects from the students (Bosanquet et al., 2015). Since some schools are reducing the amount of planning and preparation time available to TAs, in order to maximise their contact with pupils (DfE, 2019b), creative and flexible approaches are called for. Why not mentor your TA by asking them to observe how you interact with your pupils and then collaboratively identify the strategies and skills you employed to facilitate pupil thinking and learning. Then, to share the specifics of the desired learning ahead of lessons, invite them to join part of your designated planning, preparation and assessment (PPA) time. Ahead of lessons, you should prepare your TAs with the following:

- intended learning objectives and assessment outcomes
- concepts, facts and subject knowledge being taught
- skills to be learned, applied, practised or extended
- a brief description of how to model new learning when required
- key questions to prompt and assess pupils' learning
- the expected focus and nature of in-lesson pupil feedback.

Much of this detail can also be shared in advance via a lesson plan and a pre-prepared group assessment sheet, but it should also be supplemented with discussion so that TAs fully understand their role (EEF, 2018). Similarly, a combination of effective assessment and evaluation recording mechanisms and face-to-face post-lesson discussion is ideal. Perhaps moments can be grabbed near the end of a lesson by tasking the children to review their learning independently or discuss a Philosophy for Children (P4C) 'sticky question' with their partner, while you debrief with the TA. Be brave and ask your TA about your working relationship. Find out what is working well and whether there is anything you can do differently to make communications and collaboration between you even better.

Case Study 15.1

Powerful Partnerships

Helen, a highly skilled Year 6 teacher, and Tom, the TA in Helen's class, are explaining to the student teacher on placement in their class how they work so efficiently in partnership with each other:

> Helen: All TAs in this school are paid to attend staff CPD [continuous professional development], so Tom fully understands our focus on developing pupils' active enquiry and cumulative dialogue, so we both use the same pedagogic approaches when working with the children.

> Tom: In my last school, I was always working with the lowest attainers and I don't think it was good for them, as they became over-reliant on my support. Helen ensures that we both work with children across the whole attainment range, which is really important to make sure they are independent learners, ready for secondary school.

Continued

Helen: Tom does lead some carefully planned interventions and we have worked hard to schedule these at times which do not impact on lessons, so that the children involved in the intervention and Tom don't miss what is going on in the classroom.

Tom: We also plan opportunities for me to engage in one-to-one reading with each child at least twice each half-term. Obviously, this is good for their reading development, but it also provides opportunities for them to talk to me about anything that is worrying them.

Helen: We make time for regular discussion and Tom is brilliant at providing feedback from the intervention sessions and his interactions with individuals and groups in class. Between us, we have developed and refined a summary feedback sheet, which captures the names of children who excel or who struggle with any particular task, as well as any common misconceptions noted. This has also reduced my marking load, as we use these sheets to inform next-lesson 'drop-ins', where we give verbal feedback and targets to support and challenge individuals.

Tom: They are also helpful for pupil progress meetings and My Plan review meetings. I really like that Helen includes me in formal review meetings with parents, as this shows parents that we are a team working together for their child's benefit.

There are several important points to highlight from this example:

- Mutual respect and regular communication maximises a TA's impact.
- Schools that prioritise TA training and strategic involvement reap the rewards.
- Pupils of all ages can benefit from working with a skilled TA.
- Careful scheduling of any planned interventions safeguards the benefits of skilled adult input and peer interaction.
- The pastoral role of a TA is hugely important.

Of course, not all working relationships are as effective as the example in Case Study 15.1 and you will need to work hard to ensure that yours are effective, using the advice given earlier in this chapter. There may be times when relationships with TAs become strained or conflict arises. In Chapter 16, we will explore how you can navigate such situations successfully.

Response to Critical Task 15.2

Potential Reasons for Negative Impact

In Critical Task 15.2, we asked you to consider why the work of TAs might not benefit pupils in the ways we might hope. The important thing to remember is that this is largely not the fault of the TAs but the ways in which they are deployed. In Table 15.4, we have identified some potential issues and solutions.

Table 15.4 Suggested possible reasons for the negative impact of TAs

Unhelpful practice	How this might be addressed
Working exclusively with selected pupils as informal teachers	TAs partner you in delivering the whole curriculum to all pupils
Withdrawing pupils from the classroom during lessons	TAs use before-school, registration and some assembly time to run planned interventions
Spoon-feeding pupils	TAs mirror class teachers in valuing pupil learning over 'task completion'
Minimal teacher–TA liaison	Find creative and efficient ways to communicate with TAs before, during and after lessons

Working Well with Parents

Just like TAs, parents (by which we mean 'parents and carers' and other family members) also have the potential to be powerful allies in maximising children's progress, and even in curriculum delivery. It is therefore important to reflect on your understanding of the significant role they play in the success of their children in schools (Molina, 2013). Not only do they possess unique knowledge about their own children to influence your provision for school and home learning (see Chapter 10), but they can also contribute more directly to school life. Indeed, you should be optimistic about the potential of some parents assisting you in the classroom since you both desire the best educational outcomes for their children. It can, though, be difficult to entice parents into school, especially if their own experiences of school were not positive, and many schools do not have an explicit plan for how they work with parents (EEF, 2021).

Home–School Communication

The onus for cultivating effective, reciprocal parental engagement lies with teachers despite the EEF's (2021) claim that fewer than 10% have undertaken CPD in this area. Setting the right tone for home–school communication is vital. It should not only comprise of scheduled home–school meetings or difficult conversations when required. You should also cultivate regular lines of communication so that parents view you as approachable and friendly. Being present on the playground at the beginning and end of the school day allows you to interact with parents to praise their child's efforts or to address potential concerns at an early stage. Regular home–school communication via newsletters and individual reading records or homework journals provides similar opportunities. On occasion, despite your best efforts to build positive relationships with carers, you may encounter some negative responses from parents and we will explore how to handle these situations in Chapter 16.

Contributing to the Curriculum

It is common practice for schools to inform parents about forthcoming topics at the beginning of terms. I suggest you go one step further and ask whether any parents can contribute to these topics. Find out what they do for work or hobbies (without being too intrusive!), and openly invite them in to share their expertise or resources beyond being tasked with hearing children read and supervising cooking or sewing projects. For example, parents with specific knowledge of the outdoors can regularly support learning in the Forest School area by modelling how to use commonly found plants for play, making dyes and cooking. Indeed, the potential is huge. Here are other ways in which I have previously enlisted parental expertise:

- A parent and their baby illustrating a young human's needs.
- A Hindu presenting family wedding photographs, explaining the week-long celebrations and modelling a traditional wedding dance.
- A town planner judging children's presentations for a new development after we visited a local housing estate and neighbouring brownfield site.
- A grandparent recalling how it felt to live as a young city girl during World War II's blackouts and air raids, and her subsequent evacuation.
- A historian with extensive knowledge of the Roman empire leading a talk on Queen Boudica and re-enacting a battle.
- A pet enthusiast showing their wormery and their tortoise waking from hibernation to illustrate how contrasting animals adapt and behave.
- A nurse showing how to measure a pulse and how to apply basic first aid and bandages.

From plants to pet care, the list is endless. You just need the vision and desire to welcome such experts in, as well as the acceptance that you cannot be an expert in everything yourself, as explored earlier in this chapter.

Inspiration and Celebration

In many cases, visitors invited in to enrich your curriculum may also raise your pupils' future aspirations, and this has also been explored in Chapter 9. Consider the potential of amateur story writers, poets, artists, musicians and even journalists in supporting aspects of the taught curriculum and acting as role models. However, don't neglect those parents, school governors or former pupils who have performed inspirational or uplifting deeds, such as cycling across the Himalayan mountains, volunteering at a local food bank or participating in a school build-ing project in Kenya, as they may act as powerful role models for children's more holistic development.

Sharing in the celebration of children's learning is another powerful way to involve par-ents. When adopting 'project-based' curriculum design, a live audience is required to attend the end-of-topic 'exhibition' of learning held in the school hall! Imagine a Key Stage 1 topic built around the question 'Do animals have feelings?'. As well as showcasing their PowerPoint presentations, posters, news-style broadcasts, fact files and poems, your class could perform a dance inspired by viewing excerpts from the film and stage versions of *The Lion King*. Similarly, an upper Key Stage 2 pupil-led PE project prompted by the question 'How can I perform like Lebron James or Diana Taurasi?', two eminent American basketball players, could conclude with a knowledgeable parent providing feedback on the children's final outcomes.

Question Guide 15.1

Make the Most of Parents' Contributions

The *CCF* states that student teachers should:

> learn how to build effective working relationships by ... observing how expert colleagues communicate with parents and carers proactively and make effective use of parents' evenings to engage parents and carers in their children's schooling and deconstructing this approach. (DfE, 2019a: 29–30)

To help you understand how to build effective working relationships with parents and carers, use these questions to guide your discussions with an expert colleague:

- How do you establish relationships and communication with parents at the start of a new school year?
- When do parents have opportunities to see you informally?
- What sorts of things are sent home to parents and how often?
- How do you involve parents in the life of the class and school?
- How are parents' evenings organised and run in this school?
- How do you prepare for parents' evenings?
- How do you handle potentially difficult conversations with parents, either at parents' evening or in other situations?
- What do you think is the key to establishing and maintaining effective relationships with parents?
- How do you establish and maintain regular professional and respectful communication with parents?

Chapter Summary

In this chapter, we have considered the potential that other adults can play in supporting learning. The effectiveness of this approach begins with your acknowledgement that you work better in collaboration and that others can make powerful contributions. The key to working alongside TAs is to view them as skilled partners rather than just a useful 'pair of hands'. We have identified some key guidelines for effective practice, such as utilising TAs to support the full range of learners to access the entire curriculum, empowering pupils to think for themselves, and devising ways to conduct timely and meaningful communication. We have also illustrated how parents can become powerful allies in creative curriculum provision through tapping into their distinctive experiences and expertise.

Further Reading

Brown, B. (2018) *Dare to lead*. London: Vermilion.
Based on conversations with leaders in all walks of industry and public life, Brown illustrates how to put leadership ideas into practice. She explains that leadership is not about status and power, but about holding yourself accountable for recognising the potential in people and ideas, and developing that potential through empathetic and courageous connection with others.

Myatt, M. (2016) *Hopeful schools: Building humane communities*. Worthing: Mary Myatt Learning Ltd.
This book is an uplifting and important read for all aspiring and qualified teachers who want their teaching to be challenged and praised in equal measure. It provides personal observations, humane proposals and practical examples of how to develop the softer skills of making a colleague feel so valued that they want to work with you.

References

Blatchford, P., Bassett, P., Brown, P., Martin, C., Russell, A. and Webster, R. (2009) *The deployment and impact of support staff in schools: research brief*. London: Department for Children, Schools and Families (DCFS).

Blatchford, P., Russell, A. and Webster, R. (2012) *Reassessing the impact of teaching assistants: How research challenges practice and policy*. Abingdon, UK: Routledge.

Bosanquet, P., Radford, J. and Webster, R. (2015) *Teaching assistant's guide to effective interaction: How to maximise your practice*. Abingdon, UK: Routledge.

Brown, B. (2018) *Dare to lead*. London: Vermilion.

Bryan, H., Carpenter, C. and Hoult, S. (2010) *Learning and teaching at M-Level: A guide for student teachers*. London: Sage.

Claxton, G. (2021) *The future of teaching and the myths that hold it back*. Abingdon, UK: Routledge.

Department for Education (DfE) (2018) *School workforce in England: November 2017*. London: DfE. Available at: www.gov.uk/government/statistics/school-workforce-in-england-november-2017 (accessed 9 March 2023).

Department for Education (DfE) (2019a) *ITT core content framework*. London: DfE.

Department for Education (DfE) (2019b) *The deployment of teaching assistants in schools: Research report.* London: DfE.

Education Endowment Foundation (EEF) (2018) *Guidance report: Making best use of teaching assistants.* London: EEF.

Education Endowment Foundation (EEF) (2021) *Guidance report: Working with parents to support children's learning.* London: EEF.

Education Endowment Foundation (EEF) (2023) *Teaching and learning toolkit.* Available at: https://educationendowmentfoundation.org.uk/education-evidence/teaching-learning-toolkit (accessed 11 April 2023).

Kirschner, P., Sweller, J. and Clark, R. (2006) 'Why minimal guidance during instruction does not work: an analysis of the failure of constructivist, discovery, problem-based, experiential, and inquiry-based teaching', *Educational Psychologist*, 41(2), 75–86.

Molina, S. (2013) 'Family, school, community engagement, and partnerships: an area of continued inquiry and growth', *Teaching Education*, 24(2), 235–238.

Myatt, M. (2016) *Hopeful schools: Building humane communities.* Worthing: Mary Myatt Learning Ltd.

Sibieta, L. (2016) *Nuffield early language intervention: Evaluation report and executive summary.* London: Education Endowment Foundation.

Warwick, J. and Wolpert, M.A. (2018) 'Making the most of your placements', in T. Cremin and C. Burnett (eds.), *Learning to teach in the primary school* (4th edn). Abingdon, UK: Routledge, pp. 32–45.

Webster, R., Russell, A. and Blatchford, P. (2015) *Maximising the impact of teaching assistants: Guidance for school leaders and teachers* (2nd edn). Abingdon, UK: Routledge.

16
RESILIENCE, GRIT AND BRAVERY

Ben Screech

Chapter Objectives

- To define and explore the concepts of resilience, grit and bravery.
- To consider the importance of these concepts in your professional life as a teacher.
- To reflect on typical challenges that you may face in the classroom and how these can be mitigated by adopting the traits of resilience, grit and bravery.
- To consider wider questions about teacher wellbeing and its relationship to resilience.

In this chapter, we examine the increasingly important issues of resilience, grit and bravery as they relate to classroom teaching. There can be little doubt in any new teacher's mind that teaching is a profession replete with challenges. These may relate to aspects of the role as diverse as workload expectations, managing challenging behaviour, juggling multiple responsibilities and negotiating relationships with staff, pupils or parents, and may seem insurmountable at times. However, the purpose of this chapter is to introduce a range of attitudes and approaches you may find beneficial in helping to prepare for and manage such issues. The intention, therefore, is to support you in navigating the inevitable 'rough patches' in your career and ultimately to ensure enjoyment, success and longevity as a classroom teacher.

The Challenges of Teaching

The Department for Education's (DfE) research into the difficulties of retaining new teachers in England indicates that approximately 20% leave the profession within their first two years of teaching, and 33% within their first five years (DfE, 2019b). Typical reasons given for this retention problem include unsustainable workloads, negative school cultures and challenging behaviour (DfE, 2019b). Bibby (2010: 2) believes that teaching is an occupation character-ised by 'almost impossible' levels of challenge, which she relates to the 'fact that so much of what happens in the classroom is beyond our control'. Teachers and pupils are human beings, and therefore behave in ways that are liable to be multifaceted, contradictory and inconsist-ent. A classroom dynamic is predicated on its inherent unpredictability: its 'aliveness' from moment to moment. This is part of what makes teaching a vibrant and exciting job, but simultaneously, accounts for its many challenges.

Education itself is always in flux. Governments come and go, and new agendas and priorities are continually ushered in. New entrants to a career in education need to develop the kinds of skills, traits, values and behaviours necessary to help them not merely *cope* but actually *thrive* in a work environment dominated by such frequently shifting political currents and periods of significant change. They need to be able to adapt to the vagaries (and, at times, absurdities) of everyday life in education with flexibility, creativity and humour. As the actor Stephen Fry once put it in an address he gave at a teaching awards ceremony, 'new teachers are brave souls' (quoted in Ellsmore, 2005: 50).

Key Concepts and Definitions

Resilience, grit and bravery are three interrelated concepts concerned with the ability of individuals to overcome and learn from adverse experiences. Resilience is defined by one's ability to bounce back from difficulties and setbacks. Grit relates to the skills of tenacity and resolve that we gain from enduring such hardships and assimilating them meaningfully into our broader life experience. Bravery is a capacity we need to cultivate to engage with such experiences in the first place. Indeed, it is only through having the courage to face challeng-ing experiences with a positive and curious mindset that we can take on board the potential lessons they contain.

A concept that may be helpful in illustrating such beliefs and values is *stoicism*. This has, I would suggest, a particular application to teaching and learning, and as Sharpes (2013: 88) asserts, 'educators who accept the inculcation of values ... will want to know something of this philosophy'. Ancient Greek and Roman stoic philosophers, such as Marcus Aurelius, Sen-eca and Epictetus, believed that life's most profound moments of revelation and discovery happened in the midst of challenges that lay outside an individual's capacity for influence and control. Crucially, they recognised that, while we have little direct control over many of the events we are faced with on our journey through life, we are able to impact, at least to some degree, how we *think* about and respond to them. 'It is not events that disturb people, it is their judgements concerning them' (Epictetus and Dobbin, 2008: 85). For stoics, the true 'test' of an individual related to the level of adversity they could withstand, as well as their ability to unerringly (or 'stoically') employ life's previous learning in their ongoing progress through it. As we will see, part of taking a stoical approach to a career in teaching involves having an implicit understanding that dealing with adversity is 'part of the package'. Success in the role necessarily involves the ability to be humble, to view oneself as a learner as well as a teacher, and to understand that the most significant periods of struggle often contain the most crucial lessons.

Key Research on Teacher Resilience

There is an increasing body of research literature centring on teacher resilience that highlights various factors that can positively affect it. Barth (2006: 9), for example, considers the importance of new teachers having the opportunity to develop relationships that are 'trusting, generous, helpful and cooperative'. His points are suggestive of the importance of the role of others and relationships in the development of resilience, something we consider in more depth later in this chapter. Peters and Pearce (2012: 260) also highlight the cruciality of 'collaborative processes' in this regard, and proceed to consider 'the importance of building self-esteem while also developing professional knowledge and skills' in the process of building resilience. Presently, we will see how confidence and self-esteem (traits that arguably stem from resilience) arise from an early career teacher's increased ability to negotiate the demands of professionalism and its associated behaviours.

'Struggles' in education, as Johnson et al. (2015: 122) suggest, 'are often internalised and set the care of the self against duty to others'. Teaching is a caring profession and the sense of 'duty' of many teachers, while being extremely important, can, as Johnson et al. highlight, result in concerning levels of attrition when the problems they face are hidden through misguided selflessness. Contrary to this approach, learning to be resilient involves prioritising self-care through becoming comfortable to share 'struggles' as they arise, while also adopting the kinds of other key approaches to mitigating stress and anxiety, such as eating properly, sleeping well, taking time for oneself, friends and family, in addition to other factors explored later in this chapter.

Despite the ongoing contention surrounding the efficacy of its application in classroom settings (e.g., see Sisk et al., 2018), the notion of 'mindset' is a recurring theme in the literature on resilience (Dweck, 2006; Roger and Petrie, 2016; Price, 2018). I believe it has some merit in considering how trainee teachers can most effectively approach growth in their practice. 'Mindset' refers to the kinds of values and beliefs we adopt over the course of our lives that shape how we perceive, react to and comprehend the world. Luckily, our perception of things and subjectivities in general are flexible and it is entirely possible, although not necessarily easy, to change what Roger and Petrie (2016: 167) view as 'habitual attitudes and behaviour'. In this way, success in teaching becomes contingent on the way we view ourselves as learners. To become capable of resilience, grit and bravery in learning, and in life more generally, the adoption of a mindset that rejects inertia and prioritises continual movement and change is needed.

Critical Task 16.1

The Value of Developing Resilience

If we are to identify what effective practice 'looks like' in relation to resilience, we have to initially consider what we are developing this skill for. For example, considering the startling statistics regarding teacher retention discussed previously, you may simply wish to ensure your classroom career is sustainable for the 'long haul' and understand that resilience will therefore play an important role in securing this. Alternatively, perhaps you feel that resilience will relate to something specific that you find challenging in your developing teaching practice, such as behaviour management. Clearly, there are various reasons why a skill like resilience may be an asset to you as a teacher: there may, in fact, be as many reasons as there are teachers!

So, pause now to critically reflect on the question:

- What will developing greater capabilities of resilience, grit and bravery help *me* with in *my* teaching career?

Learning From, and With, Others

Carden and Bower (2018: 15) reject the idea that teachers are wholly independent entities once the classroom door shuts. Instead, they argue that, 'learning to teach … involves engaging with differing perspectives, voices and expertise'. I would suggest that this statement also represents a broader comment on the nature of professionalism and, in turn, resilience.

If we accept Carden and Bower's point that teachers do not work alone, then their success in the classroom and ability to develop skills such as resilience, grit and bravery depend on the way in which they navigate these crucial relationships. Notably too, while such relationships may, in terms of learning from the experiences of others, involve looking outwards, another key relationship that needs to be fostered in this regard is with oneself.

Case Study 16.1

The Value of a Support Network

Elle, a recently qualified teacher, describes some of the challenges she encountered in her first term in the teaching profession and how she learned to manage these:

> My first term as a teacher was really tough. At first, I thought I was doing OK, but then things started to build up and get a lot harder and I ended up really struggling to get everything done. I have always been a strong student, an independent person and a bit

of a perfectionist, so constantly feeling on the back foot was really hard for me. Honestly, I felt like quitting at one point and it took a lot of resilience to get me back on track. What helped above everything else was having a strong network of people around me to act as a sounding board when I needed it.

I lived in a house with other new teachers and really valued the way everyone mucked in when others inevitably faced similar challenges to me as the year went on. At one point, I remember everyone stayed up late, helping me create resources for a lesson the next day when I was running out of time. They also taught me the importance of compartmentalising my time more effectively and achieving a better work–life balance, by ensuring I adopted a 'done, not perfect' approach, had routine breaks from work and occasional weekends away to recharge. I would have really struggled to tackle the demands of my first year of teaching if I'd had to do it solo, so I felt very lucky to be surrounded by others who could help me to learn some of these useful lessons. Crucially, they taught me that I was not alone in this, and they were learning too.

For Elle, developing an increasing degree of resilience was initially associated with learning to mentally move away from an image of herself as an independent 'perfectionist'. Perfectionism is an enemy to resilience. This is because resilience relies on an individual's ability to embark upon challenges while accepting that things may not necessarily go to plan. Crucially, too, it involves the potential for failure. This can be a genuine concern for new teachers, many of whom, like Elle, are likely to have been academically successful in order to be awarded places on Initial Teacher Education (ITE) courses. Some may believe that this previous success will translate into success in the classroom. Therefore, to step outside their comfort zones in this way can be genuinely concerning at first, especially when it becomes clear, due to the fast-paced and, at times, overwhelming nature of the classroom, that maintaining the levels of performance demanded by a perfectionist mindset is exhausting. It can even 'result in burnout and attrition from the profession' (Glazzard and Stones, 2020: 34).

When encountering challenging situations, it can be natural to react to our present difficulty in one of a variety of ways. We might hope for a quick reprieve from whatever has derailed us, and the restoration of the status quo. Alternatively, perhaps, like Elle, we are tempted to abandon ship entirely: quitting rather than face whatever uphill struggle we have been confronted with. However, these tactics fail to pay off when we consider one of the key aspects of becoming a resilient teacher: we only experience growth when we linger for increasing lengths of time outside our comfort zone. 'A ship', as Albert Einstein famously put it, 'is always safe at the shore, but that is not what it is built for' (quoted in Wright, 2017: 93). Ships are tested by being buffeted by the ocean's waves, while teachers are tested by the daily ebb and flow of school life.

In addition to re-evaluating perfectionism, we will also be more resilient against whatever our teaching career throws at us if we are not tempted to 'go it alone', and instead understand the value of being part of a 'network' of fellow professionals. Elle's comments echo research carried out by Glazzard and Coverdale (2018: 90–93), in which they identify the importance of 'networks of support' for new teachers, comprising individuals who are able to provide both 'formal and informal' support, such as mentors, peers, other teachers, teaching assistants and parents. The authors identify this as one of a number of key factors that have the potential to influence new teachers' likelihood of 'survival' in the profession. This argument is extended by Paterson and Kelleher (2005: 144–145) in their conception of 'team resilience'. They consider how the 'collective energy' that is present when teachers 'turn to each other for support' manifests itself in a form of 'team resilience' in which team members ultimately become bestowed with increasing levels of 'credibility' and 'expertise'; this is about more than simply 'survival', as it is also related to one's ability to actively develop as a professional.

Resilience, Grit and Bravery in Situations of Conflict

We have seen how teaching is a profession characterised by relationships: this is part of what makes it an exciting and rewarding career choice. As a teacher, your role involves negotiating relationships with, for example, pupils, parents and colleagues. Although most of the time these are positive, occasionally, like all human relationships, they may become tested or frayed and you may find yourself having to engage with disagreement or conflict. Joliffe and Waugh (2017: 218) consider what they term the 'shock at the chalk face', which is inherent for many new teachers as they experience their first encounters with classroom conflicts that must be dealt with swiftly, professionally, and often without the luxury of time for reflection on possible courses of action. They consider how 'conflict, whether it is encountered in the playground or the staffroom' is an inevitable part of the 'unexpected and unpredictable nature' of school life: the inevitable collateral of 'each day being different from the one before' (Joliffe and Waugh, 2017: 218). It is here that resilience, and particularly its subskills of grit and bravery, have an important application.

Critical Task 16.2

Managing a Difficult Encounter with a Parent

In rather an assertive and accusatory fashion, a parent states their belief that their child is not receiving provision in your class that is as precisely tailored to their specific skills, interests and abilities as they would ideally like. The parent downplays your already significant levels of intervention and personalised provision that you and your teaching assistant are providing for their child, and continually pushes for far more than is realistically achievable in a classroom containing 29 other children. From your perspective, it feels like nothing you do is good enough, and no matter how hard you try, you struggle to satisfy the parent's ever-increasing expectations. In fact, their engagement with and demands of you seem wholly outside reasonable expectations, and you feel that your ability to work with them effectively is being compromised.

Pause now to critically reflect on these questions:

- What would I do in this situation?
- How would I draw on my skills of resilience, grit and bravery in de-escalating the disagreement, while respectfully maintaining my own boundaries and perspective on the situation?

The most positive response to the situation in Critical Task 16.2 would likely employ a blend of resilience, grit and bravery in the assessment and negotiation of this kind of day-to-day conflict that, for better or worse, occasionally arises in school life. Over time, you will be exposed to similar situations which will allow you to reflect on different scenarios in a measured way, before deciding on an action. You will hopefully become increasingly comfortable asking for support if you feel you need it, from a mentor or more experienced colleague, who will be able to model the most appropriate interaction merited by the situation.

Mansfield (2020: 110) identifies some key factors involved in working resiliently with others that may be useful in managing situations of potential conflict: 'Understand and identify emotions in others and demonstrate empathy; assertively communicate one's thoughts and emotions; use effective communication tools such as reflective listening'. She highlights three key skills here that are crucial tools in managing conflict in a resilient and professional manner: 'empathy', 'assertiveness' and 'communication'. Empathy and being able to see situations from another's point of view is an important aspect of resilience because it demonstrates a key stoical mindset: 'I do not hold all the answers and I have much to learn from different perspectives'. Assertiveness equates with grit and bravery in demonstrating self-possession, determination and confidence in one's values and objectives in a given situation. Communication, as we have seen, is of paramount importance in navigating any situation that requires resilience. However, I would also suggest a fourth term may be useful to consider here: compromise. Finding effective ways through challenging situations involving others almost always involves trying to find a mutually acceptable way to tackle the situation. In the situation outlined in Critical Task 16.2, this might involve, for example, demonstrating that you have taken the parent's concerns into account and are listening to them, while simultaneously, clearly communicating your own perspective on the situation and what is realistically achievable from your angle. Setting aside a weekly 'touch base' session where they can liaise with you about their child's progress can be a useful way of demonstrating that you are listening to the parent's concerns and taking them seriously, while signalling the expectation that such discussions do not extend beyond this agreed slot.

Neenan (2017: 55) considers the dangers of what he terms 'people-pleasing behaviour', and we might also consider the problems this poses to cultivating resilience, grit and bravery. New teachers have the potential to fall into 'people-pleasing', which has similar characteristics to perfectionism and is just as problematic from the perspective of resilience. When we have people-pleasing as our aim, we lose a crucial sense of our own values and feelings about a situation and are more likely to gravitate towards an uncomfortable conciliation for the purposes of keeping the peace, rather than a more wholehearted compromise. Becoming resilient is, in part, about learning to 'crystallize your thinking' in order to 'persevere with a process of change to achieve your goals' (Neenan, 2017: 55). With these thoughts in mind, I suggest that asking yourself the following questions may be helpful in considering how to keep challenging situations in perspective in a manner suggestive of a resilient mindset:

- **Am I engaging with this situation as a pragmatist or a perfectionist?** As we know from Elle's case study, as well as our discussion about people-pleasing, a mindset of pragmatism over perfectionism will pay greater dividends in the long run.
- **How long will this matter for?** Will it matter in a week, a month, a year? Will it feature prominently in my career 'in the round'? This question helps you to gain perspective on a situation by inviting you to 'zoom out' and see it as one of many inevitable 'blips' in the narrative of your classroom life that are ultimately of little consequence. It can help to lower the stakes in situations of conflict and decrease feelings of anxiety during difficult situations and phases in the life-cycle of your career.
- **What would I advise another teacher to do if they were encountering a similarly adverse situation?** This is a useful question because often the advice and counsel we give to others can be more measured and less likely to fall into the trap of unhelpful self-criticism; from an (even artificially) distanced perspective, we can glean potentially useful wisdom on a situation and perceive things more clearly.

▬ Observation Guide 16.1 ▬

Managing Conflict or Tension

The *ITT Core Content Framework (CCF)* states that student teachers should 'learn how to … build effective working relationships' (DfE, 2019a: 29).

Next time you are in school, spend some time observing how an experienced teacher manages a situation of disagreement or conflict with someone with whom they have a key professional relationship (e.g., a parent, pupil or peer). What aspects of resilience, grit and bravery can you identify in their handling of the situation?

Can you elicit any 'food for thought' in this regard, in terms of how you might manage a similar scenario in your own practice? Consider, for example, how the teacher uses their voice, the specific phrasing they employ and whether they seek any support from others in managing the situation.

Resilience and Wellbeing

In his study of *Teacher resilience*, Thom (2020: 20) identifies that, 'an all-consuming focus on one thing can make us vulnerable to mental health problems. Teachers, I have found, often face this issue.' Any discussion of resilience in relation to education perhaps inevitably needs to engage with wider considerations of wellbeing and mental health, particularly if we are to consider the ways in which we tackle the attrition rates in the teaching profession and promote strategies for new teachers' 'survivability' in their role. Resilience, as we have seen, is inextricably associated with one's ability to cope with challenging new situations, to seek advice, reframe points of view and generally find positive new ways to develop and grow into the role.

Case Study 16.2

Seeking Support and Prioritising Wellbeing

In this case study, Aaliyah comments on the wellbeing challenges she faced as an early career teacher and how tackling these head-on ultimately resulted in her developing a more pragmatic, resilient attitude to her work, as well as how her mindset shift ultimately had a positive impact on her teaching practice itself. As you are reading, consider how Aaliyah's story correlates with your own experiences of managing stress and wellbeing during your teacher training.

> Early on in my first year of teaching, I experienced a bad bout of insomnia linked to the stress of school. If you don't get enough sleep, you feel terrible and the ability to teach well is clearly linked to your overall wellbeing. It reached a point where I decided enough was enough and I decided to try counselling. I'm quite a scientific person, and I find it annoying sometimes when you're told 'you need to prioritise self-care', but, to be fair, it's true. You can't be a good teacher unless you consider yourself, your wider happiness and ability to function.
>
> Perhaps the most important lesson I learned at counselling was the need to let go of my need for control and to be proactive in rationally disputing my worries as they arose. I learnt some useful mindfulness strategies and also some different perspectives that helped me to understand that you can't control things by worrying about them. I learnt to be kinder to myself, to reframe how I saw myself as a teacher and a professional, and to remember that a teacher's job is such that it can never be truly 'done'. I think there's a misconception when you're new to this, that to be a good teacher, you just continue working and working, and then you work some more. What counselling taught me was the need to dismantle these misconceptions and draw a line under things – to basically say, that's enough for today and what I've managed to get done will be good enough.
>
> I learned to relax and go with the flow a lot more, and to react to what my pupils presented in the moment, rather than sticking to an overly ambitious plan written at

Continued

midnight the night before. These factors ultimately made for much higher quality, responsive and organic-feeling teaching, in which my pupils seemed to be far more engaged. Even more important than this, I became less anxious, started sleeping well again, and am still going strong in my role and enjoying it more and more each day!

Aaliyah's candid account of the challenges she faced early on in her teaching career has much to teach us about the value of recognising when teaching's toll is becoming overwhelming and the kinds of steps you can take to achieve a greater state of equilibrium over both your professional and personal life. As Aaliyah contends, being an effective teacher is reliant on one's ability to maintain a good level of mental health and overall wellbeing. She also notes how a resilient approach to this does not involve working endlessly to the extent that the quality of both your work and mental health suffer. Rather, considering ways to proactively manage workload and to simply know when to stop are key. An important aspect of her testimony relates to how her teaching and, ultimately, pupil outcomes benefitted from her higher levels of wellbeing. This aligns with Mansfield's (2020: 270) assertion that 'resilience supports teacher wellbeing which is associated with teacher effectiveness via students' increased wellbeing'. Teacher resilience and wellbeing are crucial, not only for the practitioner, but also for the young people for whom they are responsible.

The following are some distilled points stemming from Aaliyah's case study that comprise key food-for-thought in terms of ensuring longevity in your teaching career through managing its inevitable mental health and wellbeing challenges:

- **Be kind to yourself**: Prioritise your self-care and wellbeing above everything else.
- **Treat stress and anxiety seriously**: Do not hesitate to speak to a counsellor or similar professional if you feel your teaching role is adversely impacting your mental health.
- **Set realistic limits** to the amount of time you intend to devote to work each day.
- **Don't overplan**: Often, less is more. Adopt a policy of 'good enough'.
- **Be mindful**: Consider using mindfulness approaches to gain perspective on day-to-day classroom challenges.
- **Relax and enjoy your role**: Remember that your ability to relax and enjoy your role will impact on the kind of learning environment you are able to provide for your pupils. Happy, resilient teachers are arguably more likely to produce happy, resilient pupils.

— **Question Guide 16.1** —

Rising to Challenges

The *CCF* states that student teachers should:

> Learn how to … manage workload and wellbeing by … discussing and analysing with
> expert colleagues the importance of the right to support [and] protecting time for rest

and recovery and being aware of the sources of support available to support good mental wellbeing. (DfE, 2019a: 30–31)

Ask your teacher-mentor or another school colleague about times in their early career when they faced work-related wellbeing challenges. Use these questions to guide your discussion:

- What challenges did you face?
- How did you remain resilient in the face of these challenges?
- What strategies/approaches did you use to cope and deal with these challenges?
- Did you seek any support from others?

Consider what you can learn from others' experiences in this regard and how their accounts may influence the way you contend with similar issues as they arise in your own life in school. You can also ask about how they manage workload and wellbeing now:

- How do you maintain a healthy work–life balance while managing your workload as an experienced teacher?
- Do you find it easier to handle challenging situations now that you have more experience?
- Are there times when you still seek support from others?

Chapter Summary

This chapter has considered the interrelated traits of resilience, grit and bravery in terms of their application by new teachers in school settings. We have explored a range of illustrative case studies, reflections and examples that demonstrate the benefits of adopting a resilient mindset in approaching classroom teaching and its associated challenges. We have also seen how and when our faculties of resilience may be tested and how we can cope with issues ranging from high workload, difficult relationships and wellbeing issues. Teachers, no matter at what stage of their career, need to have grit and bravery and be willing to work extremely hard to make their career a success. Resilience is crucial in this regard, but, as this chapter has shown, it is a skill that needs to be continually cultivated and worked on. Those who are successful in this regard will be able to sustain a fantastically inspiring and exciting career in the long term. It is not easy, but by being humble, having the confidence to ask for help, being continually willing to extend yourself and step out of your comfort zone and, perhaps most importantly, not being deterred by failure, you have the ability to positively affect the lives of innumerable young people. In few other careers can the effort be said to be so worthy of the reward.

Further Reading

Bethune, A. and Kell, E. (2020) *Teacher wellbeing and self-care*. London: Sage.
This text offers practical, effective strategies to prioritise wellbeing and self-care to make a career in teaching as sustainable as possible.

Jennings, P. (2015) *Mindfulness for teachers: Simple skills for peace and productivity in the classroom*. London and New York: W.W. Norton.

This book introduces mindfulness strategies that can contribute to a greater sense of calm and resourcefulness for practitioners.

Kell, E. (2018) *How to survive in teaching without imploding, exploding or walking away*. London: Bloomsbury.

Emma Kell's book provided practical advice for stoically pursuing teaching's challenges with a view to staying the course and making it past the initial five years.

References

Barth, R.S. (2006) 'Improving relations within the schoolhouse', *Educational Leadership: Improving Professional Practice*, 63(6). Also available through the Association for Supervision and Curriculum Development at: www.ascd.org/el/articles/improving-relationships-within-the-schoolhouse (accessed 5 June 2022).

Bibby, T. (2010) *Education – an 'impossible profession'? Psychoanalytic explorations of learning and classrooms*. Abingdon, UK: Routledge.

Carden, C. and Bower, V. (2018) 'What is teaching?', in C. Carden (ed.), *Primary teaching: Learning and teaching in primary schools today*. London: Learning Matters/Sage, pp. 3–22.

Department for Education (DfE) (2019a) *ITT core content framework*. London: DfE.

Department for Education (2019b) *Teacher recruitment and retention strategy*. London: DfE. Available at: https://assets.publishing.service.gov.uk/government/uploads/system/uploads/attachment_data/file/786856/DFE_Teacher_Retention_Strategy_Report.pdf (accessed 9 Jan 2022).

Dweck, C. (2006) *Mindset: The new psychology of success*. London: Random House.

Ellsmore, S. (2005) *Carry on, teachers! Representations of the teaching profession in screen culture*. Stoke-on-Trent: Trentham Books.

Epictetus and Dobbin, R. (2008) *Discourses and selected writings*. London: Penguin.

Glazzard, J. and Coverdale, L. (2018) '"It feels like its sink or swim": newly qualified teachers' experiences of their induction year', *International Journal of Learning, Teaching and Educational Research*, 17(11), 89–101.

Glazzard, J. and Stones, S. (2020) *Staying mentally healthy during your teaching career*. St Albans: Critical Publishing.

Johnson, B., Down, B., Le Cornu, R., Peters, J., Sullivan, A., Pearce, J. and Hunter, J. (2015) *Promoting early career teacher resilience: A socio-cultural and critical guide to action*. London: Routledge.

Joliffe, W. and Waugh, D. (2017) *NQT: The beginning teacher's guide to outstanding practice*. London: Sage.

Mansfield, C. (2020) *Cultivating teacher resilience: International approaches, applications, and impact*. New York and London: Springer.

Neenan, M. (2017) *Developing resilience: A cognitive behavioural approach* (2nd edn). Abingdon, UK: Routledge.

Patterson, J. and Kelleher, P. (2005) *Resilient school leaders: Strategies for turning adversity into achievement.* Alexandria, VA: Association for Supervision and Curriculum Development.

Peters, J. and Pearce K. (2012) 'Relationships and early career teacher resilience', *Teachers and Teaching Theory and Practice,* 18(2), 1–14.

Price, I. (2018) *Headstart: Build a resilient mindset.* London: Pearson.

Roger, D. and Petrie, N. (2016) *Work without stress.* London: McGraw-Hill.

Sharpes, D. (2013) *Advanced educational foundations for teachers.* Abingdon, UK: Routledge.

Sisk, V., Burgoyne, A., Sun, J., Butler, J. and Macnamara, B. (2018) 'To what extent and under which circumstances are growth mind-sets important to academic achievement? Two meta-analyses', *Psychological Science,* 29(4), 549–571.

Thom, J. (2020) *Teacher resilience: Managing stress and anxiety to thrive in the classroom.* Woodbridge, UK: John Catt Educational Ltd.

Wright, T. (ed.) (2017) *How to be a brilliant mentor: Developing outstanding teachers.* Abingdon, UK: Routledge.

SECTION 6
PRINCIPLES OF INCLUSION

17
POSITIVE CLASSROOM CULTURES

Emma Howell

Chapter Objectives

- To explore the characteristics of positive classroom cultures.
- To consider barriers and challenges to inclusion.
- To identify practical approaches to developing positive school and classroom cultures.
- To reflect on some specific approaches in relation to children's wellbeing.

In this chapter, we explore what is meant by a 'positive classroom culture' and consider its importance for the individual child as a learner in the primary classroom. We explore why some children find the primary classroom to be a negative environment, focusing particularly on children for whom accessing the curriculum is not easy, and consider approaches to promote inclusive learning cultures for all. We discuss a child-centred approach and address some thorny issues, including anti-bullying and anti-racism, to establish how strong teacher–child and child–child relationships, founded on understanding, can lead to strong emotional wellbeing and positive social interactions. Practical ideas and approaches for the primary classroom teacher are considered throughout to illustrate the pivotal role of the classroom teacher in creating and perpetuating the classroom culture through actions and behaviours that set the classroom climate.

Positive Classroom Cultures: Characteristics and Impacts

Every school is unique and, within minutes of walking into a different school, this unique-ness becomes apparent. It is in characteristics such as the orderliness and appearance of the physical environment, the attitudes and approachability of the staff, the behaviour and work ethic of the children. The culture of a school reflects the values and beliefs of those who work in it. It is established and developed by school leaders, and it is the extent to which members of the school community share and enact these values across all aspects of daily life. These aspects create the climate in a school. Kraft and Falken (2020) note the importance of the social world of the primary school. It is through engaging and interacting in, and seeking to fit into, this social world of a school that teachers and children adapt to and contribute to the school culture. They will modify their behaviour to meet the expectations and the norms of practices in the school, learning the way things are done in the school. The established school culture thus becomes perpetuated and inevitably informs the classroom culture. That is not to say all classrooms in one school will 'feel' the same, however. The climate of each classroom is dependent on the daily actions and behaviours of the class teacher(s) and children, and the level to which they share, enact and perpetuate the wider school culture. The key is to provide positive classroom cultures and climates that enable children to thrive in school and to participate in successful learning.

The Rights of the Child

In 1992, the United Nations Convention for the Rights of the Child came into force in the UK (United Nations, 1989). In its 54 articles, it sets out the political, economic, social and cultural rights that all children are entitled to. Every child has the right to an identity, to express their views, feelings and wishes in all matters, and have these considered and taken seriously. Every child has the right to an education that develops their personality, talents and abilities to the full. While this feels wholly acceptable and fundamental to our long-established principle of education for all in the United Kingdom, Gedge (2016) reminds us that enacting these rights may not be so straightforward. We are all the product of our own experiences and upbringing and are likely to have our own unconscious bias, causing us to be blind to our own privilege and to exclude groups unconsciously. Recognising our own blind spots, taking time to genuinely understand each individual child (their needs, culture, home life, etc.) and then to see the classroom from each child's perspective can be a beneficial starting point.

Inclusive Classroom Cultures

Every child is an individual with their own experiences and background. To create fully inclusive cultures, we must recognise that all children have diverse and individual needs and, as teachers, we should aim to identify and understand these. Inclusive classrooms are spaces that accept and actively include all children. They are based on an underlying positive culture. Such spaces value and celebrate the individual child, their uniqueness and difference, enabling them to be part of the life of the classroom, wider school and society. However, what is intended does not necessarily always match what is received. While the classroom may feel comfortable and safe for the teacher, it is not always the same for the children. A school may fit with parents' desired ethos, outcome or social experience, but it can still be a bewildering, strange and, at worst, negative environment for the child. For some children, daily classroom features, such as noise level, vibrancy, or lack of fixed routine, can feel threatening. For others, a lack of regular success and attention, or perceiving themselves to be unvalued as an individual, can feel negative. As the teacher managing the classroom climate, it is important to be perceptive of each child's response to the environment you create.

Critical Task 17.1

Learning From Your Own Experiences

Think back to your own childhood/teenage school experiences. Identify one classroom environment where you felt safe, which had a positive attitude towards your learning, and where you achieved well. Identify another classroom environment where you felt less secure and motivated, and which led to lower engagement and less learning. For each, write a list of key words to describe the features.

Compare the lists and reflect on what was the same and different. What values was each teacher promoting? Which appealed to you and why? Was your response the same as all the children in the class? Draw some conclusions about what will be important for you to adopt/avoid in your own practice.

Positive Behaviour and Attitudes

The classroom approach to behaviour and attitudes, and its underpinning philosophy, is a determiner of classroom culture and climate. A classroom with a focus on control and authority can become a negative environment, even akin to a battleground, raising children's levels of fear, humiliation and shame. Such approaches can lead to children switching off from learning or responding with negative behaviour and attitudes. Building positive relationships with children and supporting them to learn through respectful interactions with teachers are more likely to lead to positive engagement and attitudes, and subsequently better learning outcomes.

Creating Inclusive Positive Classroom Cultures

Achieving a fully inclusive classroom culture is not easy, as it needs to be readily adaptable and responsive to the needs of the participants. In classroom environments with an emphasis on achievement, success, hard work and application, where all children are taught and learn uniformly, the expectation is that the child will adapt to the needs of the classroom, rather than the other way around. Classroom environments with a child-centred ethos, where the classroom adapts to the needs of the child, require more responsiveness. The teacher becomes the constant problem-solver, identifying barriers, monitoring progress and adjusting teaching to make the learning accessible to all.

School cultures take time to develop and to change. However, the primary teacher is a powerful role model and determiner of children's behaviours and attitudes and can make an immediate difference to the climate of their classroom by applying some key principles. In this section, we explore some values and practical ideas for creating inclusive and positive classrooms.

Respect

Bruce (2010) defines 'emotionally literate' schools as places where children have confidence, independence and are resilient. They are places where individuals respect each other, take pride in achievements, and engage fully in rich and creative learning experiences. All children have the right to a full and decent life with dignity and, as far as possible, independence to play an active part in the community. Simple daily classroom actions can model and promote this respect. Modelling and gaining respect involve taking time to listen to children, to allow them time to share their views and opinions. It means being genuinely courteous and polite in your interactions with others and enabling those in the classroom community to respect themselves and each other. Set the example as an honest, reliable and trustworthy teacher.

Identity

Recognising and valuing the individual identity of each child in your class is fundamental to building good relationships. It comes through getting to know each child, through valuing the child in their own right, and is not based on knowledge of a sibling or other family member. Prioritise learning names when you first meet a class and take time to get to know something about each child's interests and experiences, to enable them to feel that they belong to a class community. Providing spaces for each child and enabling them to have an identity as a member of the class is another way of making every child feel welcome and included. It can be achieved through simple strategies, such as providing a named drawer, coat peg, space to put their belongings (coats, bags, water bottles). Think carefully about how you organise this to make sure it is accessible to all.

Case Study 17.1

Respecting Individuals' Property

Aurelia, an early career teacher, is frustrated that her class is continually being blamed for a messy corridor space outside the classroom. The children's coats are often on the floor, particularly as the double row of coat pegs means some are too high for the children to reach. Her Year 1 children are unable to reach the shelf above the coat pegs designed to store lunch boxes. Aurelia's response is to rethink this organisation so that the environment enables the children's belongings to be stored carefully and respectfully. She creates cupboard space in the classroom that is accessible to the children where lunchboxes are to be stored. A large tub is found for children to store their reading book bags, and is placed just inside the classroom door. It has the added benefit of giving the class teaching assistant easy access to reading diaries to check and call children out of the classroom for one-to-one reading. A letter is sent home to ask parents to ensure PE kits are in a drawstring bag that can be easily hung from pegs, and to make sure that their child's coat has a name label inside. Aurelia then speaks with the school site manager to arrange for the coat pegs to be lowered and spread out further along the corridor. The children create their own labels for their pegs and a cloakroom monitor system is set up to give children responsibility for looking after each other's belongings.

The outcome of Aurelia's thoughtful and practical response is a tidier corridor space and each child's identity, sense of belonging and personal property are respected, valued and cared for.

Safety

Feeling safe is fundamental to children's capacity to learn. Keeping children safe in school is paramount in terms of safeguarding, which we will discuss in Chapter 19, but there are also practical elements of safety to consider in the design of your classroom. How you manage the classroom, both the physical environment and through behaviour management, will determine how safe children feel. As we explored in Chapters 2, 3 and 4, aim to manage behaviour positively, build positive relationships, and speak to children calmly at all times: children feel much safer in a calm, predictable environment, rather than when they are 'on edge' because they are never sure of how the teacher is going to react.

Safety is also about removing the fear of failure, of being able to take risks and having the self-confidence to approach new and unknown learning and tasks. The Building Learning Power initiative talks about learning-friendly classroom cultures, based on the idea that confident children are faster and better learners, concentrating more, thinking harder and finding learning more enjoyable (Building Learning Power, no date). Here, the classroom becomes a space where positive learning behaviours are discussed and promoted, and where inquiring minds, collaboration and readiness for challenge are actively promoted.

Routines

Children often feel more secure when they are in familiar contexts and daily routines can be used purposefully to help establish a feeling of safety and predictability. Bennett (2017) notes that routines create a framework of social norms which reduce uncertainty and anxiety. Routines also reduce information load on children. Visual timetables can help children cope with changes and transitions. While routines are supportive, the daily life of a primary school is often unpredictable and needs to be flexible and open to change. As a teacher, you can be proactive in modelling adaptability to change and in being active in preparing children for change. Having a reassuring and calm leader goes a long way to helping children manage anxieties in unfamiliar situations.

Observation Guide 17.1

Changes in Routines

While routines are supportive, the daily life of a primary school is often unpredictable. When observing routines in school, pay particular attention to how changes in routines are managed.

- Notice how the teacher prepares children for changes in the daily routine. Do they announce this at the start of the day or alert children to changes as the day progresses?
- Notice which children appear to show heightened anxiety or become unsettled when routines change. How does the class teacher respond to their anxiety? Which aspects of the teacher's behaviour help to calm the child?

Critical Task 17.2

Identifying Your Own Classroom Culture

The *ITT Core Content Framework (CCF)* states that 'teachers are key role models, who can influence the attitudes, values and behaviours of their pupils' (DfE, 2019: 9).

Return to your reflection in Critical Task 17.1. Revisit the conclusions you came to and make a list of the five key features of classroom culture that are important to you and that you want to promote to underpin your practice. Rank them in order. Which are most important to you and how will they benefit the children?

Addressing Barriers, Challenges and Dispositions

Every child brings their own unique life experiences, background and predispositions to the primary classroom. Some of these will be conducive to your values-led classroom culture, others will not be so. Equally, you bring to the classroom your own learning and experiences, privilege, mindset and likely conscious or unconscious bias. A barrier to supporting learners' additional needs or disadvantage is the teacher mindset that some children cannot learn (Mulholland, no date). Having confidence to say 'I can teach anyone' is a good start. It is also important to recognise that, while your classroom culture may feel safe and inclusive to you and to many in the class, it may feel alien to others. Taking time to discover and understand each child's response to your classroom culture can help you to identify barriers. A classroom that promotes the value of scholarship and continued learning (for the teacher as well as the children) is likely to be more inclusive. You will need to be responsive to individual needs and rethink your own preconceptions, and really explore how to teach everyone successfully. Having an open mindset, readiness to change and adapt your practice, and to continue to enhance your own learning are important qualities.

Disadvantage

In 2013, Ofsted's evidence report into disadvantage and achievement showed that, of the large minority of children who fail to succeed through the education system, a disproportionate number are from disadvantaged backgrounds. While the measures for this research were fairly narrow (Key Stage 2 SATs data), it does reveal a link between material poverty and low achievement, which is all too often exacerbated by low expectations.

The *CCF* states that: 'the quality of teaching is the single most important in-school factor in improving outcomes for pupils – and it is particularly important for pupils from disadvantaged backgrounds' (DfE, 2019: 3).

Seek to adopt a belief that all children can achieve and focus on developing strategies to remove barriers, rather than accepting that the barrier will lead to lower progress. Promoting high expectations for all children (as explored in Chapter 7), a 'can do' attitude and holding a genuine belief in your ability to raise pupils' and parents' aspirations are starting points for your own positive mindset towards meeting the needs of disadvantaged children.

Coe et al. (2014) tell us that great teaching comes through the quality of interactions between teachers and students, and teacher expectations – the need to create a classroom that is constantly demanding more, but still recognises students' self-worth. It also involves attributing student success to effort rather than ability and valuing resilience to failure, as identified by Dweck (2006), who talks about the power of 'yet', of valuing the ability to try and to keep trying.

Special Educational Needs and Disability (SEND)

Timpson's (2019) review of school exclusion, using data from 2017, showed school exclusion rates for children with SEND accounted for nearly half the total number of school exclusions, which he attributed to a failure to understand and properly identify children's needs and of not using this information to put in place the right support to help these children overcome barriers and engage with the curriculum. However, many learners with SEND are adept at disguising their learning difficulties and have learnt or developed tactics to 'survive' in the classroom. Such devices can be driven by their desire to 'fit in'. Gedge (2016) reminds us that taking time to celebrate and respect difference, to value everything each child brings to the life of the classroom (beyond academic achievement), and to understand each child and their learning needs will help us to create more inclusive environments. This can be achieved through adjustments to the physical space (see Chapter 18 for more information), broadening the means of communication to include pictures and signs, having clear routines and expectations, and being consistent.

Newly Arrived Children and Families

The features of inclusive practice also apply for children with English as an Additional Language (EAL), who will come from diverse backgrounds, ethnicities, cultural practices and religions, and will have their own social and life experiences. Try to become conscious of your own privilege and learn to see your classroom through the eyes and experiences of the children rather than just your own. Diverse and inclusive classrooms benefit all children for life, through the promotion of mutual respect, tolerance and understanding, as well as reducing the fear and misunderstanding of those who are different (Gedge, 2016).

Adaptive teaching approaches for children with EAL were explored in Chapter 7, but if we want children with EAL to thrive in our classrooms, we also need to consider how to make them, and their families, feel welcomed and valued as part of the school community, particularly if they are newly arrived to the country. It is important to remember that children and their families are likely to be diverse in terms of language proficiency, socio-economic background and prior educational experiences. They may have experienced traumatic situations, such as war, before leaving their home country, and we need to be sensitive to that.

The Bell Foundation (no date: no page) suggests that children 'learn best when they feel secure and valued' and that schools need 'a supportive induction process for newly arrived pupils'. It suggests taking a 'PAWS' approach:

- Prepare: Meet with the child and parents to find out about the child and create a pupil profile, provide a tour of the school and give parents the key information they need about the school. Ideally, this process can be supported by someone who speaks the family's first language.
- Alert: Before the child starts school, share the pupil profile with all staff, establish a buddy system, and prepare resources and support for the first few days.
- Welcome: Greet the child, introduce them to their assigned buddies, check they have the essentials (food, drink, know how to access the toilet facilities).
- Support: Within the first few weeks, assess language proficiency, put language and pastoral support in place, and maintain regular contact with parents.

Newly arrived children often arrive partway through the year and you may not have much notice. While this may create some additional work for you, in preparing exercise books, sourcing dual-language resources and so on, please remember that it is much more disruptive and daunting for the child and their family than it is for you: smile and appear positive and welcoming from the outset. Put the time into preparing for their first day, so that they feel like part of the class as quickly as possible. If you are really organised, when creating peg labels, drawer labels, exercise books at the start of the year, you can prepare a few spare ones, ready for this situation.

The Curriculum

The curriculum itself can be a possible tension in an inclusive classroom culture. For example, many schools place a significant emphasis on academic achievement in English and maths, and children who struggle to access learning in these subjects, or those who have a natural affinity for the more creative or physical subjects, may find the curriculum to be not very inclusive or motivating. Seek to understand how the curriculum is being received by the children so that you can tailor your teaching strategies and curriculum approach.

Children's Wellbeing

Classrooms with a positive and supportive culture can also be places that do not shy away from controversial issues. Exploring such issues openly with children can promote tolerance, respect and understanding, and equip children with the skills for living harmoniously and successfully in our diverse society.

Wellbeing

Research shows that children's mental health in the UK has been worsening in recent years (NHS Digital, 2018, cited in Bethune, 2020). This research indicates a link between higher levels of wellbeing and higher academic achievement. Schools and classrooms that focus on high levels of academic achievement can alienate children whose achievement is low and where efforts are not recognised. Resulting disengagement is often accompanied by increased negative behaviour and attitudes, and poorer mental health. Instead, in an inclusive classroom, you should seek to recognise the achievements and efforts of all, and to facilitate children to be active participants in the class community, where both independence and togetherness are valued. There is also a correlation between schools with a narrower curriculum focus and lower mental wellbeing in the children (Berliner, 2011). It is important, therefore, to raise the value of healthy subjects, such as PSHE and PE, to equip children with the skills and knowledge to develop their own mental and physical health.

Protected Characteristics

An inclusive classroom culture should, by its nature, promote equality and diversity. In the UK, it is unlawful to discriminate, either directly or indirectly, against someone with protected characteristics. It is important to become familiar with this legislation and with your own attitudes and stereotyping so that you can ensure you use and promote the language of inclusion and diversity, and design your curriculum and teach accordingly.

Schools are required to advance equality of opportunity and foster good relations between people who share a protected characteristic and people who do not share it. Be careful not to unintentionally alienate children in your classroom through lack of representation in your curriculum and resources. Children will feel they belong to your classroom if they can see that the environment values and reflects their own diversity, and if they are represented in the curriculum and resources you provide. Positive and inclusive classroom culture can also empower children to feel comfortable to talk about issues related to race, gender or other sensitive topics. In such discussions, the language and attitudes of acceptance and respect you model will be key.

Bullying

All state schools are required by law to have a behavioural policy in place that includes measures to prevent all forms of bullying among pupils. Having a clear whole-school policy is important for how you manage bullying in your classroom, as is the culture of your classroom in consistently enacting this policy. The emphasis of DfE (2017) advice is on the prevention of bullying of those with protected characteristics through creating open cultures to talk about and celebrate difference, to promote respect for each other, and to understand how our actions affect others.

Learning how to negotiate conflict and the complexity of awkward relationships with others is a part of growing up, so it is important to educate children about what we mean by the term 'bullying'. The Anti-Bullying Alliance (2023) provide this definition:

> The repetitive, intentional hurting of one person or group by another person or group, where the relationship involves an imbalance of power. Bullying can be physical, verbal or psychological. It can happen face-to-face or online.

Children will sometimes use the word 'bullying' when referring to an isolated incident, even one which was really an accident, but it is important to take all issues seriously, as the emphasis must always be on building positive relationships and prevention of bullying arising from more minor incidents. Knowing your children and having good relationships with them is fundamental to your anti-bullying classroom culture, as is an awareness of vulnerable children or groups. Foster an environment where all children feel safe to report bullying, either as a victim or bystander. Some children may feel more confident to report such issues anonymously, so consider having a box into which children can drop a short note about their concerns. Remember to check the box regularly.

When bullying does occur, it is important to take it seriously. Thoroughly investigate and ensure that appropriate action is taken, working within the school policy. It may include using a sanction to ensure that the perpetrator understands 'that their behaviour is wrong' (DfE, 2017: 13). However, as discussed in Chapter 4, it may be appropriate to use a restorative approach, so that the child who has done the bullying understands not just that their behaviour was 'wrong', but also its impact on other people. Remember that an incident of bullying is not only an issue to be 'sorted out', but also an opportunity to educate all children involved and to promote positive values.

This approach doesn't just apply to the 'perpetrator' of the bullying. It is possible that the 'victim' may benefit from thinking about how they present themselves to the world, how they interact with others and whether they can develop some assertiveness skills to support them in dealing with challenging situations in the future, as identified by Sullivan (2011: 235):

> Bullying is a dynamic rather than static process. Rather than there being bullies, victims and bystanders trapped in their roles ... assertiveness training ... can successfully be used to change the dynamics of the bullying.

Racism

Racist incidents must be taken seriously and responded to effectively, but prevention is always better than cure, so consider proactive ways in which you can create an anti-racist classroom. As the Every Future Foundation (2021) explains, British history has been recorded and told in a particular way for many years, promoting some versions or elements of history and ignoring others. Consider all elements of your classroom and curriculum to promote equality and cultural diversity through consideration of the reading books that are available, the displays in the classroom and lessons that reflect diversity and wide representation, with zero tolerance to racist language or stereotypes.

Class cultures that promote anti-racist education and values help children to understand individual children's rights, to understand the harmful consequences of racism and nurture historical literacy. The Show Racism the Red Card campaign provides many resources to help children consider the complexity of identity and to value the range of ways in which people are similar and different from each other (Show Racism the Red Card Education Hub, no date). These are complex and sometimes challenging issues, so aim to provide a safe space for children to discuss issues openly and honestly, and to learn acceptance and respect for each other.

Question Guide 17.1

Pre-empting and Responding to Bullying

The *CCF* states that student teachers should 'learn how to … respond quickly to any behaviour or bullying that threatens emotional safety' (DfE, 2019: 26).

Talk to your teacher about how the classroom culture has been designed to promote anti-bullying. Remember that this is a sensitive issue, so frame your questions professionally and positively:

- How is the culture of anti-bullying promoted in the classroom, and how are parents involved/ informed?
- How are children involved in promoting the anti-bullying culture?
- How do you ensure children feel safe to raise bullying concerns?
- What support is provided to the victim and to the perpetrator? Seek some examples here to inform your practice.

Children as Active Participants in Positive Classroom Cultures

A class culture is perpetuated through daily communication, both verbal and non-verbal, so pay attention to the language that is modelled to the children. Aim to use language that does not stigmatise or humiliate children when things do not go well or when mistakes are made. When children make poor behaviour choices, use language that addresses the behaviour rather than labelling the child. Aim to encourage and motivate each child with the use of authentic and meaningful praise. Try not to let your voice dominate the classroom: allow children time to talk and listen to them, so that they feel that their opinions are valued and that they have a say in building the classroom culture. Children will learn from you about how to communicate in calm, respectful and positive ways.

Children will gain a sense of belonging and are more likely to invest in a classroom culture if they have been involved in its development, rather than having it thrust upon them. A classroom needs to meet the needs of the people in it. Consider asking children about their values and reach joint agreement about what you will all strive for in the class. It will be important to adopt and model these values yourself, and use them to determine your teaching approach, your expectations and your interactions. Be prepared to be humble, to apologise when you get things wrong, and to model how to repair relationships when things become fraught. This may be some of the most powerful teaching you do.

Chapter Summary

In this chapter, we have considered classroom cultures as inclusive and positive environments for learners. They promote understanding and respect for the individual, and recognise and celebrate individualism and difference. The golden thread of this chapter has been relationships: how they enable us as teachers to better understand the children we work with, and for children to better understand each other. In promoting children's wellbeing, teachers should aim to develop classroom cultures that enable children to feel safe, to achieve and to contribute to the sense of belonging of others.

Further Reading

Bethune, A. (2020) 'Promoting positive mental health and wellbeing in primary schools', *Impact: Learning, Leadership and Teacher Expertise*, 9. Available at: https://my.chartered. college/impact_article/promoting-positive-mental-health-and-wellbeing-in-primary-schools/ (accessed 10 April 2023).

This article provides some insight into the link between children's wellbeing and learning, and gives a useful overview of some of the ways to promote good mental health in the children in your classroom.

Moffat, A. (2017) *No outsiders in our school: Teaching the Equality Act in primary schools*. Abingdon, UK: Routledge.

This book provides practical advice and case studies for schools to promote equality and acceptance for all.

United Nations (1989) *Convention on the Rights of the Child*. New York: United Nations. Available at: www.unicef.org/child-rights-convention/convention-text-childrens-version (accessed 30 March 2023).

This is a 'must read' for anyone working with children.

References

Anti-Bullying Alliance (2023) *Anti-Bullying Alliance* [Website]. Available at: https://anti-bullyingalliance.org.uk (accessed 10 April 2023).

Bennett, T. (2017) *Creating a culture: How school leaders can optimise behaviour*. London: Department for Education.

Berliner, D. (2011) 'Rational responses to high stakes testing: the case of curriculum narrowing and the harm that follows', *Cambridge Journal of Education*, 41(3), 287–302.

Bethune, A. (2020) 'Promoting positive mental health and wellbeing in primary schools', *Impact: Learning, Leadership and Teacher Expertise*, 9. Available at: https://my.chartered. college/impact_article/promoting-positive-mental-health-and-wellbeing-in-primary-schools/ (accessed 10 April 2023).

Bruce, C. (2010) *Emotional literacy in the early years*. London: Sage.

Building Learning Power (no date) *Building Learning Power* [Website]. Available at: www. buildinglearningpower.com/ (accessed 23 November 2022).

Coe, R., Aloisi, C., Higgins, S. and Major, L.E. (2014) *What makes great teaching? Review of the underpinning research*. London: Sutton Trust.

Department for Education (DfE) (2017) *Preventing and tackling bullying: Advice for headteachers, staff and governing bodies.* London: DfE. Available at: https://assets.publishing.service.gov.uk/government/uploads/system/uploads/attachment_data/file/1069688/Preventing_and_tackling_bullying_advice.pdf (accessed 10 April 2023).

Department for Education (DfE) (2019) *ITT core content framework.* London: DfE.

Dweck, C.S. (2006) *Mindset: The new psychology of success.* New York: Random House.

Every Future Foundation (2021) *Every Future Foundation* [Website]. Available at: https://everyfuturefoundation.co.uk/anti-racism-school-programmes/ (accessed 11 April 2023).

Gedge, N. (2016) *Inclusion for primary school teachers.* London: Bloomsbury.

Kraft, M.A. and Falken, G.T. (2020) *Why school climate matters for teachers and students.* Alexandria, VA: National Association of State Boards of Education.

Mulholland, M. (no date) 'SEND and the art of detection: an evidence-based approach to supporting learners', *Early Career Hub.* Chartered College of Teaching. Available at: https://my.chartered.college/early-career-hub/send-and-the-art-of-detection-an-evidence-based-approach-to-supporting-learners/ (accessed 10 April 2023).

Ofsted (2013) *Unseen children: Access and achievement 20 years on.* London: Ofsted. Available at: https://assets.publishing.service.gov.uk/government/uploads/system/uploads/attachment_data/file/379157/Unseen_20children_20-_20access_20and_20achievement_2020_20years_20on.pdf (accessed 23 November 2022).

Show Racism the Red Card Education Hub (no date) *Show Racism the Red Card Education Hub* [Website]. Available at: https://theredcardhub.org (accessed 10 April 2023).

Sullivan, K. (2011) *The anti-bullying handbook* (2nd edn). London: Sage.

The Bell Foundation (no date) *New arrivals.* Cambridge: The Bell Foundation. Available at: www.bell-foundation.org.uk/eal-programme/guidance/diversity-of-learners-who-use-english-as-an-additional-language/new-arrivals/ (accessed 21 March 2023).

Timpson, E. (2019) *Timpson review of school exclusion.* London: HMSO/Department for Education. Available at: https://assets.publishing.service.gov.uk/government/uploads/system/uploads/attachment_data/file/807862/Timpson_review.pdf (accessed 10 April 2023).

United Nations (1989) *Convention on the Rights of the Child.* New York: United Nations. Available at: www.unicef.org/child-rights-convention/convention-text-childrens-version (accessed 30 March 2023).

18
SPECIAL EDUCATIONAL NEEDS AND DISABILITY

Lynda Kay and Tristan Middleton

Chapter Objectives

- To explore the importance of inclusive values to underpin positive practice for learners with Special Educational Needs and Disability (SEND).
- To consider the implications of key legislation in relation to SEND.
- To explore how teachers can meet the individual and diverse needs of pupils with SEND.
- To understand the role of the Special Educational Needs Co-ordinator (SENCo).

The *ITT Core Content Framework (CCF)* (Department for Education (DfE), 2019) sets out the principle that quality-first teaching is a vital factor in improving outcomes for all pupils. In this chapter, we consider how our values and the legislative framework for special educational needs and disability (SEND) shape everyday inclusive classroom practice. We explore the importance of working effectively with others, including the Special Educational Needs Co-ordinator (SENCo), to develop your inclusive practice.

Inclusive Values: A Starting Point for Effective SEND Practice

Effective practice in providing for the needs of learners with SEND needs to start from a position of inclusive values. In Figure 18.1, we have developed a framework through which you can understand the key dimensions of inclusion and the values that underpin all aspects.

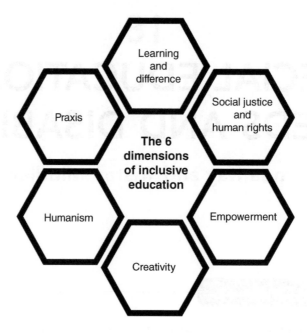

Figure 18.1   The six dimensions of inclusive practice (adapted from Middleton and Kay, 2020: 68)

Copyright (2020) From *Using an inclusive approach to reduce school exclusion: A practitioner's guide* by Middleton & Kay. Reproduced by permission of Taylor and Francis Group, LLC, a division of Informa plc.

The framework in Figure 18.1 starts from the principle that all children have the right to education, and it is our role as teachers to contribute to developing a just world where all can access this right. To enable access for each of our learners, we need to understand their needs, which can only be fully achieved if we empower learners to have their say in their learning and to be part of the process in planning for the learning opportunities they experience. It is also important to value difference in and between learners and to recognise that diversity can be a learning opportunity for all. Your approach to teaching all children will be underpinned by your values.

Critical Task 18.1

Inclusive Education and Diversity

What diversity will learners with SEND bring to the classroom and how can you value all learners?

Think about the spectrum of needs you may have experienced or read about, as well as your own needs, and how this influences your perspective.

Understanding Legislation

The *CCF* states that you should learn 'how to use the *SEND Code of Practice*' (DfE, 2019: 20), published by the Department for Education and Department of Health (2015). In this section, we aim to help you to understand this guidance document and the two key pieces of legislation which sit behind it.

The Equality Act 2010

The Equality Act 2010 (UK Government, 2010) identifies nine protected characteristics: age, disability, gender reassignment, marriage and civil partnership, pregnancy and maternity, race, religion or belief, sex, and sexual orientation. It is worth noting that, in this context, disability is understood to include special educational needs and disability. The Equality Act places a duty on all schools and local authorities to be proactive in eliminating discrimination against learners with these characteristics. As a teacher, you will need to consider how your planning and teaching removes the potential for discrimination against those with protected characteristics.

Critical Task 18.2

Seeking to Eliminate Discrimination

What discrimination might learners identified with SEND experience in their school lives and how might it be eliminated or mitigated?

The Children and Families Act 2014

The Children and Families Act 2014 (UK Government, 2014) provides the legal background for the *SEND Code of Practice* (which we will explore further below) and, in section 20, sets the definition for special educational needs:

> A child or young person has special educational needs if he or she has a learning difficulty or disability which calls for special educational provision to be made for him or her.
>
> A child of compulsory school age or a young person has a learning difficulty or disability if he or she:
>
> (a) has a significantly greater difficulty in learning than the majority of others of the same age, or

(b) has a disability which prevents or hinders him or her from making use of facilities of a kind generally provided for others of the same age in mainstream schools or mainstream post-16 institutions.

The Act also has these key areas which are important for you to understand in the context of SEND:

- Education professionals must work together with those from health and social care to improve outcomes.
- Professionals must share information with children and their families.
- Children and their families should have an active role in the planning of their provision.
- A young person, their parent or their school can ask the local council for a formal assessment of their special educational needs. If this assessment identifies that the learner does have significant special educational needs, then a legal document, an Education Health Care Plan (EHCP), will be issued.
- Children and young people with medical needs have a right to access education and schools have a responsibility to enable this access.

The Special Educational Needs Code of Practice

The *Special Educational Needs Code of Practice* (*CoP*) (DfE and DH, 2015) gives schools and other organisations guidance on how to carry out their duties as set out in legislation.

Key to the *CoP* is the principle that all teachers have a responsibility for the learning of children and young people identified with SEND and should set high expectations for all learners. The *CoP* outlines the four areas of special educational need which should inform practitioners as to the provision that is needed. These areas of need are:

- communication and interaction
- cognition and learning
- social, emotional and mental health
- sensory and/or physical needs.

The *CoP* also states that when planning for learners with SEND, schools should follow the 'graduated approach'. This is a four-stage cyclical process: 'assess, plan, do and review' (DfE and DH, 2015: section 5.38).

- **Assess**: a range of information is gathered to establish the pupil's needs in relation to both learning and wellbeing.
- **Plan**: the class teacher, SENCo, parent(s)/carer(s) and the child agree outcomes, provision and expected progress.

- **Do**: the class teacher is responsible for the child's learning, progress and curriculum planning.
- **Review**: the class teacher reviews the impact of SEND support termly, with the parent(s)/carer(s) and the child, and uses this to inform further planning for SEND support.

How to Support Learners Identified with SEND

Effective inclusive practice that enables all learners to participate and make progress starts right at the beginning of our planning for learning and teaching. This means that we think about the pupils with SEND, as well as all the other pupils in our class, at the beginning of the planning process, rather than considering adaptations for learners with SEND afterwards. In this way, we act in an anticipatory way, as required by the Equality Act 2010 and the *SEND CoP* (DfE and DH, 2015). Careful planning in advance of the lesson will support you to maintain high expectations for all learners, remove barriers to participation and progress for learners with SEND, and build positive working relationships with pupils. Next, we will explore three elements that help this anticipatory approach: classroom environment, high-quality teaching and knowing your learners.

The Classroom Environment

Careful reflection on three dimensions will support you to design an inclusive classroom environment: the socio-emotional environment, the physical environment and the sensory environment. All three dimensions will help you to shape a culture in which all children feel they belong and that supports their engagement and motivation in learning.

Social-Emotional Environment

A review of research conducted by Allen et al. (2020: 8) highlighted the vital role played by positive relationships between school staff and pupils in shaping a feeling of connectedness and sense of belonging to the school that in turn positively influences engagement and academic achievement. Indeed, feelings of stress and anxiety, or of not being valued, impact negatively on learning and development. Inclusive approaches to building relationships are underpinned by an ethos that all children are important and have the right to education.

As we explored in Chapter 4, it is important to make conscious efforts to develop connections with children through attentive listening to their views and interests. This may be through conversations with pupils as well as through observations of pupils' actions in learning activities and of their interactions with others. You should also aim to create a culture in which it is safe to make mistakes. Teachers can model making a mistake and how to respond in a positive way to mistakes made by themselves and others.

Aim to identify and authentically celebrate each child's strengths and steps of progress in order to develop their self-belief, confidence, self-esteem and a positive view of themselves as learners (Glazzard et al., 2019: 165). You will need to consider all of the curriculum, not just a few subjects, and remember that what may appear to be tiny incremental steps of progress may be huge leaps forward for some children.

The social-emotional environment is also influenced positively and negatively by the interactions and relationships between pupils in the class. Many learning activities involve children working collaboratively with a partner or small group. Teachers can develop an inclusive environment through explicitly teaching children positive strategies for working and socialising cooperatively and supporting one another in positive ways. For example, teachers can model the socially expected behaviours and language that support working successfully with a partner and group. Visual prompts showing the actions and language to use can be particularly helpful for children who have communication and interaction difficulties or social-emotional or mental health (SEMH) needs.

Physical Environment

Careful planning of adaptations to the physical environment can help to meet the diverse needs of learners. The Equality Act requires that adaptations are made for accessibility, for example for wheelchair users or for those with visual impairments. An audit of the learning environment can support you to identify what is working well and what needs to be changed; it is not only about improving accessibility and participation, but also about the ideas that are communicated to pupils about diversity and inclusion, for example through the displays.

Well organised and clearly labelled resources support ease of access and independence, as these can be easily found and tidied away after use. Using pictures or symbols with text on the labels enables all children to be able to identify the resources regardless of the level of reading ability or understanding of language.

Visuals are a powerful way of communicating key ideas with clarity, to aid understanding and to support memory. They provide support for a range of needs. Imagine that you are visiting a country and do not speak the language used there. This situation can make us feel anxious and we may need help to navigate around the area or communicate our needs. Visual support relates to the visual representation of information. It may be in the form of real objects, photographs, symbols, written text, drawings and videos. For example, imagine you are going to read a text with the class that includes hurricanes. Photos and videos of hurricanes will illustrate for children what hurricanes are and help them understand your verbal explanation. These visual supports can be part of whole-class teaching or group teaching to support children who have speech, language and communication needs (SLCN), for example.

At times when we are struggling to understand or to remember key information, our levels of anxiety might increase, which can further hamper our ability to think, to process information and to resolve problems. Information presented visually can help us to understand what is happening or where something is. There are a variety of needs that benefit from the use of visual supports in the learning environment, including:

- literacy and reading difficulties
- language and communication needs
- anxiety
- memory difficulties
- rigidity of thinking/difficulty with managing change (for example, autism).

Visual supports can enable pupils to:

- Understand new concepts and vocabulary through, for example, using real objects, photographs and videos to support verbal explanations.
- Communicate their thoughts, needs, desires and answers to questions, through using drawing, pictures, photographs or signing to communicate visually.
- Decode and comprehend text and produce written text through using symbol-supported text.
- Understand the routine of the day and expectations of a task through the provision of visual timetables and task schedules.
- Become more independent because the pupil does not need to repeatedly ask an adult or peer what they should be doing.
- Manage memory difficulties through the provision of word mats and memory mats with reminders for key information, spellings or number bonds.
- Sequence and plan writing or an activity such as a science experiment.

Make sure that all key information is presented at an appropriate height for all children and in a format that is appropriate to the developmental stage of the pupils.

Sensory Environment

Our brain continually receives and processes sensory information (what we see, hear, smell, taste and feel) in an automatic and unconscious process which determines our body's response to those stimuli (Yack et al., 2002). Some children are hypersensitive (highly sensitive) or hypo-sensitive (decreased sensitivity) to sensory stimuli from the environment they are in. These sensitivities may trigger heightened levels of anxiety or distress, which may lead to angry outbursts or difficulties with sustaining attention. Such behaviours can disrupt the learning of the child and the class. Therefore, teachers should consider sensory sensitivities in their planning and reviewing of the learning environment, to identify ways to reduce anxiety and stress and support children to focus on their learning.

The Autism Education Trust (AET) has produced a sensory audit for classroom environments and a sensory checklist that teachers can use to identify potential areas of difficulty for pupils and potential issues within the environment (Autism Education Trust, no date). Adaptations to the environment can then be made, such as changes to seating so that a child sensitive to bright light is away from the window, or pre-warning a child who is sensitive to loud noise before a fire drill and allowing them to wear headphones to help reduce classroom noise levels.

Observation Guide 18.1

Inclusive Environments

The *CCF* states that student teachers should 'learn how to … provide opportunity for all pupils to experience success' (DfE, 2019: 20).

During your next placement, observe how an inclusive learning environment is provided for pupils with SEND. In particular, look out for the following:

- Notice how supportive resources and visuals are used to aid understanding and memory.
- Notice how pictures, photos and real objects are used.
- Notice how the teacher communicates with children about what will happen during the day.
- Notice how instructions are given. Are instructions given in small sequential steps? Are visual cues used to support instructions?
- Notice the expectations that the teacher has for the learners with SEND. How are they communicated? How do the expectations align with those for other learners?

High-Quality Teaching

The *SEND CoP* (DfE and DH, 2015) places a strong emphasis on the importance of high-quality teaching that is personalised to meet the needs of pupils with SEND and facilitate good progress. Several elements should be considered in the planning of high-quality teaching. Research published by Education Endowment Foundation (EEF) (2020) and Skipp and Hopwood (2017) has identified some key elements:

- A flexible approach to grouping children for learning activities in order to take account of differing strengths in different curriculum areas and to support opportunities for collaborative learning.
- Using metacognitive strategies to explicitly teach children skills to self-manage their thinking and approach to learning activities.
- Scaffolding is an approach in which temporary visual, verbal or written support is provided to support pupils with learning tasks (EEF, 2020). The support can be removed in incremental steps.
- Pre-teaching is a strategy in which a child is taught vocabulary, concepts or skills before a lesson to enable them to understand the lesson's content, to participate

and make progress. It works to provide the child with a preview of the lesson and knowledge that will help reduce frustration, and increase their confidence and engagement. To implement this strategy effectively, you will need to identify the skills, concepts or vocabulary that the child has not yet mastered.

- Explicit teaching is an approach that teaches new concepts and skills in small sequential steps using clear explanations and with demonstrations from the teacher (e.g., modelling thinking aloud as they work through a task or problem). It is followed with activities for the children to practise skills and work independently on tasks. The teacher will work to anticipate potential areas of misunderstanding in their planning of the activities but also to be responsive to issues that arise.
- Technology can provide helpful support for learning and teaching for children with SEND (EEF, 2021). Examples include apps that provide opportunities to practise skills or to aid learning (such as to support note-taking) or to augment communication for children who have communication difficulties.

For some children, there may be a need for additional intervention, but it should not replace the high-quality teaching implemented in the classroom (EEF, 2020). Interventions should be carefully and systematically planned and informed from a holistic assessment of the child and discussion with the SENCo. The intervention should make explicit links between the knowledge and skills taught in the intervention and in the classroom (EEF, 2020) and provide opportunities for the children to practise and apply skills.

Supporting Children with SEND with Developing Independence

It is important for teachers to identify ways in which they can support the development of independent skills for learning in children with SEND (Table 18.1). It can serve to empower learners and improve motivation, confidence, self-awareness, self-regulation and progress with academic skills. It can also enable the teacher to explore a wider variety of types of learning activities that are set for children that are well matched to their needs and offer challenge to their learning.

Table 18.1 External and internal factors that shape the development of independent learning

External factors influencing success	Internal factors influencing success
Trustful relationships between children and teachers.	Development of cognitive skills: memory, attention, problem-solving.
Teachers plan flexibility in the amount of time for children to work on specific tasks.	Development of metacognitive skills: awareness of factors that positively support their own learning.
Positive and inclusive learning environment: anticipatory approach to planning to meet learning needs.	Development of emotional understanding and skills that positively support learning: motivation, self-esteem, resilience, perseverance.

Approaches to help develop children's independence through your inclusive practice include:

- Modelling how to be an independent learner and how to work collaboratively with a partner or group.
- Mentoring children through feedback and explicit discussion of strategies used for independent learning.
- Scaffolding learning tasks through gradually reducing the amount of support offered.
- Teaching thinking skills and ensuring that children have opportunities to practise these skills.
- Listening to pupil voice to understand factors that positively support their learning, and to draw on it in your planning of learning and teaching.
- Teaching children skills to self-monitor their learning and emotional responses, and to practise strategies to support this.
- Providing specific feedback to support self-reflection.

It is important for you to be flexible and to monitor new strategies and interventions carefully and be ready to make changes or adjustments as the child makes progress, or to respond if there is no positive impact. It is important that we allow time for these strategies to work positively, with space for feedback and practice, in order to support children to securely grasp the intended concepts, skills or behaviours.

Know Your Learners

In order to have a good understanding of the barriers to participation that children with SEND may experience, you will need to have a good knowledge and understanding of each pupil's profile of strengths, interests and needs. This approach of using information gathered from assessment aligns with the graduated approach required by the *SEND CoP* (DfE and DH, 2015).

Adopting a holistic approach to assessment with a focus on academic attainment *and* social-emotional development can support the building of a deep understanding of each child's profile (EEF, 2020), and enables you to fulfil the requirements of the graduated approach. One example of a holistic assessment tool is the Interactive Factors Framework (IFF) (Frederickson and Cline, 2015), as explored in Chapter 2. The IFF tool can be used as a working document to support you to gather and record evidence over time about factors that may be influencing learning and development. It supports discussions with others (e.g., parents/carers and colleagues within the school) about the child and informs planning.

The United Nations Convention on the Rights of the Child (UNCRC) (United Nation,1989) laid the foundation for the principle in the *SEND CoP* (DfE and DH, 2015) that schools must listen to children's views and involve them in decision-making about learning and other aspects of school. This practice is supportive of building positive working relationships with children and encouraging their sense of belonging (Middleton and Kay, 2020), in addition to supporting information-gathering for holistic assessment. Pupils with SEND often have valuable insights that can empower us to understand more about the nature of their specific difficulties and the strategies and resources that are supportive to their learning (Middleton and Kay, 2020).

There are a range of approaches you can use to elicit pupils' views that can inform your assessment and planning. Try to listen attentively to your pupils during learning conversations and everyday discussions within the academic and social aspects of school life. Any specific approaches that you decide to use to gain insights into the children's views need to be carefully matched to their development and communication needs. For example, you may need to modify your language or use visual approaches, or ask children to draw or take photographs of their school experiences, or provide them with pictures and use these as stimuli for conversations.

Case Study 18.1

Reflecting on the Things Children Find Challenging

Krishna is a postgraduate primary student teacher, who is undertaking his final school placement:

> Krishna has Sam in his Year 4 class. Sam has speech, language, and communication needs (SLCN). During a whole-class explanation and instructions, Sam becomes fidgety. They are unable to answer a question that Krishna asks. Krishna thinks that this is because Sam is not listening carefully.
>
> Krishna has created a word bank with pictures and photos of key words to help Sam during the independent task. However, Sam does not sustain attention on the task, and becomes disruptive.

It is good that Krishna has provided visual aids for the task, as these support Sam to understand more of the information being shared and thus help them to sustain attention for longer. It is possible that providing a visual task schedule for the steps of the independent task will support Sam's understanding and memory of what they need to do, and will thus support their independence and attention on task.

Krishna might reflect on any other reasons, beyond poor listening, that may have caused Sam to be unable to answer the question that was asked. Working with the SENCo, Krishna could investigate this further to identify appropriate strategies.

Response to Critical Task 18.2

Seeking to Eliminate Discrimination

In Critical Task 18.2, you considered what discrimination learners with SEND may experience and how it may be eliminated or mitigated. In Table 18.2, we suggest some possible answers.

Continued

Table 18.2 Seeking to eliminate discrimination

Possible discrimination	Possible actions to work towards eliminating discrimination
Learners with dyslexia who have not scored highly enough in their English results miss out on the opportunity to take part in a story-writing contest.	Consider a range of criteria which may qualify a learner to be a successful story-writer. Consider enabling a range of formats for stories to be presented to the competition (e.g., audio submission or a pictorial presentation).
A learner with autism receives a punishment for refusing to complete a surprise test paper.	Ensure that neuro-divergent learners, who may find change from routine difficult, are given outlines of the expectations for the day in advance and support them to understand changes in the usual routine.
Learners with mental health difficulties that impact attendance miss out on school rewards for 100% attendance.	Work with school leaders to recognise attendance achievements which consider medical needs.

The Special Educational Needs Co-ordinator

Legislation since 2008 has stipulated that all state-funded schools must have a SENCo and that they need to be a qualified teacher. The Children and Families Act 2014 (UK Government, 2014) stipulated that SENCos must achieve the National SENCo Award (NASENCo), which is due to be replaced by NPQ SENCo from October 2024.

What Can You Expect from the SENCo?

The SENCo in your setting will be an experienced teacher. They should have completed additional training and have a range of experiences to equip them to take on the role. However, this does not mean that they will be an expert in all aspects of SEND or know all the answers of what to put in practice. What you can expect is that the SENCo will work supportively with you as a teacher to identify the needs of your pupils, to plan and implement approaches to support those learners and to monitor the effectiveness of those approaches.

The SENCo will also have a whole-school overview of SEND, including learner needs and provision, in terms of resources and staff skills. This leadership overview will be a support to all teachers in planning for the needs of those they teach and help ensure you fulfil all the requirements of the paperwork and accountability for your learners with SEND.

The SENCo is also responsible for maintaining positive relationships with external professionals who support the school's SEND provision, such as educational psychologists, speech and language therapists, occupational therapists, play and drama therapists and advisory teachers. The SENCo will be able to advise you on how and when to access external support and will signpost you to resources and professional development opportunities to support you in your work to provide the best opportunities for learners with SEND.

Supporting learners with SEND can be challenging for the adults who work with them and the SENCo is often a source of support to parents and other staff. In addition to offering professional and practical support, the SENCo is often someone who offers an understanding ear and emotional support and care for the adults they work with (Middleton and Kay, 2021). If you find yourself struggling or feeling overwhelmed with the work you are doing to support learners with SEND, do talk to your SENCo about it.

Question Guide 18.1

Meeting with the SENCo

The *CCF* states that student teachers should 'learn how to … build effective working relationships by … [understanding] how to work closely with the SENCo and other professionals supporting pupils with additional needs' (DfE, 2019: 29–30).

To help you to understand the role of the SENCo and how the needs of pupils with SEND are met, use some of these questions to guide your discussion with the SENCo:

- How does this school define inclusion?
- How does this school identify SEND?
- How do you support teachers with planning or provision?
- What else does your role entail?
- Do external colleagues contribute to the provision for any of the children with SEND in the class I am placed in?

What Can the SENCo Expect from You?

A key element of the SENCo's role is that they are accountable, along with the governors and senior leaders, for the way in which provision for learners with SEND is planned and delivered. However, they are not responsible for planning or delivering the provision: this is something that each teacher is responsible for. The SENCo will expect you, as a teacher, to be aware of the expectations set by legislation and guidance and those set by the school leadership and the SENCo. They will expect you to keep appropriate and up-to-date paperwork relating to the graduated approach taken in planning and delivering provision for individual learners with SEND. You will need to be reflective in your approach to your understanding of learners' needs and the planning and reviewing of provision: there is no 'one-size-fits-all' solution, rather the SENCo will expect you to engage in professional reflective discussions about your practice.

The SENCo will also expect you to work in partnership with all those involved in the education of learners with SEND. This will include the learner themselves, their parents or carers, teaching assistants and other professionals in the school, as well as external professionals. This aspect of practice is discussed in more depth in Chapter 15.

Case Study 18.2

Taking Responsibility for All Children's Progress

Max, an early career teacher, is talking about one of the learners with SEND in his class of Year 3 pupils:

> I plan a programme of interventions for Samira each week, which her allocated TA works through and at the end of the week the TA records Samira's achievements on her Personal Education Plan. When Samira's Annual Review meeting was due, I summarised the achievements she had made over the year and provided some examples of her work for the meeting.

It is good that Max is planning for and assessing Samira's progress, but he needs to ensure that he is taking responsibility for Samira's learning and not relying on the TA to carry out the majority of the teaching and assessment. He should reflect on his whole-class teaching and how it can be adapted for the needs of all learners in the class.

It is not clear if Max is using the graduated approach. He should ensure that he reviews the effectiveness of his provision and develop the involvement of the children and their parents in the graduated approach. This means keeping parents informed about the targets set and their child's achievements as well as involving the children and their parents in planning the provision.

Chapter Summary

Children are not a homogeneous group; for children with SEND, we need to consider their individual specific needs rather than expecting them to conform to a one-size-fits-all approach. Reflecting on this will support you to respond sensitively and flexibly to your diverse learners, helping you to create a positive, inclusive learning environment.

In this chapter, we have considered the importance of starting from a foundation of inclusive values to help you construct effective inclusive classroom practice. We have explored the requirements of the legislative framework for schools and the expectation that schools, and teachers, will work with an anticipatory approach to meet the needs of children with SEND. We have explored how quality-first teaching approaches will help to meet the diverse needs of all pupils. While the responsibility for the children with SEND lies with you as class teacher, you will work as part of a team to support the children in your class.

Further Reading

Department for Education (DfE) (2014) *The Equality Act 2010 and schools: Departmental advice for school leaders, school staff, governing bodies and local authorities*. London: DfE. Available at: www.gov.uk/government/publications/equality-act-2010-advice-for-schools#full-publication-update-history (accessed 23 March 2023).

This document gives a clear and concise summary of the most important elements of the Equality Act that schools need to be aware of. It will help you to start addressing equality and discrimination in your setting.

Education Endowment Foundation (EEF) (2020) *Guidance report: Special educational needs in mainstream schools*. London: EEF.

This guidance report will help you to consider elements of practice in relation to supporting learners with SEND. It provides resources and case studies to guide your thinking and offers practical ideas about how to develop practice in your setting.

You may also consider joining the National Association for Special Educational Needs (NASEN), the national charity for SEND, and subscribing to *Special Needs Jungle* (www.specialneedsjungle.com/), to keep up to date with recent developments in the field of SEND.

References

Allen, T., Riley, K. and Coates, M. (2020) *Belonging, behaviour and inclusion in schools: What does research tell us?* London: National Education Union. Available at: https://neu.org.uk/media/13036/view (accessed 11 May 2023).

Autism Education Trust (no date) *Sensory resources*. London: Autism Education Trust. Available at: www.autismeducationtrust.org.uk/sensory-resources (accessed 11 May 2023).

Department for Education (DfE) (2019) *ITT core content framework*. London: DfE.

Department for Education (DfE) and Department of Health (DH) (2015) *Special educational needs and disability code of practice: 0 to 25 years. Statutory guidance for organisations which work with and support children and young people who have special educational needs or disabilities*. London: DfE and DH. Available at: www.gov.uk/government/publications/send-code-of-practice-0-to-25 (accessed 23 March 2023).

Education Endowment Foundation (EEF) (2020) *Guidance report: Special educational needs in mainstream schools*. London: EEF.

Education Endowment Foundation (EEF) (2021) *Using digital technology to improve learning*. London: EEF. Available at: https://educationendowmentfoundation.org.uk/education-evidence/guidance-reports/digital (accessed 23 March 2023).

Frederickson, N. and Cline, T. (2015) *Special educational needs, inclusion and diversity: A textbook* (2nd edn). Buckingham and Philadelphia, PA: Open University Press.

Glazzard, J., Netherwood, A., Hughes, A., Neve, L. and Stokoe, J. (2019) *Teaching and supporting children with special educational needs and disabilities in primary schools*. London: Sage.

Middleton, T. and Kay, L. (2020) *Using an inclusive approach to reduce school exclusion: A practitioner's guide*. Abingdon, UK: Nasen Spotlight/Routledge.

Middleton, T. and Kay, L. (2021) 'Uncharted territory and extraordinary times: the SENCO's experiences of leading SEN during a pandemic in England', *British Journal of Special Education,* 48(2), 212–234.

Skipp, A. and Hopwood, V. (2017) *SEN support: Case studies from school and colleges.* Research Report. London: Department for Education. Available at: https://assets.publishing.service. gov.uk/government/uploads/system/uploads/attachment_data/file/636465/DfE_SEN_ Support_Case_studies.pdf (accessed 23 March 2023).

UK Government (2010) *Equality Act 2010, c. 15.* London: HMSO. Available at: www.legislation. gov.uk/ukpga/2010/15/contents (accessed 19 July 2022).

UK Government (2014) *Children and Families Act 2014, c. 6.* London: HMSO. Available at: www.legislation.gov.uk/ukpga/2014/6/contents/enacted (accessed 19 July 2022).

United Nations (1989) *Convention on the rights of the child.* New York: United Nations. Available at: www.unicef.org/child-rights-convention/convention-text-childrens-version (accessed 30 March 2023).

Yack, E., Sutton, S. and Aquilla, P. (2002) *Building bridges through sensory integration.* Arlington, TX: Future Horizons.

19
SAFEGUARDING

Debbie Innes-Turnill

Chapter Objectives

- To explore safeguarding and the life-changing impact it can have on children.
- To consider how to identify and report safeguarding issues, and make safeguarding decisions.
- To reflect on the importance of making your classroom a safe space.

In this chapter, we explore why 'safeguarding is everyone's responsibility' (Department for Education (DfE), 2018: 11). We define what safeguarding is and the responsibilities teachers and school staff have, as detailed in the statutory guidance, *Keeping Children Safe in Education* (DfE, 2023). This includes what to look for, how to report concerns and how to make decisions about safeguarding. While all those who work with children must accept these responsibilities, it can be difficult for busy teachers to prioritise the safeguarding needs of children in their class. We therefore also look at how safeguarding issues impact on children and their behaviour, and hence their engagement in learning. We also discuss why you should and can make it your key priority through your relationships with the children and their families, making your classroom a safe space in which children can thrive.

What is Safeguarding?

Safeguarding is defined in *Working Together to Safeguard Children* (DfE, 2018) as:

- protecting children from maltreatment
- preventing impairment of children's health or development
- ensuring that children are growing up in circumstances consistent with the provision of safe and effective care
- taking action to enable all children to have the best outcomes.

284 INTRODUCTION TO PRIMARY SCHOOL TEACHING

This wide-ranging responsibility must be met by all those who work with children. The safeguarding and welfare of children has been based on this multi-agency approach, in which, since the *Children Act 1989* (UK Government, 1989), schools have a key role. A report by the National Audit Office (2019) shows that education is second only to the police in making referrals to children's social care, making almost a fifth of all referrals.

Research by Baginsky et al. (2022) shows that education is increasingly responsible for the safeguarding and wellbeing of children. Changes in policy and practice have put schools at the forefront of not only keeping children safe from harm but also providing an education that understands the impact of Adverse Child Experiences (ACEs) (Felitti et al., 1998) and trauma-informed practice (Pence et al., 2013), as explored in Chapter 4. Since the introduction of the DfE's first *Keeping Children Safe in Education* in 2014, the requirements of schools have grown and developed. In addition to statutory referral, they are now required to offer 'Early Help'. The NSPCC (2021: no page) explains that early help is 'also known as early intervention [and] is support given to a family when a problem first emerges. It can be provided at any stage in a child or young person's life'. Schools often find themselves offering these early help interventions in increasingly diverse ways to children and families who are experiencing difficulties but who do not meet the rising thresholds for children's services support.

The Impact of Safeguarding Issues on Children and the Difference Schools can Make

Safeguarding issues can have a significant impact on children in school (Wilkinson and Bowyer, 2017). Impacts can include poor achievement (Crozier and Barth, 2005), behaviours that lead to suspension or exclusion, low attendance and increased incidence of special educational needs (Jonson-Reid et al., 2004). Issues of abuse, risk or vulnerability can also inhibit learning, as well as damaging long-term self-worth and resilience (Burr, 2022).

How is Safeguarding Managed in Schools?

There are two key documents that you need to read before taking responsibility for working with children in a school. All school staff have to read the first part of the latest *Keeping Children Safe in Education* (DfE, 2023) document. This document is usually updated annually, so do ensure you are reading the most recent version. You also need to read the school's safeguarding policy, which should be published on the school's website. If you are unable to find it, make sure you ask for it. It might use terminology that you are unsure of; again, make sure you ask for clarification.

Every opportunity should be taken to improve children's wellbeing, and to prevent them from being at risk of, or experiencing, abuse, and this is why you will often hear the statement 'safeguarding is everyone's responsibility' (DfE, 2018: 11).

The Role of Designated Safeguarding Leads

The role of designated safeguarding lead (DSL) was introduced in the Children Act 2004 (UK Government, 2004). Since then, DSLs have taken an increasingly significant role in managing the safeguarding and wellbeing of children in schools. This person (or persons: some schools have several, or they have additional deputy designated safeguarding leads or DDSLs) is key to leading and implementing the school's safeguarding policy. They should be trained to a higher level than the rest of the staff and are usually more experienced in child protection and safeguarding issues.

Question Guide 19.1

Meeting with the DSL

The *ITT Core Content Framework* (*CCF*) states that student teachers should 'learn how to ... build effective working relationships by ... knowing who to contact with any safeguarding concerns and having a clear understanding of what sorts of behaviour, disclosures and incidents to report' (DfE, 2019: 29–30).

Make sure you ask who the DSL and DDSLs are and about how you contact them. If possible, you should ask to meet them. If you do, then the following might be useful initial questions to ask:

- What is your advice to a new member of staff in relation to managing safeguarding effectively in this school?
- Can you explain how you would like me to record and report any concerns I have about children?
- What are the most prevalent safeguarding issues I am likely to come across?
- Are there any children in the class that I am going to be working with that have particular safeguarding concerns that I should be aware of?

You can also ask the previous question of the class teacher you are working with. In addition, it will be useful to ask the class teacher:

- How do the safeguarding issues for children in this class affect their behaviour or learning and what strategies do you use to manage them?

The Role of Student Teacher/Class Teacher and Safeguarding

In addition to your safeguarding role, you will also be responsible for the implementation of elements of the school's offer of early help. It will vary widely from school to school but always begins with the relationship you have with the children in your class and their families. The class teacher is often the person who knows children and families best and is therefore best placed to communicate with them about issues and concerns. As a student teacher, you should be supported to do this, particularly if the communication is of a challenging nature. Ask for help if you are not sure, as it is important to get safeguarding messages right.

Remember, getting it right for children who are experiencing challenges can have a life-changing impact on them. The rest of this chapter will help you to understand how to recognise when a child may be experiencing abuse, what to do about it, how it may affect their learning and how you can provide a safe space for them in your classroom.

Identifying Safeguarding Issues, Reporting and Recording

In *Keeping Children Safe in Education* (DfE, 2023), you will see many different types of safeguarding issues that children may experience. It is impossible to detail all of them here, but it is important that you understand the main categories of child abuse and how they, and other safeguarding issues, may manifest themselves so that you can identify them, report and record them. Much of safeguarding and child protection is about assessing risk. It becomes easier with experience but you should *never*, even when you are really experienced, disregard a concern without first discussing it with other safeguarding colleagues.

Categories of Child Abuse and their Indications

Physical abuse: Any hitting or physical punishment is considered to be physical abuse. It might also be evident in bite marks, cigarette burns or fabricated symptoms of illness, for example. This is the abuse that you are most likely to actually see, because if a child in your class is suffering, there may be evidence of injury.

You should be vigilant when children are changing for PE and look out for children who seek to keep themselves fully covered (e.g., not wanting to take off their jumper). If you see evidence of an injury, always ask the child how it happened and report it to the DSL.

Sexual abuse: This type of abuse can be very distressing to think about and we know that many more children are being sexually abused than have been identified by professionals (Jay et al., 2022). Any sort of sexual activity with a child is abuse. It can be penetrative or non-penetrative, or children witnessing sexual acts, either in person or through pornography. It is very difficult to identify when a child is being sexually abused. Sometimes there will be physical symptoms, such as frequent urination or urinary tract infections (but, of course, there may also be many other reasons for these symptoms). There may be some signs in their play, either with toys or with their peers. Concerns about possible sexual abuse should always be referred to the DSL.

If a child discloses to you, then you should support them by listening and understanding. However, if they have not said anything and you just have suspicions, you can do more harm by asking them about anything directly before you have sought advice. Further advice as to what to do if a child tells you about abuse that is happening to them is included later in this chapter.

Emotional abuse: If children are being belittled, if they are being required to take responsibilities beyond their developmental capabilities, if they are being bullied or if they are witnessing others being subjected to violence or abuse, then they are being emotionally abused. Again, this type of abuse is often difficult to see. You may witness an adult in the child's life treating them indifferently, they may tell you that no one loves them, or more likely, they will behave in ways that suggest that their life is not a happy one.

Get to know the children in your class and observe and monitor the actions and reactions of the adults who care for them. If you suspect emotional abuse, record the evidence with dates and discuss it with the DSL. How to record your concerns is covered later in this chapter.

Neglect: This is where a child's needs are not being met. Think about what a child needs to thrive. They need to be fed, clothed, kept clean, kept warm and loved. When this does not happen, they are experiencing neglect. It is an extremely difficult area of abuse to prove and teachers are key in providing evidence over time to ensure things improve. You may notice that a child is frequently dirty or often hungry. You may also notice behavioural indications, which are covered in the next section.

Ensure that you make a note of your observations, and date them. You can also talk to the child about their home life. These notes should be shared with the DSL so that you can agree what happens next. If a child is hungry, it has a negative impact on learning, so it is important to provide something to eat. There may be a school strategy in place for this scenario, so find out quickly: a hungry child should not have to wait.

The Reality of Identifying Abuse

In reality, abuse within these categories can be difficult to identify and children tend to communicate what is going on in their lives through their behaviour, rather than distinct disclosures of what has happened to them. You need to be sensitive to these behaviours, and those of their parents or carers, to spot when a child may be being abused or experiencing welfare issues at home. Make sure you build relationships so children know they can trust you and can talk to you if anything is worrying them. If you do identify something that you think is concerning, you will need to find out more, either through talking to the child or by asking colleagues for advice.

These are things to look for and explore further, thinking about what may be causing them:

- lack of self-assurance or confidence
- struggling to control emotions
- difficulty making or maintaining relationships
- lack of social skills
- fear of people or a person they know
- language or sexual behaviour you would not expect the child to know
- having nightmares or bed-wetting, which may be reported to you by the child or perhaps noticed during a residential trip
- self-harm
- changes in eating habits or developing an eating problem
- changes in their mood or behaviour and showing themselves to feel irritable and angry
- health issues, such as decaying teeth
- being left alone at home for long periods of time.

You can see how difficult it can be to determine what is causing these behaviours and issues. The experience of home life for many children who are experiencing safeguarding issues may be:

- **Chaotic**: For example, the frequent changing of phone numbers, inability or apparent reluctance of parents to attend parents' evenings or class assemblies and the lack of equipment needed in school.
- **Lacking in boundaries**: For example, children who appear to be 'out of control' when in their parents' care or children who cannot adhere to boundaries in school.
- **Lacking in routines**: For example, children who are late to school or appointments, children who do not have breakfast before school, children who are not in uniform or uniform that is regularly unclean.
- **Unstable relationships**: For example, parental relationships that are 'on/off' and/or demonstrate domestic abuse, family members who are present and then not present, or where parents frequently change partners.
- **Lack of consistency**: Boundaries and routines are maintained for short periods of time but cannot be sustained, so children are not able to rely on their parents. For example, after support, children arrive at school on time for a couple of weeks but then slip back into habitual lateness.
- **Lack of persistency**: Parents are not able to be steadfast in boundaries or applying routines firmly. For example, parents who are able to understand the damaging nature of playing computer games until late at night but are not able to insist that their children switch off the computer.

Be alert to these things and make sure that you record anything that you observe.

Case Study 19.1

Identifying Concerns

Milly, a postgraduate primary student teacher, has become concerned about Fred, one of the pupils in her placement class.

> Fred is 6 years old and often arrives at school angry and not able to engage with his class teacher or peers. His mum often brings his lunchbox to school later in the morning and his clothes frequently have mud and yoghurt on them from previous days. One Monday morning, when Fred is changing for PE, Milly notices that his vest is stained, slightly damp and smells of urine. Milly asks Fred about the vest. Fred tells her that he had wet the bed the night before and could not find a clean vest that morning. Milly speaks to the DSL, who asks her to upload a record of her concerns to the school's online child protection management system (CPOMS). She is asked to log each event so that the school can build a picture of neglect. The DSL arranges to speak to Fred's mum and asks Milly if she would like to be part of the conversation to learn about how to challenge and support parents with issues of neglect.

In this example, Milly noticed some early signs of neglect. She did the right thing in speaking to the DSL and was given the opportunity to learn about what happens next when there are these sorts of concerns about a child.

Taking a Disclosure

The school's safeguarding policy will give you guidance as to what to do if a child talks to you about being abused or about a welfare issue. It is crucial that you do not promise a child confidentiality; you cannot keep anything of concern 'a secret', however much the child may want you to. You must not ask leading questions and you must not discuss the issue with anyone other than the DSL. Listen carefully to what the child is saying, let them know that they have done the right thing by telling you, tell them it is not their fault, tell them you are taking them seriously and explain what you will do next.

Make sure you pass this information on to the DSL *immediately*. It cannot wait until the end of the day, so ask other staff to help you do this if you are in charge of the classroom. If the child has told you who the abuser is, do not talk to that person unless you are asked to do so by the DSL.

Reporting and Recording

If you are concerned about a child, then you must make a report. In the first instance, it can be a discussion with one of the safeguarding leads in your school. You may be asked to evidence why you are worried and what you think the risks are. The safeguarding policy is, again, the 'go to' document for how a particular school records and reports concerns.

When it comes to providing a written record of the concern, many schools now require you to do this through an online child protection management system: CPOMS, My Concern and Sleuth are some of the most popular systems. While each system has slightly different requirements, key principles remain the same. You need to be clear, concise and factual about the concern you have and make sure you upload it to the correct child's record:

- **Be clear**: Make sure that your report is not confused by comments that mean it is difficult to identify who did what and when. For example, you might write, 'Emily told me that her mum hurt her before school this morning when she was at home; her sibling was not present.' *not* 'Emily said that she was at home when she was hurt but he was not there'.
- **Being concise**: Try to summarise what has been happening for the child without too much narrative. For example, 'Emily told me that her adult brother hit her.' *not* 'During an activity in our lesson this morning Emily was doing a maths problem when she said that her big brother hit her'.
- **Be factual**: This means not giving your opinion about what is happening for the child but giving evidence. For example, 'Emily says she has not eaten breakfast for the last two weeks.' *not* 'I think Emily is not being fed at home'.

Critical Task 19.1

Being Clear, Concise and Factual

Take a look at the following entry to a safeguarding online management system. Think about what you have just read about reporting and recording to consider how this entry could be improved.

> Just one that I'm concerned about. She mentioned that she is meeting her new dad today. The reason I'm flagging is I know mum is a little strange and aunty used to collect her regularly. Anyway, I haven't seen her for a while but she had a bruise on her wrist today, I don't know how it got there.

The Impact of Safeguarding Issues on Children

Children who experience safeguarding issues are often considered to have experienced trauma. These are sometimes referred to as Adverse Childhood Experiences (ACEs), although trauma is a more inclusive term. Trauma is likely to have an ongoing impact on a child's engagement with learning and their behaviour in school. Children may be worried about what is going on at home and not be able to concentrate. Lack of self-esteem and resilience may manifest themselves in a lack of progress or poor behaviour. Being hungry, dirty, tired or in pain is also likely to lead to poor concentration and social difficulties in school.

Case Study 19.2

Acting on Your Observations

In this example, Tyrone, an undergraduate student teacher, notices that Jenny is not concentrating on her work.

> When Tyrone looks at Jenny's book at breaktime, he sees that she has scribbled on the page and not completed any of the tasks, which is unusual for her. At the start of the next lesson, Tyrone asks Jenny what is wrong. Jenny gets upset and says that she is worried about her mum. She tells him that her dad had 'got mad last night' and she had heard shouting. She says that her mum was crying and this morning she had a mark on her face which she had tried to cover up.
>
> Tyrone knows that this is an urgent concern, so he asks the teaching assistant to keep an eye on the class while he goes to tell the DSL what Jenny has said. The DSL comes to speak to Jenny and then calls Jenny's mum. With her consent, the DSL makes a referral to Children's Services and the local domestic abuse support service. Tyrone is asked to upload his concerns to My Concern so that the DSL can update Jenny's records with the subsequent actions.

In this example, a serious safeguarding concern was only disclosed because Tyrone noticed that Jenny was not engaged in her learning that morning. He asked her what was wrong (not 'if' anything was wrong) in a non-threatening manner. Jenny felt safe enough to tell Tyrone what had happened at home, and he immediately recognised and referred this information to the DSL, knowing it could not wait until later in the day.

Observation Guide 19.1

Working with Parents/Carers

The *CCF* states that student teachers should 'learn how to … communicate with parents and carers proactively' in relation to safeguarding (DfE, 2019: 30).

If possible, it is helpful to observe the DSL or other experienced member of staff when they are speaking to parents/carers about a safeguarding issue. It may be a formal meeting, such as a child protection meeting, or a teacher speaking to a parent when there has been a concern. Ask

Continued

if you can observe, making it clear that you will be a neutral observer and won't contribute to the meeting. You will also need to make sure the parents/carers are happy for you to be there in an observational capacity. While you are observing, consider the following questions:

- What is being discussed?
- Who is leading the meeting?
- Who gets the most 'airtime' and what impact does it have?
- How does the person leading the conversation ensure that the focus is kept on the child/children?
- What is the body language of those involved?
- How anxious or hostile are those involved?
- How is it made clear what will happen next?

After the meeting, it will be helpful to speak to the person you observed. If appropriate, ask the following questions, taking care to avoid sounding critical in any way:

- How do you think the meeting went?
- How do you think it will improve things for the child/children?
- Is there anything you might do differently if you were to have this meeting again?

Making Your Classroom a Safe Space

> More than anything else, being able to feel safe with other people defines mental health; safe connections are fundamental for meaningful and satisfying lives. (Van der Kolk, 2014: 352)

Children need to feel safe in order to learn. You need to create a safe environment in your classroom in order for learning to happen, as we explored in Chapters 4 and 17.

Trauma-informed practice is a good place to start in making sure that your classroom is safe for all children and particularly those who have experienced safeguarding issues. Implementing trauma-informed practice involves understanding how trauma affects children, particularly what might trigger them, and providing support as a result. It is built on five core values:

- **safety**: both physical and emotional
- **trustworthiness**: consistent and persistent expectations
- **choice**: enabling the victim of trauma to take control
- **collaboration**: ensuring the sharing of power over what happens
- **empowerment**: developing skills and resilience for the future.

(Adapted from Wilson et al., 2013)

The implications of these core values for your practice are explored below:

Emotional safety: Let children know that you like them and care about them. Children need to feel loved and those with safeguarding issues in their lives often don't feel loved. Research indicates that the presence of resilience-promoting relationships in their lives is a key factor in supporting children to 'cope with and rebound from adverse experiences' (Wilkinson and Bowyer, 2017: 19). It does not contradict the need to maintain boundaries for children; instead, it enhances the experience of children feeling safe with you as their teacher.

Physical safety: Ensure that children know they are safe from outside influences but that they can get out should they need to. Sometimes physical safety involves giving a child a hug or holding them. Make sure you know your school's policy on physical contact with children and ensure that you follow the guidance carefully.

Trustworthiness: Trustworthiness can be defined as the ability to be relied on as honest or truthful. For children, it means always doing what you say you are going to do. One way you can do this is to not make promises. If a child asks you to do something for them, then saying that you will try your best or do what you can, explaining that you cannot promise because there are other factors which might prevent it from happening, is an honest and truthful answer, which a child can rely on. The same goes for if you are not sure about how to answer a child's question. Telling them that you don't know the answer is honest and truthful. Over time, these sorts of responses show the child that you are reliable. It is from this base that trust is built. It is why, in a safeguarding situation, you must not make promises. Children are most vulnerable when they are disclosing or talking about abuse or welfare issues. Honesty and truthfulness are key.

Choice: Children who have been abused will not have chosen or had control over what has happened to them. Ensuring that your classroom offers children the opportunity to make choices will teach them how to do this safely.

Collaboration: Collaboration links closely to 'choice'. Children who have been abused or about whom there have been welfare concerns are often not included in the decision-making process about what happens next. Providing opportunities for children to co-design their own learning/environment or how to approach the learning will enable them to learn about agency and how to think about the future. Collaborating with you will help them to understand that adults are there to support their lives, not just make all the decisions for them.

Empowerment: Teach children, implicitly and explicitly, about resilience, strength-building and what their rights are. It will help them to become empowered, both in their lives now and also for their futures. Think about how you can include children's rights in your teaching. UNICEF (no date) has a helpful one-page document that summarises the United Nations Rights of the Child.

Case Study 19.3

Lasting Impact

Obviously, I can't share any details of this case, but the following message, from a former pupil of mine, who is now an adult, demonstrates the significant and long-lasting impact of acting compassionately and prioritising children's safety and wellbeing:

> I wanted to message to tell you that I am so grateful I had a figure like you in my life. I'm glad I had a role model and someone that understood me and didn't gaslight me about what I was going through. You were one of the few adults in my life that made me feel safe, loved and validated and I'll never forget that.

Your Own Emotional Safety

Safeguarding and child protection is a key part of your role. Teachers take it very seriously. It can be very challenging and often distressing. It is important that you learn to manage this emotional load by sharing your worries and concerns with the DSL or with your line manager. Some schools will have an official 'supervision' or 'reflective practice' process. If your school does not have such a process in place, make sure you find ways of managing your own emotions and have an outlet to ensure that your mental health is not adversely affected by the abuse or safeguarding issues the children in your class are experiencing, while remembering the need to maintain confidentiality. If you are not emotionally healthy, you will not be able to support the children who need your support.

Chapter Summary

In this chapter, we have considered what safeguarding is and how to recognise and report concerns about a child. We have also looked at the potential impact of safeguarding issues on children's learning and how you can mitigate that by ensuring your classroom is a safe space. We have also considered the importance of looking after your own wellbeing. Safeguarding is a challenging aspect of a teacher's responsibilities, but it is one in which acting with compassion and courage can make a significant and life-changing impact on the lives of children.

Further Reading

The following texts may be helpful in further developing your understanding of effective safeguarding:

Baginsky, M., Driscoll, J., Purcell, C., Manthorpe, J. and Hickman, B. (2022) *Protecting and safeguarding children in schools*. Bristol: Policy Press.

This helpful book explores some of the most recent research into how schools manage safeguarding.

Department for Education (DfE) (2023) *Keeping children safe in education.* London: DfE. https:// www.gov.uk/government/publications/keeping-children-safe-in-education–2 (accessed 30 August 2023).

It is mandatory that everyone who works in school reads Part 1 of the most recent version of this document.

McGovern, W., Gillespie, A. and Woodley, H. (2022) *Understanding safeguarding for children and their educational experiences.* Bingley, UK: Emerald.

This book is useful to support your learning about a range of different safeguarding issues, including how children become vulnerable and what you can do to support them.

References

Baginsky, M., Driscoll, J., Purcell, C., Manthorpe, J. and Hickman, B. (2022) *Protecting and safeguarding children in schools.* Bristol: Policy Press.

Burr, R. (2022) *Self-worth in children and young people: Critical and practical considerations.* St Albans: Critical Publishing.

Crozier, C.C. and Barth, R.P. (2005) 'Cognitive and academic functioning in maltreated children', *Children and Schools,* 27(4), 197–206.

Department for Education (DfE) (2018) *Working together to safeguard children.* London: DfE. Available at: www.gov.uk/government/publications/working-together-to-safeguard-children--2 (accessed 9 November 2022).

Department for Education (DfE) (2019) *ITT core content framework.* London: DfE.

Department for Education (DfE) (2023) *Keeping children safe in education.* London: DfE. Available at: www.gov.uk/government/publications/keeping-children-safe-in-education--2 (accessed 30 August 2023).

Felitti, V.J., Anda, R.F., Nordenberg, D., Williamson, D.F., Spitz, A.M., Edwards, V., Koss, M.P. and Marks, J.S. (1998) 'Relationship of childhood abuse and household dysfunction to many of the leading causes of death in adults: the Adverse Childhood Experiences (ACE) Study', *American Journal of Preventative Medicine,* 14(4), 245–248.

Jay, A., Evans, M., Frank, I. and Sharpling, D. (2022) *The report of the independent inquiry into child sexual abuse.* London: HMSO. Available at: www.gov.uk/government/publications/iicsa-report-of-the-independent-inquiry-into-child-sexual-abuse (accessed 30 March 2023).

Jonson-Reid, M., Drake, B., Kim, J., Porterfield, S. and Han, L. (2004) 'A prospective analysis of the relationship between reported child maltreatment and special education eligibility among poor children', *Child Maltreatment,* 9(4), 382–394.

National Audit Office (2019) *Pressures of children's social care.* London: National Audit Office.

NSPCC (National Society for the Prevention of Cruelty to Children) (2021) *Early help (or early intervention).* London: NSPCC. Available at: https://learning.nspcc.org.uk/safeguarding-child-protection/early-help-early-intervention (accessed 30 March 2023).

UK Government (1989) *Children Act 1989, c. 41*. London: HMSO. Available at: www.legislation.gov.uk/ukpga/1989/41/contents (accessed 9 November 2022).

UK Government (2004) *Children Act 2004, c. 31*. London: HMSO. Available at: www.legislation.gov.uk/ukpga/2004/31/contents (accessed 9 November 2022).

UNICEF (no date) *A summary of the U.N. Convention on the Rights of the Child*. New York: UNICEF. Available at: www.unicef.org.uk/wp-content/uploads/2019/10/UNCRC_summary-1_1.pdf (accessed 30 March 2023).

Van der Kolk, B.A. (2014) *The body keeps the score: Brain, mind, and body in the healing of trauma*. New York: Penguin Random House.

Wilkinson, J. and Bowyer, S. (2017) *The impacts of abuse on children; and comparison of different placement options*. London: Department for Education. Available at: https://assets.publishing.service.gov.uk/government/uploads/system/uploads/attachment_data/file/602148/Childhood_neglect_and_abuse_comparing_placement_options.pdf (accessed 30 March 2023).

Wilson, C., Pence, D.M. and Conradi, L. (2013) 'Trauma-informed care', in *Encyclopaedia of Social Work*. Oxford: National Association of Social Workers and Oxford University Press. Available at: https://doi.org/10.1093/acrefore/9780199975839.013.1063 (accessed 30 March 2023).

20
STARTING YOUR CAREER AND ENJOYING YOUR TEACHING

Rachel Eperjesi, Colin Forster and Ruth Hollier

Chapter Objectives

- To consider how to secure your first teaching post.
- To consider how to prepare for the start of your teaching career.
- To explore ways to really enjoy your teaching over the long term.

In this chapter, we look forward to your new career as a teacher, beginning with a consideration of how to secure your first teaching post. We explore some key issues related to preparing for your first term and consider how you can prioritise your professional development
during the early stages of your career. Finally, we consider ways in which you can stay well and
positive about your teaching over the long term.

Achieving Your Goal of Teaching … and Enjoying It

It is often said that teaching is one of the best jobs in the world. We believe this to be true,
but it doesn't change the fact that teaching is also a challenging and, at times, difficult job.
In this chapter, we want to help you look ahead to a long and positive teaching career, in
which the enjoyment and satisfaction you derive from your work far outweighs any short-term
challenges or problems you may face.

In Chapter 1, we considered the values that drive great teachers. As you prepare to enter the profession and experience the roller-coaster that is the first year or two in teaching, remember to hold those values tightly. These are the driving forces that brought you into teaching: keep them in sharp focus to help you remember why you wanted to teach and the difference that you hope to make, every day, to the children in your care.

— Critical Task 20.1 —

Your Values and Motivation

In just a sentence or two, write a statement that you can read every morning that will remind you of the life-changing impact you are trying to achieve in your teaching each day.

As we identified in Chapter 16, teaching is not an easy job, but it is a hugely rewarding one. Many teachers find it challenging in the first few years, so hold onto what drives you, develop a resilient approach, and don't forget to search for the joyous moments that make teaching such a privilege.

Securing Your First Teaching Post

As you approach the end of your journey to achieve Qualified Teacher Status, a new, and challenging, hurdle looms: securing your first teaching post. Remember, throughout, that this is a two-way process: of course, you are hoping that a school will choose to employ you, but you also have an element of choice about which schools you apply to and whether, ultimately, to accept any job offers that are made to you.

Before the Application

When you first see a teaching post advertised, there are a few issues to consider about whether the school will be a good match for you. Some are practical, such as where the school is located and how far you will have to travel, and some are related to the type of school it is (church school, academy trust, free school, local authority, infant, junior, primary, first or middle) and how it will 'fit' with your own values and aspirations as a teacher. It is therefore important to find out as much as you can about the school before deciding to apply. The school website will give you an idea about the school ethos, curriculum and approaches to teaching and learning. Another way to get a good 'feel' for a school is to visit, which will enable you to look into the headteacher's eyes and decide if this is someone for whom you would like to work ... or not.

The school will be able to provide you with applicant information, which should include both a job description and a person specification. The job description should set out the main requirements of the role of the class teacher and is likely to be quite similar for many schools. The person specification is very important for you as an applicant, as it sets out what kind of person the school is looking for in terms of skills, prior experience and personal attributes. In effect, the person specification forms a set of criteria against which your application will be judged.

The Application

Once you have decided that you like the look of a particular school, the next step is to complete the application. There are normally two parts to the application: the rather functional 'box-filling' part, in which you state your name, address, qualifications, etc., and the very important 'personal statement', in which you make a clear case as to why you are an excellent candidate for the job.

It is important to ensure that you provide accurate information about your qualifications and previous employment, as the school will want to check these details later if they offer you a contract of employment. So take your time to check your certificates and fill in the form with care. Then keep a copy of all this information so that it is easier to fill in another application later.

The 'personal statement' may be called different things but is the part of the application in which you write about 800 words that communicate what a great teacher you are and, importantly, how well your skills, experience and personal attributes match what the school is looking for, as set out in the person specification. The use of short examples throughout your personal statement can help the headteacher or governor reading your application to build a picture of what the teaching and learning looks like when you are in charge of a class.

Teaching a Sample Lesson

If you have submitted a strong application and have been shortlisted by a school, they are likely to invite you to teach a sample lesson. It is a key part of the recruitment process because it enables the headteacher and governors to 'see you in action' in the classroom. It is likely that the school will ask you to teach for about 30 minutes; sometimes they will define the lesson content and objectives for you and sometimes they will give you a good deal of choice about the focus of your lesson. In either case, the key thing to remember is that this is your opportunity to demonstrate what you know about teaching and learning and how to have a great impact on learning. It is not a time to 'play it safe', but to teach a creative and purposeful lesson that excites the children about their new knowledge and inspires them to want to know more. At the end of the lesson, take a moment to reflect on how it went and what you might have done differently, as these things may form the basis for a question in the interview.

Doing Well in an Interview

Interviews are nerve-racking but here's an important and often overlooked fact that might help: you probably won't be the only nervous person in the room. An interview panel is often made up of three or four people and a common group might be the headteacher, another senior leader, a staff governor and a parent governor. The headteacher will know that the single most effective way for them to improve their school will be to appoint the best teacher they can, so they may also be feeling a bit of nervous tension about making the right choice. The parent governor might not be experienced as an interviewer and so might be feeling nervous about the whole process. So, if you're feeling a bit shaky, you probably won't be alone! You can make everyone in the room (including you) feel calmer by giving each person a warm smile and a positive greeting.

When you are being interviewed by a panel of three or four people, it is likely that they will share out the work and each ask a few questions, and you can be left wondering who you should look at or address your answers to. The usual rule of thumb is that you should mostly address your answer to the person who asked the question, but also glance around the other panel members to make a little eye contact with everyone if you can. However, don't be surprised if this is tricky, as most members of the panel will be furiously making notes about your answers.

Remember that the panel will be trying to get the best out of you, but they are also trying to work out which candidate they think will be the best fit for their school, so they may ask some tricky questions. If you are not sure about what the question is getting at, don't be afraid of asking for it to be rephrased or to take a few moments to think about how you might answer it. As with the personal statement, it is useful to try to include examples from your recent experience in your answers, to illustrate your understanding of effective practice and to give further insights into your excellent teaching.

Be Ready for a Quick Decision

Throughout the selection process, remember that you are choosing the school as much as the school is choosing you. At the end of the interview, you are likely to be asked if you are still a firm candidate for the job. If you have thoroughly enjoyed your day and would be happy to accept a job at the school, then the answer is easy. If you have decided you would rather not work there, it is best to be clear about it at this point in the interview.

Sometime in the afternoon or evening following the interview, it is likely that the headteacher will phone the preferred candidate and offer them the job. It is therefore important to be ready with your answer, as it is very unlikely that they will give you much time to think it over. If they are unable to appoint their preferred candidate, they will want to quickly make the offer to their second candidate, before another school snaps them up, so be ready with your answer if you are offered a job!

Preparing for Your First Term

Preparing to start your first teaching job is undoubtedly exciting, and there is much to prepare. Even at this stage, remember to look after yourself: there is no point starting the year feeling exhausted and anxious because you have spent the entire summer holiday planning every lesson for the entire year.

Before the Start of the Academic Year

During the summer holiday, you will want to spend some time in your classroom, making yourself at home and developing your confidence for September. One important thing to remember is that the classroom might go through a deep clean at some stage over the summer, so check with the caretaker when this will happen: you don't want to spend hours setting your room up in the first week of the summer holiday, only to come back three weeks later to find all the furniture piled up in one corner of the room.

Once you have the go ahead, you will want to consider how best to arrange the classroom furniture. Remember that there is no one 'right way' to arrange the tables and chairs in your room, but a golden rule is that you should avoid any arrangement that ends up with some children having their backs to the board. It may be worth discussing classroom arrangement with other teachers in your school to see what they do.

You may find that your classroom has a lot of 'stuff' in it that just needs throwing away. Teachers tend to be hoarders, so there may be some old resources that are of no use now: check with a senior member of staff and then, if approved, throw out anything that looks unusable.

You may want to prepare the display boards, using some to show resources that will be useful for your early topics, while keeping others blank, ready to be filled once the children are in school. The important thing, as with all aspects of your preparation, is to hold your values close. Do you want this room to be 'my classroom' or 'our classroom'? If you want the children to have a sense of shared ownership of the room, then make sure you create good opportunities for this in your planning of the space.

You will also want to make a start on planning some of your early lessons and topics. It's probably not worth planning too much, as you will have to make adjustments depending on how the children progress, but you will feel more confident starting the year if you have some planning under your belt.

In Your First Term

The top priority in the first few weeks of your first year must be to get to know the children. Find out about their hobbies, their interests, their families. Observe them in the classroom and on the playground: work out what they enjoy and with whom they work well. Give the children good opportunities to talk about themselves and their lives outside school. Try to identify how you might tailor your approach to teaching and learning to take account of the children's interests as well as their individual needs.

You will also want to make a good impression on the parents and carers of your children. One important piece of advice here is to keep an eye on the weather! If it is raining, make sure that your children are ready to go, with coats on and bags packed, as soon as the school day ends: don't leave the parents standing in the rain a moment longer than necessary! Take every opportunity to build relationships with parents, as we explored in Chapter 15, so that you have a good foundation on which to build when you need to have difficult conversations about behaviour or other issues.

It will also be important to invest in relationships with the wider team, including midday supervisors, cleaners, the caretaker and administrative staff. You will want to work closely with your immediate teaching colleagues to share planning or ideas for teaching, to solve problems together and to explore ways in which you and your classes may collaborate.

In all you do, aim to make a positive impact: you are a professional and a member of the school team, so seek to make a contribution to the community from day one. This doesn't have to be grand actions like running a staff meeting or organising the Christmas concert (but go for it if you feel you want to). Small actions are powerful and cumulative, so seek those small opportunities that will help to embed you into the team: check in with the school administrators to say hello, offer to cover playground duty for a colleague who is not feeling great, or share a joke with a midday supervisor.

Professional Development and the *Early Career Framework*

As a teacher new to the profession in England, you will be known as an Early Career Teacher (ECT) and will be supported through a two-year induction programme, which is designed to continue the education and training that began in your Initial Teacher Education (ITE), and which led to you having gained Qualified Teacher Status (QTS). As a student teacher engaging in ITE, your training programme was underpinned by the *ITT Core Content Framework* (CCF) (DfE, 2019b) and complied with the required criteria around which your provider planned your development programme. Similarly, in your ECT years, the induction programme which you undertake will follow the *Early Career Framework* (*ECF*) (DfE, 2019a).

The *ECF* builds on the *CCF* and forms part of 'a "golden thread" of high-quality evidence underpinning the support, training and development available through the entirety of a teacher's career' (DfE, 2022: 5). It is framed around the *Teachers' Standards (England)* (DfE, 2011: 5), which 'apply to the vast majority of teachers regardless of their career stage'. The ECT induction programme combines support from a mentor in your school with an expectation that you engage with professional development discussions, tasks, sessions and activities both within and beyond your own school. In order to complete your induction period successfully and become a fully-fledged member of the profession, you need to show that you have engaged with the induction programme successfully and your teaching has continued to develop in quality.

If you are starting your teaching career in other countries of the UK, or if you have chosen to work abroad, different standards for teachers apply and there are different arrangements for induction into the profession. In Wales, for example, the *Professional Standards for Teaching and Leadership* (Welsh Government, 2019) apply, with a matching induction programme for Newly Qualified Teachers (NQTs).

Wherever you start your career, there is likely to be an induction programme which focuses on developing your knowledge and skills in your early years as a teacher, as well as supporting you to understand how to continue your own professional development beyond the end of the programme. One of the ways in which you can do this is to continuously engage with self-evaluation, just as you have done as a student teacher. It will become more and more intuitive with time and will give you ideas as to how you can target your focus for your own development. You will also be part of more formalised, school-wide appraisal systems, which may involve you being observed by, and in observing, other colleagues at work in the classroom. Such experiences can provide you with valuable opportunities to learn from and with your colleagues, prompting professional discussions that will enhance your skills and understanding of the teaching and learning process.

Whenever you teach a new topic, or revisit one you have taught before, it will be an appropriate time for you to extend your subject knowledge by undertaking your own research. It is also useful to look out for more formal opportunities to develop your knowledge in particular subjects by engaging with subject associations or working with organisations such as the Maths Hubs (www.ncetm.org.uk/maths-hubs/). Beyond that, many teachers find great value in undertaking further study, undertaking Master's degrees or National Professional Qualifications (in England), which provide a more academic and formal framework for continuing professional development.

In Chapter 14, we learnt that taking control of your own professional learning provides you with a solid platform for becoming a critical and adaptable teacher who will be constantly learning about yourself as a teacher and as a learner. You can refer to that chapter to explore those ideas further. However, the key point here is that while there will be induction and support for you as you enter the profession, only you can really make your continuing professional development (CPD) your own. Time is precious as a teacher, so you need to make sure you tailor your CPD activity to make the best possible use of the time you have, seeking to have the maximum impact on your practice, and on the children's learning. You should engage with your own learning as keenly as you engage with that of your pupils because one of the joys of teaching is that you will be learning and developing throughout your career.

Wellbeing and Joy

Remember that no one expects you to be a brilliant teacher straight away, apart from, perhaps, you! Try not to put too much pressure on yourself and utilise some of the practical steps to maintain your own wellbeing that we discussed in Chapter 16, such as making time for yourself, catching up with friends, engaging in personal hobbies and other 'unrelated-to-teaching' activities, and seeking support when things are getting hard. Every experienced teacher started as a novice, and most will understand the challenges you are facing and will be more than willing to share their knowledge and expertise to help you solve those knotty problems.

Teaching is undoubtedly hard work, but it is also full of moments of fun, laughter and silliness, so make sure that you notice and enjoy these elements too. Jot down some of the funny things that children say, as well as some of the profound insights they provide about the important things in life. Savour those 'lightbulb' moments children sometimes have in their learning or those times of 'awe and wonder' when they experience something amazing for the first time. Bottrill (2018) identifies that children see the world differently from adults, and recognising and even joining in with the 'magic' of childhood can open our eyes to a whole new world of play and joy.

Question Guide 20.1

Drawing Inspiration From Colleagues

While on placement, or in your early career, take opportunities to ask colleagues about how they stay motivated and positive about teaching, even during the challenging times.

Chapter Summary

In this chapter, we have considered how to secure your first teaching post, exploring the processes involved and recognising that, while the school will be looking for a teacher who is a 'good fit' for them, you also need to find a school that feels right to you. We have explored how you might prepare for your first term of teaching, so that you can make a confident and organised start, as well as identifying some priorities for those first few weeks in your new role. We have considered the role that the *Early Career Framework* (DfE, 2019b) will play in your induction and professional development in the early stages of your teaching career. We also reflected on the importance of prioritising your own wellbeing and sense of joy at all stages of your career as a teacher. If you are to have a life-changing impact on the children that you teach, it starts with valuing yourself.

Further Reading

Bottrill, G. (2018) *Can I go & play now? Rethinking the early years.* Los Angeles, CA: Sage. Although this book is about good early years practice, teachers of all ages will benefit from reading it. It challenges us to see the world from the children's point of view and to question many of the 'adult world' school conventions that can prevent us from connecting effectively with our learners.

Department for Education (DfE) (2019) *Early career framework.* London: DfE. As this document will play such an important role in your induction period, you need to familiarise yourself with it before starting in your first teaching post.

References

Bottrill, G. (2018) *Can I go & play now? Rethinking the early years.* Los Angeles, CA: Sage.

Department for Education (DfE) (2011) *Teachers' standards.* London: DfE.

Department for Education (DfE) (2019a) *Early career framework.* London: DfE.

Department for Education (DfE) (2019b) *ITT core content framework.* London: DfE.

Department for Education (DfE) (2022) *Delivering world-class teacher development: Policy paper.* London: DfE.

Welsh Government (2019) *Professional standards for teaching and leadership.* Cardiff: Welsh Government. Available at: https://hwb.gov.wales/professional-development/professional-standards#professional-standards-for-all-school-practitioners (accessed 23 November 2022).

INDEX